THE PLACE OF BREATH IN CINEMA

THE PLACE OF BREATH IN CINEMA

Davina Quinlivan

EDINBURGH
University Press

For Lambert

© Davina Quinlivan, 2012

Edinburgh University Press Ltd
22 George Square, Edinburgh EH8 9LF

www.euppublishing.com

Typeset in 10/12.5 pt Sabon
by Servis Filmsetting Ltd, Stockport, Cheshire

A CIP record for this book is available from the British Library

ISBN 978 0 7486 4899 3 (hardback)
ISBN 978 0 7486 4900 6 (webready PDF)
ISBN 978 0 7486 6474 0 (epub)
ISBN 978 0 7486 6473 3 (Amazon ebook)

The right of Davina Quinlivan
to be identified as author of this work
has been asserted in accordance with
the Copyright, Designs and Patents Act 1988.

CONTENTS

List of Illustrations	vii
Acknowledgements	viii
Introduction: Troubling Invisibility and the Breathing Body	1
Thinking about Breathing: Towards a Philosophical Enquiry	6
The Place of Other Breaths: Discourses on Breath Outside of Film Theory	13
Inherited Places: Engaging with Sobchack and Marks	17
'The Sound of Thought Itself': The Place of Territory and Voices	22
Irigaray's 'Le temps du souffle'	27
Thinking with Irigaray, Sobchack and Marks	31
1 The Haptic Logic of a Breathing Body: Elemental Topographies of Memory and Loss	41
Existing Criticism of Egoyan	43
The Breathing Child: The Sweet *Hereafter*	45
Escaping Haptic Logic and the Sensory Refrain	53
'Whispering on the Threshold of the Body': Breathing Sounds	59
The Place of Stillness	62
Felicia's Journey: The Orality of the Place	65
Lost Breaths: Archival Spaces and Absent Bodies	73
Exotica: Asphyxiating Geographies	77
Intimate Dwellings	79
Pastoral Visions and Suffocation	80
Concluding Thoughts on Egoyan	84
2 An 'Air in Flesh': An Anatomy of Breath, Carnality and Transcendence: The Breathing Bodies of David Cronenberg	90
Filmic 'Flesh', Filmed Bodies and Irigaray	92
Breath Becoming Body in *Spider*	94
Suffering	97

Olfactory Trauma	100
Bad Air	102
Film's Breathing Body	104
The Lungs of the Film	109
Breathing Objects in a Video World	112
Respiring Interfaces	114
Feminine Transcendence	117
Reflecting on Cronenberg	119
3 Towards Inter-subjectivities of Breath and the Breathing Film Viewer: Lars von Trier's 'Gold Heart' Trilogy	124
A Prelude: von Trier's Element	126
Golden Hearted	129
Empathetic Images: *Breaking the Waves*	131
Hearing the 'Grain'	137
Love and Sorority	141
'If Living Is Seeing, I'm Holding my Breath': *Dancer in the Dark*	146
'I've Seen It All': Breath, Motion and Emotion	150
'My Favourite Things': Troubling Objects	153
The Idiots: Engendering Breath through Silence	157
Karen's Theme	161
Concluding Thoughts	162
Conclusion	168
Bibliography	173
Filmography	185
Index	189

LIST OF ILLUSTRATIONS

Figure I.1	*Gray's Anatomy*	7
Figure 1.1	*The Sweet Hereafter*	48
Figure 1.2	*The Sweet Hereafter*	48
Figure 1.3	*Felicia's Journey*	68
Figure 1.4	*Evidence*	76
Figure 1.5	*Exotica*	81
Figure 1.6	*Exotica*	83
Figure 1.7	*Exotica*	83
Figure 2.1	*Spider*	98
Figure 2.2	*Spider*	98
Figure 3.1	*Breaking the Waves*	135
Figure 3.2	*Breaking the Waves*	135

ACKNOWLEDGEMENTS

I am truly grateful to those who have put their faith in this book and supported my dedication to it. I am most grateful to Sarah Cooper, for everything she has taught me and for her meticulous advice and support. I also thank Martine Beugnet, Claire Thomson and Kristi McKim for their helpful comments on earlier drafts of this book. I owe a great debt to peers, colleagues and friends who have pointed me in particular directions; here, I especially give thanks to Laura U. Marks, Emma Wilson, Jenny Chamarette, Liz Watkins and Markos Hadjioannou. I am also grateful to Richard Dyer, Ginette Vincendeau and Mark Betz for their helpful advice on material which features in the introduction to this book. I am also indebted to several institutions which enabled me to carry out research by providing access to archived material. In this respect, I wish to thank the Institute of Contemporary Arts, Canada House and Modern Art Oxford. I would also like to thank The University of Liverpool and The University of Leeds for providing generous bursaries in order for me to participate in conferences and present earlier drafts of the research undertaken for this book.

This book would not have been possible without the support of my husband Dylan, Lambert and Patricia Quinlivan, Loretta, Adeline and Selwyn.

The section on *Breaking the Waves* first took the form of a book chapter in *Realism and the Audio-Visual Media* (Palgrave Macmillan, 2009) and I am grateful to the editors of this volume and Palgrave Macmillan for granting me their permission to draw on this material here. Henry Vandyke Carter's beautiful illustration of the lungs, originally featured in the second edition of *Gray's Anatomy*, would not have found its way into this book without the help of Ruth Richardson and the Wellcome Library. Atom Egoyan very generously granted me permission to reproduce stills from his films and I am grateful to Marcy Gerstein at Ego Film Arts for making this possible.

INTRODUCTION: TROUBLING INVISIBILITY AND THE BREATHING BODY

Something that is invisible and impalpable fails to be simply absent, simply *not there*. Rather, it insinuates itself within the very present that excludes it, or haunts the corporeality to which it cannot be reduced. It is an excess, or a residue.[1]

Steven Shaviro

I could not go abroad in snow – it would settle on me and expose me. Rain, too, would make me a watery outline, a glittering surface of a man – a bubble. And fog – I should be a fainter bubble in a fog, a surface, a greasy glimmer of humanity. Moreover, as I went abroad – in the London air – I gathered dirt about my ankles, floating smuts and dust upon my skin.[2]

H. G. Wells

Breath can become part of a story and as my body reproduces the gait of that story, so my mind embraces its meaning.[3]

Claude Lévi-Strauss

How can we start to think about something we cannot see? This book explores the place of breath in the cinema and it begins with the question of borders between visibility and invisibility. Thus the notion of breathing stimulates new ways in which to question the nature of seeing, perceiving and sensing things which are not always entirely visible in film. My concern with the interstices between visibility and invisibility in film can be seen to represent an interest in the way in which sound serves to stimulate our perception beyond what is visible on screen. For example, voices and sound effects in film are often 'invisible', untraceable in the diegetic image. Yet human bodies that *are* represented on screen can also hold the potential to imply a diegetic, bodily absence. Indeed, the spectre or ghostly figure in the 'haunted house' film genre 'appears' as a blur or flickering light wandering through the filmic diegesis and the transparency of such bodies reinforces this paradox: they are elusive bodies whose presence is only partial. In this sense, the interstices between visibility and invisibility that are evoked through film can be seen to play with our viewing expectations. Certainly, thinking through the relations between visibility and invisibility tends to raise questions that are invariably pertinent to the viewing experience of the filmic medium and its particular viewing pleasures. The model of viewing pleasure posited by the film theorist Laura Mulvey, in her groundbreaking 1975 essay 'Visual Pleasure and Narrative Cinema', demonstrates how film is a visual medium which gratifies us through its spectacle,[4] but I would argue that this pleasure lies just as much in what we cannot wholly perceive. Indeed, a particular pleasure of the cinema is the joy of its allusions and its gesturing towards the borders between the seen and the unseen, both literally and symbolically.

Borders between the seen and the unseen in film relate especially to the human body, as my examples of the voice-over's articulation of invisibility and the spectre's 'transparent' presence suggest. The breaking down of bodily borders unsettles the relations between the seen and the unseen in a way that is dominantly visceral according to the feminist film theorist Barbara Creed. In her seminal book *The Monstrous Feminine*, Creed examines the significance of the interior of the body – blood and viscera – and the ways in which it breaks the external, border-surface of the skin in the horror genre. For Creed, the horror genre features excessive visual imagery which draws attention to the fluidity of the contained 'inside' of the body and its dramatic expulsion. Thus, Creed suggests that the representation of the human body in film can be usefully analysed as a place in which borders collapse, where boundaries separating bodily matter become unstable.[5] However, as my examples of the voice-over and the figure of the spectre demonstrate, the presence of the human body in film also raises questions about the borders that exist between visual and non-visual realms or, more precisely, the unsettling of the oppositions that exist between sound and image in film. The title of this book, *The Place of Breath in Cinema*, underscores my main aim to draw attention to a particular activity of the human body whose foregrounding in film calls into question the boundaries between invisibility and visibility and, especially, the relationship between sound and invisibility. While Creed argues that it is the particular presence of blood and viscera of the body in the filmic diegesis that represents a breaking of bodily boundaries, it is my aim to investigate how breathing represents a subtle dimension of our bodies that can be seen to be both inside and outside of ourselves (as we inhale and exhale), whilst the borders of the skin remain intact. Our skin and, indeed, all our other organs depend upon breathing in order to function; breathing is part of our existence as human beings, but it is not something we tend to think about and its presence is rarely considered in film. While the argument that is put forward in *The Place of Breath in Cinema* will be primarily concerned with the locus of breath in film and the unique configuration of embodied gestures in the filmic diegesis, this book also bears broader implications for the theorisation of the interstices between visibility and invisibility that are called into play by the very place of breath in the film experience.

Breathing is neither completely visible, nor invisible – it troubles this opposition. For example, we might be able to 'see' our own breath as it forms a patch of vapour in the air when we exhale into a cold atmosphere, but this glimpse of breath soon vanishes and therefore it is particularly difficult to think about breathing in terms of vision – a task that is vital given the context of the visual medium of film within which I situate my exploration of breathing. It might be more accurate and appropriate to come to think of breathing as an '(in)visible' dimension of the human body. My adoption of the term '(in)visible' calls attention to the way in which boundaries of visibility and invisibility become blurred when thinking about the very nature of breathing as it is foregrounded in film throughout this book. Indeed, the term '(in)visible' is particularly useful as a way of describing the conditions of visuality that emerge as a result of my enquiry into breathing in film. This is to say that we engage with a kind of visuality sensitive to our breathing bodies and, in this way, breathing and vision are connected. In this book, my use of the term '(in)visible' connotes, in shorthand fashion, the partial, yet undeniable role of processes, sounds, actions and movements in film which are evocative of breathing; more broadly, my theoretical interest in breathing considers the human body's involvement in creating such conditions of (in)visibility in film.

While the term '(in)visible' is helpful in emphasising the particular unsettling of boundaries between vision and the unseen that breathing corresponds with, a term is needed in order to foreground the ambivalent dimensions of physicality and materiality that breathing also calls into question or the kind of bodily activity that breathing is involved in. In this respect, it is appropriate to liken breathing to a kind of '(im)materiality', a term which will also be key to my theorisation of breathing and its particular suggestion of a different kind of bodily matter. While the term 'immaterial' can refer to something of inconsequentiality, my adoption of the term '(im)material' refers to a mode of duality between the material and the incorporeal that breathing specifically suggests. My particular interest in the (im)materiality of breathing in *The Place of Breath in Cinema*, then, reflects a concern with bodily matter that is different from the analysis of blood, viscera and skin pertinent to Creed's work. While Creed's book draws much on the viewer's experience of watching the mutilated and traumatised human body in the horror genre,[6] the human body in film can also evoke a kind of visuality that tends to operate within an (in)visible mode of perception. Though the (in)visible will be involved in my theorisation of the locus of breath in film, it is the (im)material which will offer a more appropriate means through which to underscore my interest in the embodied film experience.

While the terms (in)visible and (im)material clarify my interest in breathing, it is important to suggest how the human, breathing body can first become 'filmic' in order to orient ourselves towards further contemplation of this physical process and its involvement in film. Returning to my earlier point of departure when thinking about the filmic medium, the particular example of the voice-over in film suggests a dimension of the viewing experience that is motivated towards the unseen, but the specific foregrounding of breath as a sonic motif prompts a different perspective on the unseen presence of the human body in film.

The sound of breathing – air being inhaled and breathed out as gasps or as a constant rhythm of noise – has been most notably theorised by Michel Chion and Jodi Brooks, whose analyses are focused on a thematic concern with the aural experience of breathing. In his discussion of *The Elephant Man* (David Lynch, 1980), Chion suggests that the terrible, troubled wheezing of John Merrick (John Hurt) serves as a sort of sonic narrative: Merrick's asthmatic, distorted breathing presents a continuum between his distressed, suffering body, machinery and the film's portrayal of industry.[7] Yet Chion's discussion of breathing in the cinema is ultimately short-lived. More broadly, my theoretical analysis of sound echoes Chion's concern for the audio-visual, that is, a theory that intends to think both sound and image together as a dual entity, what he terms 'the audio-visual contract'.[8] Building on a similar approach to Chion, the work of Brooks in her rich article 'The Sound of Knocking: Jacques Becker's *Le Trou*' argues that the sound of breathing in the film emphasises the rhythmic nature of Becker's visuals.[9] The work of Chion and Brooks, then, already suggests that breathing occupies a considerable position within the construction of mise en scène and the sonic textures of film. Although breathing is implicit to their argument, Chion and Brooks only become aware of it through the presence of the voice or the suggestion of a body in the diegesis, and this is crucial to the way in which questions of the seen and the unseen become complicated through the place of breath in film.

One of the most complex examples of a diegetic body in film that is associated with the sound of breathing is featured in a film that has been seen by millions and viewed by generations of cinema-goers: George Lucas's *Star Wars* (1977). In 1977 cinema-goers across the world flocked to their local movie theatres to experience for themselves what was to become not only one of the largest-grossing epics of all time, but also an enduring figurehead of popular Western culture. While it is certain that the awe-inspiring special effects, operatic scale and overall dynamism of *Star Wars* beguiled many adults and children alike, a large part of such enchantment stems from a simpler, yet rarely told story which takes place on and off screen. This narrative occurs between bodies both real and imagined – some *thing* which strikes beyond our psychical perception and hooks into the very heart of visceral being. Such a filmic encounter begins with one single sound: a murmur of breath. As with Brooks's and Chion's views on *Le Trou* and *The Elephant Man*, breathing is also a thematic concern of *Star Wars*, but in a way that is much more obvious.

If we consider *Star Wars*'s iconic antagonist, the character Darth Vader, the subject of breathing is already an implicit part of film history. *Star Wars* occupies a considerable position within our collective, cultural memory and it is the strange, 'whooshing' sound of breathing associated with the Darth Vader character that is at the core of this iconic film. It is important to begin with the example of Darth Vader since it is one of the most universal, associative links between film and breathing. Furthermore, I want to consider how *Star Wars* works on various levels to privilege the role of breath. While *Star Wars* is not the focus of this book, it provides a useful point of departure for thinking about breathing as a filmic presence and emphasises the productiveness of addressing the role of breath in the film experience.[10]

The character Darth Vader is undeniably associated with the diegetic sound of breathing. Indeed, the persistent sound of breathing in *Star Wars* (conceptualised by the film's sound designer Ben Burtt) is synonymous with the film's antagonist and definitive of his presence throughout. Burtt's creation of Darth Vader's 'whooshing' breaths combine low, deep gasps and muffled, rhythmic sighs of exhalation and it is this specific perception of Darth Vader as a breathing body which has become synonymous with the film itself, reflected in the popularity of the film's extensive merchandise. There are several versions of a Darth Vader voice-changer or 'breathing device', all of which are still widely available.[11] Rather ironically, these 'voice-changers' enable users to create or enhance the very noises that they already, although more naturally, make. One can argue, then, that Darth Vader's imposing and deeply affective, unsettling portrayal within the film owes much to the fact that we can hear his breathing, and through this we gain a particular impression of embodiment, peculiarly more so than with any other character in the film. Indeed, I will return to the issue of Darth Vader's embodiment and its implications for the spectator later in this introduction. Ultimately, Darth Vader's breathing is apparent in a way that is unnatural and inhuman, primarily since the physical act of respiration is not normally overtly audible unless the body is physically exerted or the sound is deliberately exaggerated, and thus substantially amplifies the character's threatening persona. Certainly, the sound of Darth Vader's breathing functions as a prominent reminder of his physical weakness since it is explained in the film that his body, wounded from battle, was rebuilt as a cyborg, his face now covered by a mask that functions as a respiratory apparatus.[12] Yet, in spite of this knowledge, the particular feelings of discomfort that may be experienced by the viewer as a result of hearing Darth Vader's continuous, stifled breath contained within the mask remain difficult to explain.[13] One can argue that Darth Vader's breathing is part of the narrative trajectory, implying a constant awareness of the plot that serves to suture the audience into the world of the film. However, the role of breathing in *Star Wars* clearly also works on a much deeper level to elicit feelings of unease that may haunt the viewer long after the film has ended. Darth Vader's breathing emphasises the living, suffering human body which underscores the issue of mortality in the film. Indeed, one can argue that it is the representation of mortality foreshadowed through the foregrounding of breath that audiences find most troubling and associate with their experience of the film's villain.

As *Star Wars* shows us, when breathing is foregrounded in film, it has the potential to shape our viewing experience and, as the sales of Darth Vader-related merchandise suggest, it can haunt the very moments we take home with us once our experience of the film is over. For *Star Wars*, it is the particular use of diegetic sound that offers a literal example of the way in which breathing can be understood as an extremely powerful narrative device and aural signifier. Indeed, Darth Vader's breathing represents an (in)visible dimension of the diegesis since breath is heard rather than seen and it reveals something about the *inside* of the body that is visible on screen. But, while a significant aspect of this foregrounding of breath owes to the film's use of sound, this book aims to re-view cinema's bodies as they 'breathe' within an audio *and* visual field of perception. We might thus call the audio and visual experience of breathing in film a kind of 'filmic encounter' with a breathing body, a term which foregrounds the filmic realm of possibility which compels viewers to engage with the locus of breath in film. This book's study of embodiment proposes a series of filmic encounters in which new light is shed on film's mysterious and enigmatic reflection of the embodied human subject, an exploration of what is communicated through images not only of the *breathing* body in the frame, but of the place of breath in the cinema.

While *Star Wars* offers an example of breathing that is especially conveyed through the film's soundtrack, the actual act of breathing as a purely biological process is also registered in film through images of the lungs, as we shall see. However, before I reflect on the actual images of respiration which appear in film, it is useful to consider the strictly biological processes involved in respiration.

Thinking about Breathing: Towards a Philosophical Enquiry

Respiration is the term used to describe the act of taking oxygen into the lungs and releasing it. Other than humans, mammals and other living creatures, indeed most living organisms, also depend on various types of respiration to sustain life. For example, plants and trees also breathe through photosynthesis, and other organic substances like soil and clay also respond to the oxygen in the air through processes of oxidisation. However, it is human biology that is the focus of my particular enquiry into breathing. In the early medical textbook *Anatomy of the Human Body*, Henry Gray identifies the respiratory apparatus (*apparatus respiratorius*) as a set of five organs: the larynx or organ of voice, the trachea or windpipe, the bronchi, the lungs and the delicate membrane of each lung, the pleurae.[14] When we breathe through our mouth or nose, oxygen

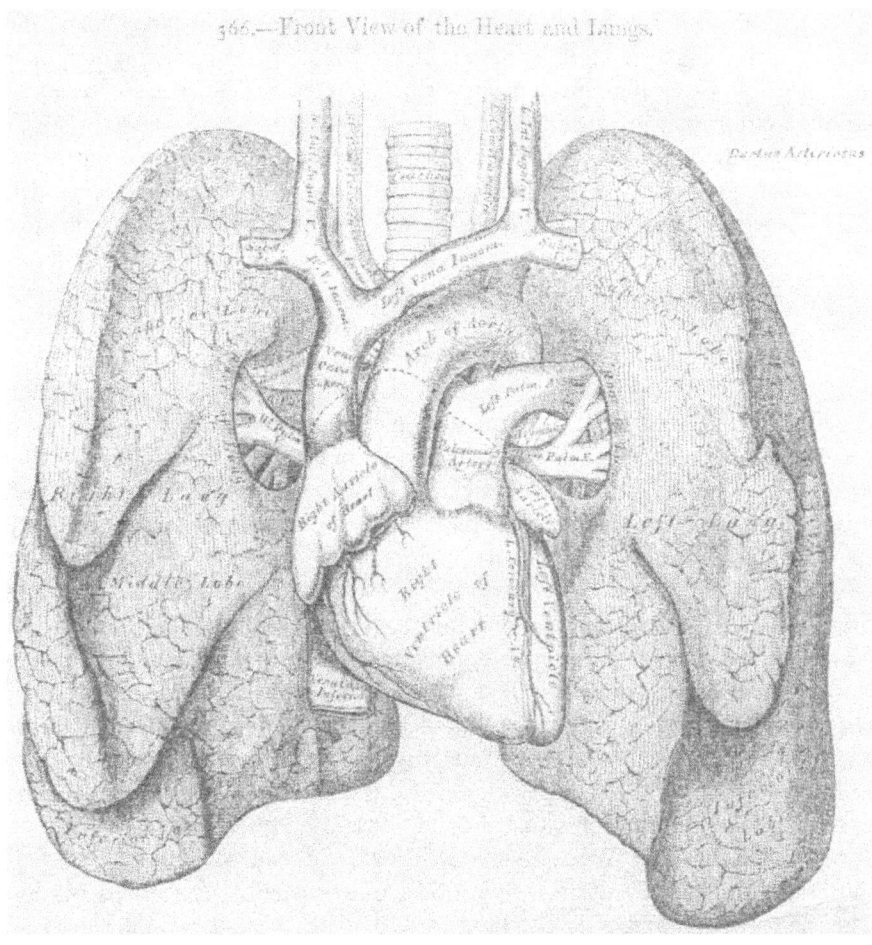

Figure I.1 Gray's anatomy of the lungs. Illustration by Henry Vandyke Carter in Henry Gray's *Anatomy: Descriptive and Surgical* (London: John W. Parker and Son, 1860), p. 686.

passes from the larynx to the trachea, bronchi, lungs and pleurae in order to oxygenate blood cells and release carbon dioxide from the body, each breath enacting a constant exchange of gases that ensures cellular activity and, thus, sustaining life itself.

While the focus of this book is not limited to the actual representation of the biology of respiration, it is important to consider how film might illustrate this process. X-ray images and microscopic photography of the human body are frequently used in film to create various dramatic and aesthetic effects and this includes the imaging of human lungs. I am especially drawn to a series of microscopic images of the lungs which appear in Paul Thomas Anderson's

1999 feature film *Magnolia*. Unlike the use of breathing in *Star Wars*, the images of the lungs in *Magnolia* are exemplary of how breathing might appear in film as a purely biological process that is actualised on screen, recalling Gray's anatomy of the lungs.[15]

Early on in *Magnolia*, Anderson's highly mobile camera zooms into the dying protagonist Earl Partridge's (Jason Robards) softly breathing, wrinkled mouth before cutting away to a high-speed montage of animated graphics and microscopic images. These images track a cancerous cell in Partridge's lungs through to diagnosis via an X-ray of his chest and the urgency with which these shots are used in the film as we are first introduced to the character is unmistakable. The images do not simply contribute towards Anderson's post-modernist aesthetic, since this implies a tendency to draw attention to the surface of things; rather, the microscopic hub of cellular activity serves to encapsulate the diegesis: it becomes part of a moment that is intangible. While my earlier example of Darth Vader shows us how the sound of breathing can unsettle the film viewer, and even remind us of our own mortality, the very speed of the film footage in *Magnolia* emphasises breathing as a particularly temporal process, that is, the increased awareness of time passing with each breath. This temporal notion of breathing will be explored in this book with regard to bodily time, the slowness and speed of breath and, in particular, the relations between memory and the filmic memorialising of the breathing body. However, while time is important to Anderson's imaging of the (dying) breathing body and its associations with time, my main reason for drawing attention to *Magnolia* is to highlight an example of the filmic, pictorial rendering of the breathing, human body's biological conditions.

In contrast to *Star Wars*, *Magnolia*'s detached and scientific imaging of the human body shows how respiration can be visually represented in film. The microscopic images of the lungs reveal to the viewer the interiority of Partridge's body and serve as evidence of his terminal illness. Furthermore, *Magnolia*'s representation of respiration at a molecular level reveals the hub of biological activity which takes place as we exhale and inhale oxygen. Yet, despite the visual impact of Anderson's microscopic images of respiration, they ultimately offer limited scope for reflection beyond the representational qualities of such images, and, as my discussion of *Star Wars* suggests, I want to develop the experiential and intellectual ways of treating the subject of breathing in feature films. Indeed, it is the sonic presence of breathing in *Star Wars*, rather than the clinical image of breathing in *Magnolia*, that invites a more complex theoretical approach. Furthermore, my interest in the experience of the role of breathing in film requires some consideration of the theatrical release of films and their cinematic qualities and thus the study of scientific images is beyond the scope of this book.

It would seem that the potency of breath in *Star Wars* lends much to the film's significance as a cultural phenomenon pertinent to Western popular culture and therefore the cultural specificity of breathing appears to be an issue that is key to my particular interest in the role of breath in film. Examining the cultural specificity of breath may lead to a greater understanding of the questions of mortality, suffering and human subjectivity that have been foregrounded during my analysis of *Star Wars*. Furthermore, it is useful to consider cultural perceptions of breathing from a diverse range of traditions as well as Western views since they tend to share one particularly wide-ranging belief: breath is the 'soul'. This relationship between breathing and the soul enables me to build on the biological conditions of breathing and explore the role of breathing in the context of philosophical thought.

Etymologically speaking, the word 'breath' invokes the presence of the soul throughout many cultural traditions; Greek philosophy conceives of breath as the *pneuma*, while the Ancient Greek poet Homer also wrote of the psyche as the 'life breath'.[16] Indeed, the recurrent appearance of primordial deities Aether (God of the upper-air and light) and Zephyr (God of the west wind) in Greek mythology underscores the importance of air and wind as metaphors for ethereal being, elemental mysticism and the cosmos. The divine significance of breathing is also reflected in ancient tribal mythology; for example, the story of Creation that belongs to the Hopi Native Americans refers to *Síkangnuqua*, the yellow light of the second phase in the dawn of Creation in which breath first entered the body. Similarly, Buddhist traditions view breath as the *prāna* or 'life force', but it is their belief that breath must be controlled (*prānāyāma*) in order to achieve mastery over the body.[17] Yet a last breath is also exhaled before death and this is a view widely held by many cultures; as the last breath passes from the lips of dying, the soul is 'not in the breath, it is the breath'.[18]

If breath evokes the soul, then, its foregrounding in *Star Wars* makes this meaning explicit, but the fact that it is the film's villain whose 'soul' we are most reminded of is particularly troubling since it implies knowledge about a character that we are, at least conventionally, least likely to identify with. The philosophical interpretation of breathing as the essence of the spirit or soul offers a rich and intriguing line of enquiry, but a broader theoretical framework is required in order to encompass and reflect my concern with the question of human subjectivity that the locus of breath in film tends to foreground. While it is certain that many cultural traditions offer a wide range of perspectives on the symbolic meaning of breathing, it is the philosophy of Luce Irigaray which is most appropriate to my interest in the place of breath in cinema.

Both Buddhist and classical Greek philosophy stimulate a multifaceted theoretical concern with breath in the French feminist thought of Irigaray. Irigaray's philosophical engagement with breath is one of the most sustained and wide-ranging studies to have thought through the importance of breathing to human existence beyond its purely biological significance. Thus, while my exploration of the subject of breathing in film could fruitfully build on scientific discourses in film studies, as my discussion of the microscopic imagery in *Magnolia* implies, my main interest in Irigaray's philosophy leads me to focus on questions less ordered by a strictly scientific perspective on film.

One of the foremost thinkers of modern French philosophy, Irigaray is well known for her work on sexual difference in her 1974 publication *Speculum of the Other Woman*.[19] Irigaray's early work sought to critique the phallocentric order upheld and perpetuated throughout Western continental philosophy, namely the classical Greek thought of Plato and the psychoanalytic models of Sigmund Freud and Jacques Lacan. *Speculum* targets the foundations laid by continental thought for a phallocentric order which denies the presence of sexual difference. According to Freud's totalising, patriarchal ideology, female subjectivity is appropriated and denied; it performs only within a 'realm of semblance',[20] to quote the model of thought offered by Irigaray's foremost commentator Margaret Whitford. Thus, phallocentrism appropriates all other forms of difference, above all sexual difference. Since *Speculum*, Irigaray has continued to build on a conceptual framework which posits a theory of sexual difference based upon the critique and deconstruction of Western continental philosophy, while also attending to the wider social and political relevance of such thinking. In recent years, Irigaray has embarked upon a re-examination of her own personal inheritance of particular Western traditions, especially Judeo-Christianity.[21] Coming to terms with questions of sexual difference which emerge through her readings of Judeo-Christian ideology, Irigaray's later work reflects on non-Western traditions, namely Buddhism, culminating in her philosophical and practical interest in the subject of breathing which develops from Eastern teachings and the practice of yoga.[22] Most importantly, Irigaray's critical examination of Eastern philosophy synthesises Buddhist ways of looking and thinking about the world in order to suggest how breathing might preserve sexual difference in the body.[23]

Irigaray's philosophy of breath can be seen to reflect a new concern within her overarching project of sexual difference, but the key stages of her discourse on breathing also mark distinctly new territory in her corpus of work. Irigaray's philosophy of breath is divided into three theoretical areas of concern: firstly, the sensory and contemplative nature of breathing; secondly, the spiritual and sensible awakening of the body; and thirdly, the body's relationship with the environment and air which comes to represent the communality of sharing breath and living within a shared space of air. These three areas of concern in Irigaray's philosophy represent a framework that is structured according to an investigation of corporeality, spatiality and inter-subjectivity which will lead my own exploration of breathing in this book.

Irigaray's philosophy of breath, her envisaging of a *'temps du souffle'* (culture of breath), is particularly useful for developing thought on the issue of embodiment in relation to the film experience, given her conceptual engagement with the philosophical writings of Maurice Merleau-Ponty and the way in which this dialogue has shaped her thinking throughout her corpus of work. Merleau-Ponty's phenomenological concept of the 'lived-body' makes sense of the world through means of 'lived perception' or the body's involvement in everyday thought and experience.[24] A growing interest in Merleau-Ponty's philosophy, especially his writings on film itself, has prompted a major shift in contemporary film theory, originating with the pioneering film theory of Vivian Sobchack in her book *The Address of the Eye* in which the filmic apparatus is theorised as a differentiated 'body' in the viewing experience.[25] Irigaray's critique of phenomenological thinkers such as Merleau-Ponty, as well as Martin Heidegger and Emmanuel Levinas, shifts emphasis from paradigms of embodied 'vision' to the 'interiority' of the sexed, sensing body.[26] Her theorisation of breathing as a key motif of such an 'interiority' of the body is most pertinent to my interest in the sensory experience of film and the ways in which embodied vision becomes complicated through the presence of breathing.

While it is Irigaray's philosophy which prompts me to consider how the locus of breath in film orients our perception of the film experience, my contribution to the theorisation of filmic embodiment also owes a particular debt to the models of embodied spectatorship and sensuous theory offered through the work of Sobchack and the multisensory thinking and haptic theories of Laura U. Marks.[27] Both Sobchack and Marks directly engage with filmic interpretations of Merleau-Ponty's phenomenology, but I am particularly interested in how their subjective treatment of film adopts an approach to the viewing experience which closely resonates with Irigaray's critique of phenomenology and the way in which she calls upon a vision that is 'interiorly constituted',[28] to quote Catherine Vasseleu's use of the term. Indeed, the kind of inner reflection or contemplation that Irigaray writes of is precisely implicated in her philosophical treatment of the subject of breathing and its meditative connotations. Furthermore, while Marks and Sobchack do not explicitly situate their work within a feminist context, their formulation of film viewing and its appeal to the senses, especially their reflection on the sense of touch offered through Marks's model of haptic perception, calls to mind some of the strategies at work in Irigaray's texts to show how the sexed body is implicated in bodily perception. This common ground of shared interests between Irigaray, Marks and Sobchack will provide a basis for my exploration of breathing in embodied film theory.

My analyses of *Star Wars* and *Magnolia* suggest that the locus of breathing, as implied through the bodies of characters in the diegesis, is bound up with the viewer's experience of bodily trauma and mortality in film. However, the thought of Irigaray, Marks and Sobchack shapes my interest in breathing not only as it appears in the filmic diegesis, but through the formal properties of film and the apparatus itself, leading me to consider how multiple aspects of film form and the cinematic apparatus become suggestive of a breathing 'body' in addition to those that are represented by the diegetic bodies on screen. These various ways of thinking about breathing in film also open up questions about the viewer's breathing body and his or her response to the medium, as well as the diegesis. Thus, the question of the breathing body's mortality must be posed in the context of the medium, the apparatus, viewing relations and the diegesis. While we have seen how *Star Wars* and *Magnolia* evoke breathing in terms that relate to loss and mortality, the engagement with these issues that is suggested through the Western contemporary filmmaking of Atom Egoyan, David Cronenberg and Lars von Trier is especially relevant to my overarching concerns with the breathing body in film.

Before elaborating further on the specific issues of loss and mortality which lead my discussion of the films of Egoyan, Cronenberg and von Trier, it is important to acknowledge that my interest in the work of three male filmmakers might be seen to reflect Irigaray's strategy of examining patriarchal structures from the inside, as it were. While it might appear that I have deliberately drawn on the work of male directors in order to mirror Irigaray's methodology, the main reason, in fact, for my engagement with Egoyan, Cronenberg and von Trier is my fascination with their unique evocations of breathing. While I certainly do not wish to undermine the importance of sexual difference, given Irigaray's position on this issue, my interest in breath begins with the filmic diegesis and it is from this point through which questions of sexual difference will be addressed.

The films of Egoyan, Cronenberg and von Trier that I turn to in this book are Egoyan's *The Sweet Hereafter* (1997), *Felicia's Journey* (1996) and *Exotica* (1994); Cronenberg's *Spider* (2003) and *Videodrome* (1986); and von Trier's *Element of Crime* (1984), *Breaking the Waves* (1996), *Dancer in the Dark* (2000) and *The Idiots* (1998). The themes of Egoyan, Cronenberg and von Trier's films can be seen to collectively reflect on the troubling nature of loss and the public and private collapse of personal identity. Indeed, identity and the real, as well as existential, experience of mortality haunt the subject matter of Egoyan, Cronenberg and von Trier's films. While Egoyan, Cronenberg and von Trier deal with issues of loss and personal identity in separate ways and probe their subject matter through various styles and genres, their work shares an interest in pushing representational and cultural boundaries in order to delve more deeply into the nature of mortality and human experience. Each filmmaker's figuring of mortality shores up various stylistic and narrative allusions to the human body which shapes different film experiences compelled by the foregrounding of breathing. These filmic evocations of breathing not only embody what we hear but cannot see, but also prompt questions of how the filmic medium is involved in processes that may operate alongside more tangible, proximal gestures of filmic embodiment privileged by Marks and Sobchack. With the thinking of Irigaray, the films of Egoyan, Cronenberg and von Trier inspire ways to envisage the move from the strictly material to the (im)material that breathing implies, as well as enabling me to theorise the important role breath can play as part of the film experience as a whole.

In this book, questions of the role of breathing in film will be specifically posed through each facet of Irigaray's tripartite schema of spatiality, corporeality and inter-subjectivity, taking each dimension of Irigaray's thought as the overarching conceptual model for each chapter. While the first chapter shows how Irigaray's thoughts on the 'space' of air as a place of habitation bear implications for Egoyan's diegetic depiction of filmic topographies, the second chapter envisages a shift towards the gendering of breathing in Irigaray's philosophy in order to rethink the physicality of Cronenberg's formal aesthetic. The third chapter adopts the Irigarayan ethics of sharing breath in order to demonstrate how the viewer's responses to the protagonist's diegetic breathing in the films of von Trier prompt theorisation of a new viewing relation.

While the theoretical focal point of this book considers how breathing is foregrounded in film, existing scholarly analyses tend to focus on the broader implications of such a bodily process, thus avoiding fuller analyses of its implications. The next section of this introduction will present an overview of the work that has sought to think about the subject of breathing and its relevance to critical discourses in the humanities. My subsequent investment in existing analyses of breathing will then lead me to shift focus from the work of scholarly thinkers to the practice of artists whose projects reflect a key fascination and concern with the representational possibilities of breathing. My analysis of the ways in which the subject of breathing has stimulated critical thinking in the humanities and the involvement of breathing as a feature of contemporary art draws attention to the aural implications and the modes of perception that are made available through breathing. Most importantly, my foregrounding of the key issues and questions surrounding the role of breathing in art and scholarly criticism will be vital to my theorisation of its filmic possibilities.

The Place of Other Breaths: Discourses on Breath Outside of Film Theory

The wide range of ways in which the subject of breathing has been explored outside of the parameters of film studies emphasises its importance as a distinct line of enquiry that is emerging within the broader context of embodied discourse and the theorisation of the body in the arts. The existing treatments of the subject of breathing that I discuss in this section not only resonate with the expanding filmic discourses on embodied subjectivity and sensory media which have undoubtedly shaped studies of corporeality in recent years, but also show exactly how the subject of breathing illuminates the theorisation of film experience.

While this book is primarily interested in the ways in which feature films hold the potential to shape Western ideology, as my earlier discussion of *Star Wars* demonstrated, this section of my introduction argues that key critical engagements with the notion of breath are predominantly concerned with the paradoxical nature of breath as both a visual and a non-visual concept in areas of study beyond the discipline of film. Most notably, work by the cultural theorist Steven Connor suggests that the role of breath in literature is to evoke potent imagery, while the thought of Mike Lloyd considers how the figure of the swimmer and their respiring torso engenders a visible form of bodily difference.[29] However, while cultural theory offers an exploration of the subject of breathing from the broader perspective of embodiment, contemporary artists, especially those working with the medium of installation, have been inspired by the paradox of breath's oscillation between visibility and invisibility or, rather, (in)visibility: its proposal of new means in which to think about liminal and ambivalent notions of vision. Works by the Korean feminist artist Kimsooja, the British installation artist Anthony McCall and the German conceptual artist Werner Reiterer negotiate a (real, lived) space evocative of breath in order to delineate visual as well as aural textures for the perceiver's body and gaze. While the contemporary artwork of Kimsooja enables me to re-view issues of embodied sound pertinent to my theorisation of the sound of breathing, McCall prompts questions about the relationship between breath, light and colour that are applicable to the specificity of the filmic medium. Finally, Reiterer's exploration of the relations between breathing and its spatiality are resonant with the space of the cinema, as well as its representation of filmic space.

The most recent and comprehensive engagement with the subject of breathing to date is offered through Connor's cultural criticism of the social and symbolic significance of breath, developed in conjunction with his overall concern with air, recently published as *The Matter of Air: Science and Art of the Ethereal*.[30] Over the course of several substantial essays, Connor devotes his attention to breath and its peripheral, metaphysical, linguistic and mythical kinship with air, often teasing out the irreverent, subversive and magical associations with the role of air in twentieth- and twenty-first-century culture.[31] Connor's approach examines largely under-theorised tropes of the invisible such as gas, smog and ether in the Victorian novel, pointing to the relevance and centrality of air as the least solid and tangible of the elements.[32] The literary source is privileged in Connor's writings on breath, although his exploration of air also includes an address of the radio (airwaves), architecture (spaces of air) and ventriloquism (pneumatics).[33] Although it can be argued that Connor's lively and inventive treatment of breath invokes a plethora of imagery, as with his evocation of the lungs as 'windbags and skinsongs',[34] his overall project tends to be more concerned with the invisible realm, as it may be suggested through air, than its relationship with the (in)visible which I situate at the heart of my filmic discussion. Certainly, as I have emphasised in the previous section, my term '(in)visible' highlights the audio as well as visual elements that are unsettled and destabilised by the foregrounding of breath in film, an area of enquiry that remains unexplored by Connor in his analyses.

This mode of indeterminacy and oscillation, of being 'in between' visual and non-visual perception, has featured prominently in a study situated within the field of sociology. In Lloyd's article 'Life in the Slow Lane: Spectacular Body Modification', the swimmer's body is the object, and site, of subtle, physical modification as breathing alters the conditions for changes in the contours and shape of the body.[35] In his contemplation of the swimmer, Lloyd draws attention to breathing as a form of body modification that, unlike the tattoo or the piercing, relies less on the perception of dramatic changes in the appearance of the body. Change is, then, the subtle flow of breath itself where the only visible trace of difference must be observed in close-up, as it were; close enough to see the quietly alternating image of the respiring torso as it conveys movement from inside to outside, through the surfaces of the skin. Lloyd's thought underlines the possibility of registering breath as a partially visible process that is detected through very small changes in the appearance of the body.

While Lloyd highlights the significance of breathing as a physical movement that can be seen, a number of video and conceptual artists have taken this line of thought even further and have evoked breath through various imaginative and abstract visual forms. Most notably, Kimsooja's recent installation, entitled *To Breathe* (2006), invites a comparison between breathing and weaving where the object being woven is exchanged for air itself, flowing through her body or what she describes as the 'weaving factory'.[36] Kimsooja displaces the dominant mythology surrounding weaving as a form of female expression. Indeed, Kimsooja offers an example of the way in which breathing can be gendered, a key issue explored throughout Irigaray's philosophy of breath.

Kimsooja's haunting, beautiful piece places emphasis on the female body as itself a ubiquitous site of creation repossessed through breathing and refusing its commodification through labour. The installation consists of a projection of colour which is accompanied by the sound of Kimsooja's breathing, employing a 'textural' aurality in which the voice symbolises a weaving tool. The projected spectrum of colours corresponds with the quivering sonic frequencies of Kimsooja's breath, but it is the use of sound which ultimately shapes the viewer's perception of the piece. Indeed, during her discussion of the work featured on her website, Kimsooja describes breath as a material object – an 'invisible needle'[37] – which threads through flesh and exterior world, a movement emphasised by the projection of colours which are manipulated and distorted by the vocal intensity of the piece. Kimsooja's comparison of breath with a needle, a tool which implements creation, also calls to mind the Greek notion of *technë*, a concept based upon understanding the value of craftsmanship, not only as an activity but as a 'manner of knowing', as Sobchack writes: a bringing forth of a greater truth.[38] Kimsooja's 'needle' of breath informs a view of *technë* as a 'practice' of carnality, an assertion of the self, and of the body, as an instrument of truth itself. Furthermore, it is the human, breathing voice which heralds such enlightenment. Unlike the *Star Wars* merchandise whose pleasure lies in replicating 'scary' sounds from the movie, Kimsooja subverts the commodification of a (literally) labouring, breathing body by transplanting it to a theatre, an arena for the production of art rather than objects, emphasising the embodied subjectivity of the women working in the factories of Kimsooja's homeland.

As with Kimsooja's elegant reflections on bodily noise and self-expression, my own endeavour to understand the significance of breathing and its Irigarayan resonances with selfhood will lead me to trace several links between vocality and breath throughout this book. For Roland Barthes in his 1977 publication *Image, Music, Text*, the grain of the voice is the materiality of the body speaking its mother tongue.[39] Yet, although breath is acknowledged by Barthes as an aspect of the voice, it is not included in his *tangible* notion of vocality. Kimsooja's invocation of weaving suggests the 'tangibility' of breath, and air, likening it to a kind of fabric. My interest is in how the filmic medium can provoke, further still, a tangible dimension of breath that might also be ordered by the gendered body in film.

While Kimsooja's *To Breathe* utilises the ornate design of Venice's opera house La Fenice in order to demonstrate the changes which occur when she breathes within a particular space, the interactive work of Reiterer organises space as a kind of breathing room or 'chamber' that is not 'empty' but rather full of potential encounters. Reiterer's *Breath* (2006) makes full use of the space of Paris's Pompidou Centre where it was originally installed, asking the viewer to breathe 'on' various panels which in turn, through the use of sensors, cause a change in the lighting or colour of the room.[40] Breathing thus prompts a visual response, but unlike Kimsooja's projection of colour which emphasises the intense vibrations of her breathing, Reiterer's installation depends upon the interaction of the viewer, whose breathing body becomes involved in the process of creation.

While Reiterer's installation encourages the viewer to think about their own breathing in order to involve themselves in the creation of art, another example of breathing as an interactive feature of contemporary art is implied by McCall in his installation *A Line Describing a Cone* (1973).[41] Unlike the changes in light that are activated by the viewer's breathing in Reiterer's installation, light is the very medium through which air is foregrounded by McCall and its presence is one that appeals to the inquisitive viewer whose body intermingles with the space it creates. On screen, McCall's film projects a small dot which then becomes a line before finally arching into a circle. While the image of the increasing circle is shown throughout the duration of the film, a beam of (spherical) light emerges between the projector and screen – a 'cone' formed through particles in the air illuminated by the projector. While McCall's work calls to mind the very nature of the filmic apparatus and its dependence on light in order to project images, it also draws attention to the space of air. Certainly, as the title of my book suggests, spatiality will be a central concern in what follows and will emphasise the importance of place, namely the elemental 'place' of air, as well as its significance as a real, lived environment. However, while Reiterer, Kimsooja and McCall attempt to situate breathing within a partially visible context (Reiterer's panels sensitive to breathing, Kimsooja's colourful light display, McCall's solid light film), it is not breath itself which we view during their pieces, but rather the pieces present to us some *sense* of it.

While the contemporary art work of Kimsooja, McCall and Reiterer emphasises the range of visual and aural possibilities that breathing suggests within the context of the visual arts, the theoretical studies offered by Connor and Lloyd provide useful contexts in which to situate my own analysis of breathing.

The particular modes of visuality pertinent to breathing that were explored throughout this section will be reconsidered in the next section in order to focus on the embodied discourses in film theory that are specifically involved in my theorisation of a filmic visuality of breath. Most notably, Kimsooja, McCall and Reiterer's art prompt interactive responses from its viewers, but such an invitation is framed differently by the filmic medium and this, above all, bears implications for the way in which breath is involved in the film experience. The work of Marks and Sobchack orients my discussion of breathing towards the specificity of visual perception that film offers us, especially as embodied viewers. Their work on the nature of embodied film viewing illuminates and complicates notions of visuality, which tend to oscillate between seeing and *sensing*, and the ways in which the viewer's body responds to film.

Inherited Places: Engaging with Sobchack and Marks

Such rich and stimulating works within visual art and cultural studies provide essential thinking in order to approach the subject of breathing in the cinema, particularly with respect to the positioning of this act within a visual economy. Furthermore, these works are particularly pertinent since they offer precious insight into the possibility of theorising the visuality of breathing in filmic terms. The main trajectory of this section explores Sobchack's concept of the 'film's body' and her citation of the apparatus as a breathing subjectivity which effectively serves to introduce breath to the medium itself. Drawing on more recent work, Sobchack's latest thoughts on breath and her neologism of the *cinesthetic subject* also propose important questions regarding the embodied viewer. While Sobchack's thought leads me to consider the film viewer's breathing body, the second half of this section draws on the recent haptic enquiry offered through the work of Marks. The Marksian concept of *haptic visuality* raises questions about acts of visuality and proximal relations which breath complicates through its resonances with sound and bodily intimacy.

Sobchack has not dedicated an entire article to the role of breath in the context of embodied film theory, but it is clear that breathing is implicitly in her thoughts, from her earliest work on the reversible dialectics of embodied vision between film and viewer to her present critical shift towards 'carnal thought' and sensual cinema. Most importantly, Sobchack's phenomenological rethinking of the filmic apparatus usefully likens its material mechanism to a figural, breathing 'body' in her seminal book *The Address of the Eye*.[42] While Sobchack's earlier work, then, focuses on the apparatus, her recent work draws more on the nature of the image itself, developing a view that also reflects on transcendence and the viewer's subjectivity. In her article 'Embodying Transcendence: On the Literal, the Material and the Filmic Sublime', Sobchack makes important links between heightened, embodied viewing and breath, reflecting on a kind of filmic, breathing consciousness.[43] Sobchack's thought on consciousness and the breathing body specifically calls to mind Irigaray's philosophical position on breath, especially its spiritual associations. Furthermore, Sobchack's conceptualisation of the apparatus as a differentiated, breathing body opens up questions of materiality, rhythms and temporality, as well as formal suggestions of breath, all of which must be addressed prior to any further discussion of diegetic concerns if we are to first acknowledge the very specificity of the medium itself.

In *The Address of the Eye*, Sobchack's theorisation of the 'film's body' marks an important shift in thinking beyond the literal image of the body within the film's diegesis: 'the "film's body" is not visible in the film except for its intentional agency and diacritical motion'.[44] This filmic 'body' possesses its own anatomy, for Sobchack, and this is made most evident in her comparison of cinema's shuffling flow of images to a 'breathing body',[45] its rhythmic articulation according with a respiratory process:

> Indeed, we could liken the regular but intermittent passage of images into and out of the film's material body (through camera and projector) to human respiration or circulation, the primary bases upon which human animation and being are grounded. The lungs fill and collapse before they fill again. The valves of the heart open and shut and open again. Both respiration and circulation of blood are not continuous but segmented and rhythmic activities.[46]

Sobchack suggests that images are like a continuous flow of oxygen, their flickering vitality each like an individual breath flowing into and out of the 'body' of the filmic apparatus.[47] Images are drawn into the apparatus's actual corpus (mechanisms and spools which celluloid pulses through) and 'exhaled' both on to the screen and out of its internal mechanisms. Most importantly, Sobchack's thoughts on breathing relate to the technological specificity of the apparatus.

Sobchack's acknowledgement of breath and the bloodstream accomplishes a substantial leap in Film Studies, exploring the philosophical resonances between sight, envisioned being and the embodied subject in film through the phenomenological thought of Merleau-Ponty. While the images which Sobchack suggestively designates as 'breaths' in the 'film's body' take into account the film itself as part of the apparatus's embodied subjectivity, a close consideration of such 'breaths' may lead to questions surrounding the filmic diegesis, as well as the apparatus itself. Surely, if one is to consider breathing, one must also consider the conditions, terms and specificity of each diegetic moment. While *The Place of Breath in Cinema* is concerned with the presence of breath within images, that is, in the films themselves, film's formal attributes, the materiality of the images themselves, and the technical processes of film are also important to my analysis and the questions I will pose regarding the viewer's positioning as a differentiated breathing body.

While Sobchack posits a theory of the materiality of filmic mechanisms and their suggestion of a 'breathing' body, her recent work in 'Embodying

Transcendence' gestures towards a kind of heightened, embodied consciousness felt by the viewer, resonating within their own, breathing body. Drawing on the closing moments of *The Last Temptation of Christ* (Martin Scorsese, 1988), Sobchack observes a connection between breathing, the experienced vision of abstract patterns of colour and light, and her body's response to such visual impressions:

> This figural strategy finds its sensual correspondence in what is perhaps the least material regime of corporeality: the contraction and expansion of breath. Felt sensually on the cinesthetic subject's body, respiration—the expansion and yet aching constriction of the chest, suspended and thus swelling breath—thus becomes phenomenologically transfigured as the expansion of being, as spiritual uplift, indeed as inspiration . . . I have not suggested a programmatic or deterministic use of the sensual correlations between the cinesthetic subject and filmic figuration but, instead, simply heightened awareness of their myriad—and ever dynamic and context bound—sensual possibilities.[48]

Sobchack's recent thought constitutes an important shift away from the apparatus and towards the figural relations produced on screen: these take us towards the diegetic and formal attributes of the film with which I am more concerned. While I am interested in the filmic diegesis, I also want to draw attention to the way in which film's formal attributes can become suggestive of breathing, especially the rhythms of editing techniques, composition, colour and camera movement. Furthermore, I also want to examine film's materiality such as its graininess, which is the focal point of Marks's analysis. My definition of the 'film's body' synthesises both Marks's and Sobchack's analyses, taking into account the formal attributes of the image and the materiality of the film itself; this approach allows me to examine the filmic medium in its entirety.

While Sobchack's argument rests on correlations between figural, formal attributes of the image and the breath of the viewer, she is careful not to frame it in particularly material terms, acknowledging breath as 'the least material regime of the body'.[49] For Sobchack, filmic abstraction, as offered through her example from *The Last Temptation of Christ*, suggests a dimension of the film experience in which breath can be literally and suggestively felt or 'sensed' by the viewer or rather, in her case, 'on the cinesthetic subject's body'[50] – her neologism which suggests that film viewing is not only organised through embodied sight but also informed by the knowledge of the other senses. Indeed, Sobchack describes the cinesthetic subject as a viewer who not only *has* a body but *is* a body and, through an embodied vision, is informed by the knowledge of the other senses.[51] Thus, Sobchack's kind of 'breathing', a form of embodied sight, takes place at an interval between representation and meaning; it is in between such relations, but it is also undeniably part of a visual regime, thus inviting further questions regarding the visuality of breath. Although Sobchack's thought introduces her neologism of the cinesthetic subject to the notion of breathing, it is still unclear how breathing might serve the senses or, indeed, operate *prior* to sensation. Such complexities of inter-sensorial being and the nuanced fleshing out of embodied breathing must be further examined in order to truly estimate the potential of breath as a filmic, embodied gesture. For example, to recall Merleau-Ponty's exemplary metaphor for illuminating his concept of 'flesh' or lived experience,[52] we see our hands in front of our eyes prior to seeing the world they are placed before. If I enact this example, raising my hands to eye level, arms outstretched, and breathe deeply in and out, my hands will also feel the rise of my chest and move gently, in accordance with my breaths: this is the relation between vision, sensation and breathing which must be explored further. Embodied sight is always already lived through a breathing body and I am interested in film's potential to remind us of this fact, as well as to encourage us to think beyond its literal meaning.

Eight years after Sobchack's groundbreaking work in *The Address of the Eye*, Marks's phenomenological treatment of the film experience places special emphasis on intercultural relations, the senses and memory to articulate epistemological concerns regarding the communication of knowledge embedded in the senses. Building again on the thought of Merleau-Ponty but also, more crucially, engaging with the post-structuralist thinking of Gilles Deleuze and Félix Guattari, Marks's writing on cinema, especially diasporic filmmaking, embodiment and the senses uncovers traces of the emotive potential of film in a way that might be regarded more as a study of intimacy than a general response to the sensuousness of film.[53] The valuable thinking Marks brings to phenomenological film theory is primarily her adoption of haptics as a concept that she emphasises as richly applicable to the cinema. Marks's approach borrows from existing haptic discourses, namely that of Deleuze and Guattari's thought on the *optical image* and *smooth space*,[54] as well as the formalist thinking of Alois Riegl,[55] in order to conceive of the term 'haptic visuality': a mode of seeing that responds to the texture of the image. For Marks, this mode of vision occurs when 'the eyes themselves function like organs of touch'[56] and thus it is not only the image of a body that is considered, but rather the image itself as a sensuous object. Embodied knowledge is embedded in the senses. A film image might, then, communicate embodied 'thoughts' in a way that corresponds with psychoanalytic discourse, as a pre-linguistic, pre-symbolic exchange, but such psychical ramifications are not Marks's main concern. For Marks, the haptic is characterised by an interplay of surfaces which comes to stand for 'the skin of the film', a movement in which 'all our self rushes up to the surface to interact with another surface'.[57] Yet breathing is not only felt on the surface of things, as Lloyd's example of the swimmer's breathing torso suggests: breathing engenders a form of bodily difference from the *inside* as one breath is inhaled and another exhaled.

Marks's model of film viewing emphasises touch as an embodied exchange between viewer and image that takes place on the surface of things, but my work envisages this point of contact according to the ways in which breathing unsettles borders between the inside and outside. Importantly, breathing suggests a relationship with the image that involves the *mind* of the viewer as well as the body. This new dimension of film viewing is articulated through my analysis of diegetic and non-diegetic proximal relations, evocations of air as a place within the image, either through the sound of the human body (breath as a different aspect of vocality), silence and interpretations of 'emptiness' or the elemental as an ambient presence within the mise en scène. If, as Daniel Frampton argues of his conceptual approach to film thinking, 'the idea, the "filmosophy", is to ask what the images and sounds are saying',[58] then my attentiveness to breathing questions not only what the film is showing us as a 'breathing encounter', but also what we, as breathing human beings, are mimetically, ontologically sharing with the film. A visuality that accords with breath refers to the relations that exist between human subjects and films, as shifting and fluid as breath itself.

Crucially, my theoretical model differs from Marks's since her work tends to privilege the image over the soundtrack, a 'silence' which is also acutely felt in Sobchack's work. As we have seen in my discussion of *Star Wars*, sound is a vital aspect of my conceptualisation of breathing in film and my interest in Marks's haptic visuality lies in her focus on close-range vision which I rethink in terms of close-range sound and the viewer's aural proximity to film. Marks's treatment of Shauna Beharry's *Seeing Is Believing*[59] focuses on imbalances between sound and image which do have an impact upon the ways in which haptic visuality is produced, but ultimately her argument foregrounds the visual rather than sonic implications of such imbalances. In her analysis, Marks draws attention to the photographed folds of a sari belonging to Beharry's recently deceased mother which are looked at 'ever more closely'[60] by the camera. While Beharry's voice describes the difficulty of mourning, of remembering her mother through such images, it is the camera, for Marks, that gestures towards a way in which it is possible to remember, conveying the tactile memory of the mother's skin (recalled through her sari), moving over the lush fabric as if to brush over it, evoking an embodied memory through touch that her words, her voice, cannot even begin to express. Marks's haptic visuality thus 'emphasises a disparity between the searching movements of the camera and Beharry's wishful voice on the soundtrack'.[61] My model of thought draws attention to a different kind of disparity that takes place between the audio and visual image created through breath, as well as exploring possible concordances registered through both the image and sound of breathing. While the applicability of Marks's model to breathing, filmic encounters will certainly be tested during the course of this book, my model's increasing investment in issues of sound will inevitably prompt a shift away from haptic visuality and towards 'haptic hearing', reconciling the act of listening to the proximal gestures of touch which pervade Marks's thinking.

While Marks's and Sobchack's thoughts on the embodied nature of film viewing raise questions about the inscription of the body in the film experience that are essential to my theorisation of breathing in film, my concerns with film sound and the foregrounding of breath in the space of the film also require me to pay particular attention to narrative and the way in which it informs the aesthetic of each film I analyse. Indeed, in addition to film form, my interest in the locus of breathing in film places special emphasis on the film's content, the filmic diegesis and the film's mise en scène.

As we have seen in my analysis of *Star Wars*, the content of the film functions as a space in which to diegetically embed the breathing body, namely the concretely visible bodies of the film's subjects as embodied by the performance of the actors on screen. Importantly, I have suggested how the sound of breathing contributes towards the viewer's experience and their engagement with the film's content. Yet questions still remain about the relationship between filmic subjectivity and the role of filmic, breathing subjectivity. The next section will show how the content of the film is pertinent to the locus of breath in the film experience.

'The Sound of Thought Itself': The Place of Territory and Voices

Star Wars and *Magnolia* have shown us that film foregrounds breathing in ways that are not exclusive to one particular genre or specific style of filmmaking. Indeed, the meaning attached to the locus of breath changes according to the specificity of the film, its diegetic content as well as its style, and the narrative context through which it is evoked. In this section, a range of genres and experimental cinemas is analysed from the perspective of the notable presence or foregrounding of breath in the diegesis of the film. In the previous section it was made clear that the presence of breathing in the filmic diegesis is not independent of any other object within the image since it 'insinuates itself'[62] within the very presence of other signifiers and, consequently, this bears implications for the viewer's experience of the mise en scène. The filmic examples discussed in this section are necessary in order to consider the most notable ways in which breathing 'surfaces' in film. Yet, while this section's textual analyses enable me to explain how breathing is involved in the diegetic aspects of the film experience, what emerges through this analysis is the question of subjectivity that foreshadows some of the most significant examples I discuss, leading me to think beyond the filmic representation of breathing and towards the mind and body of the breathing subject that is the focus of Irigaray's philosophy.

This section will first analyse formal as well as pictorial and figural evocations of breath in the mise en scène of the science fiction genre, drawing especially on the filmed environment of air and the suggestion of space that the role of breath tends to foreground. While *Star Wars* has shown us how sound is used effectively to gesture towards the presence of breathing, this section will explore the possibility of seeing breath beyond the microscopic images of lungs in *Magnolia*. While I evaluate the 'sight' of breath according to its increasingly emotive potential, the heard and not seen presence of breath is then explored in relation to the horror genre. Earlier, I suggested that the horror genre, especially the 'haunted house' movie, invariably suggests figures whose physical absence is central to the diegesis – the haunted space depends upon the figure of the ghost – but my treatment of Wes Craven's *Scream* (1996) and Jonathan Demme's *The Silence of the Lambs* (1992) will explore the significance of breathing as it calls into play a different kind of unsettling filmic experience invested in absences and the unseen. I continue to examine the way in which breathing accords with a kind of strangeness, drawing on the pictorial and sonic rendering of breath in David Lynch's psychological drama *Blue Velvet* (1986).

Alternatively, the films of Chris Marker and Wim Wenders, notably *La Jetée* (Marker, 1962) and *Wings of Desire* (Wenders, 1987), seem to evoke breath in ways that are more complexly woven through the diegesis and formal gestures, especially editing and the indication of off-screen space. The final concerns of this section draw attention to the technological advancements in film which effect changes in the way that breath emerges through the diegesis, drawing on the use of digital sound in two recent films: *Zidane: A 21st Century Portrait* (Douglas Gordon and Philippe Parreno, 2006) and *Rosetta* (Jean-Pierre and Luc Dardenne, 1999).

Returning to issues of genre posed implicitly through my earlier exploration of *Star Wars*, air, as well as breathing, is frequently alluded to in the science fiction film, particularly through its thematic reference to the air-lock or lack of oxygen, as well as in the horror genre's exploitation of heavy breathing, silence and the repression and final release of the scream. The air-lock, an airless chamber, is a prominent feature of the science fiction film. Protagonists of the science fiction genre are often fated to be sealed inside such a space, forced to endure the effects of decompression, if not suffocation, in films such as *Supernova* (Walter Hill, 1999) and *Event Horizon* (Paul W. S. Anderson, 1997) where each slow and violent death is graphically conveyed to the viewer. The pressure chamber also appears in numerous well-known canonical science fiction films such as *2001: A Space Odyssey* (Stanley Kubrick, 1968) and the *Alien* series,[63] often signifying a potential threat of entrapment and death. Indeed, the threat of suffocation is thoroughly evoked in the *Alien* films, where the parasitic 'face-hugger' attaches itself to its victim so as to pacify and appropriate their silent body. Here, the image of passive suffocation is consumed by the viewer as iconic spectacle, Kane's (John Hurt) body functioning as a vessel for incubation where his mouth is a site of entry that fuses with the body of the alien. While the quest to find supplies of oxygen is also a recurring theme in recent films such as *Sunshine* (Danny Boyle, 2007) and *Stranded* (María Lidón, 2002), it is a form of poison in Andrei Tarkovsky's classic science fiction film *Solyaris* (1972), when the lead protagonist's lover Hari (Natalya Bondarchuk) attempts to commit suicide by drinking it in its liquid form. Indeed, the irony of *Solyaris* is that oxygen is used to extinguish life rather than sustain it.

If science fiction cinema is preoccupied with oxygen then the horror genre's foregrounding of breath is defined in terms that relate to a rather more emotional expression, or what could be understood as a heightened emotional realism. Filmed in a knowingly post-modern fashion (a notable characteristic of Craven's film and television work), *Scream* opens with a telephone conversation taking place between a murderer and his victim. As the initially playful tone of the discussion becomes increasingly fraught, the viewer's awareness of Casey's (Drew Barrymore) quickening breath increases. Craven limits his use of ambient sound in order to create a tense atmosphere and snatches of dialogue appear to be punctuated with the sound not only of Casey's breathing body but of the murderer's body, heard as a mere whisper on the end of the telephone line. Casey's final scream is literally cut short as the murderer severs her vocal cords, thus the earlier sound of her breathing is even more poignant since it emphasises her fragile embodiment of a corporeal subjectivity. While Craven opens his film with the sound of breathing, *The Silence of the Lambs* presents an almost unbearably tense dénouement set within the home of the murderer where Clarice Starling's (Jodie Foster) breathing is the only sound heard as she treads through a dark pit, viewed only partially through night-vision surveillance goggles. The film's poster also evokes the iconography of suffocation, recalling the alien's attack of Kane's face in *Alien*, with its central image of Foster whose mouth is obscured by a moth (the moth is a central motif of the film, but its head is here made up of numerous naked figures in order to resemble a skull). The spiritual realm also possesses a relationship with breathing in William Friedkin's *The Exorcist* (1973), where the sound as well as image of Regan's breathing body conveys the lapses between herself and the spirit that has entered her: breath is, then, the soul that is split in Friedkin's film and resonates with the presence of the other, the unseen. Overall, breathing in the horror film is much more bound up with issues of affect than the science fiction genre, with the exception of *Star Wars*. Although both genres foreground the breathing body within their mise en scène, the horror film does not refer explicitly to breathing, unlike the science fiction film through its thematic concern with oxygen, and therefore what surfaces is a filmic experience that is *felt* within both the mind and body of the viewer.

A particular manifestation of breathing that cannot easily be categorised within generic conventions is David Lynch's *Blue Velvet*. The film has been described as the representation of an 'Oedipal Netherworld' by Mulvey and her analysis draws on the film's central themes of transgression and forbidden desire, but the bizarre, ritualistic performance of male sexuality tests the limits of perversion suggested through Oedipal discourse.[64] Although much has been made of the film from a psychoanalytic perspective, a focus on breathing registers a different concern which might be more appropriate to my interest in embodied discourses. The male protagonist Frank (Dennis Hopper) holds Dorothy (Isabella Rossellini) captive in the confines of his apartment. When the young male protagonist Jeffrey (Kyle MacLachlan) follows Dorothy one evening he is forced to hide inside a closet and watch Frank asphyxiate on amyl nitrate, an erotic stimulant that precedes a masochistic sexual encounter with Dorothy. The plastic, misted gas mask that Frank holds up to his gasping face many times throughout his encounter with Dorothy is an object within the mise en scène which literally shows Frank's breathing materialise as well as affecting a shift on the audio track as his voice becomes muffled and extremely unnatural. Recalling, yet in more ambiguous and perverse terms, the inhuman suggestion of breathing in *Star Wars*, one can argue, then, that the strangeness of *Blue Velvet* also owes a considerable amount to its foregrounding of breath.[65] Indeed, 'breath', or the singular notion of breathing, tends to relate to an isolated moment in film, as my analysis of *Blue Velvet* suggests, while 'breathing' refers to a series of moments or a plurality that is ongoing and, often, a trope of the film.

The plurality of breathing or rather the sound of a whisper, diluted and obscured to the point of being neither speech nor gasp, is also evoked as a kind of strange or notable foreignness, a trope which turns the bodies of the film inside out in Wim Wenders's *Wings of Desire* and Chris Marker's *La Jetée*. In Wenders's *Wings of Desire*, angels are impassive observers, walking the streets of Berlin unseen and able to listen to the multiplicity of thoughts and desires of mortals. In one scene, the angel Damiel (Bruno Ganz) enters a library and, through its silence, hears only the pure thoughts (and breaths) of those present within its space. Breath is conveyed through the soundtrack as a whisper that also accords with the sound of thought itself: a kind of inner consciousness. The inside is *outside* of the image, as it were. In my earlier analysis of the dynamic use of breath in the art of Kimsooja, the body becomes an instrument of truth where breath compels an enlightened perception; Wenders's film offers a community of bodies or chorus of breathing voices whose subjectivity is, in a sense, objectified: implying the fascinated 'hearing-body' of the angel Damiel. Certainly, given Wenders's emphasis on Damiel's closed eyes when entering the library, audition is paramount to this scene and perhaps, given his inability to touch the living, the breathing voices might offer access to a different kind of sensory pleasure.

The whispers of *Wings of Desire* are articulated through sharp intakes of breath and sighs, but in *La Jetée* such vocal exhalations represent not the interiority of a community, as in the library of Wenders's film, but the embodied trauma of a man whose thoughts are being used in an experiment to 'give birth' to a new future after the devastation of a nuclear holocaust. A collective of voices, representing the scientists who snatch the protagonist from his dreams, is conveyed as a layered aural presence on the soundtrack. We hear German-language whispers, recalling the occupation of World War II, that are amplified through Marker's still photography of images embodying a blinking gaze, as if waking from consciousness. While the unnerving heartbeat of Marker's editor Jean Ravel plays over the image-track, reminding us of the examination of humanity at the heart of Marker's film, the whispers of *La*

Jetée embed a different kind of tension in the film experience, conveying the uncanny sound of a familiar yet undesired external reality.

La Jetée signals a specific shift from the 'representation' of breathing to the 'feeling' of breathing and its sensorial concordances. The visuality of Marker's film plays with notions of temporality and the dream-like qualities of cinema through its use of monochrome photographic stills, embodied movements in time which appear to disintegrate before our eyes, breaths and whispers rousing us from this slumber. *La Jetée* complicates its foregrounding of filmic and spectatorial subjectivity, issues which are pertinent to my theorisation of the place of breath in film. The whispers and their breathing noises work in tandem with the medium itself, becoming intertwined with the diegetic bodies on screen so as to enfold each other in a shared, breathing 'consciousness'. However, while *La Jetée*'s particular engagement with breath as it surfaces precisely through aurality, diegesis and film form works to complicate our perception of the filmed subjects, it offers only a handful of moments in which to analyse the role of breath in film, limiting its usefulness to the concerns of this book.

While *La Jetée* highlights the analogue workings of the filmic apparatus through the aurality and synchronicity of breath, film's digital evolution almost eradicates such formal gestures and replaces them with distinctly sonic possibilities. In *Zidane: A 21st Century Portrait* experimental filmmakers Douglas Gordon and Philippe Parreno set up seventeen cameras to follow Real Madrid footballer Zinedine Zidane through the course of an average game. The detail of such images, including many close-ups, is stunning, but it is the sound which sets it apart from any other digital photography. The combination of silence, movement and deep breathing, the tap of a booted heel on the ball, a hand wiping away sweat from a damp forehead, produces a remarkable, contemplative cinema – a cinema of extra-materiality produced through noise.[66] While Gordon and Parreno's contemporary portraiture offers a particularly gendered depiction of a filmic, breathing body (a strange, paradoxical combination of warrior and ethereal deity), Jean-Pierre and Luc Dardenne's film *Rosetta* evokes a far more subtle portrayal of a youthful energy. The grainy images of the Dardennes' hand-held aesthetic combined with the use of Dolby SR, a digital process which improves the dynamic range of analogue recordings, draw attention to the sound and vibrant image of a constantly moving, breathing body. The troubled yet impassioned Rosetta (Émilie Dequenne) is filmed moving through desolate urban landscapes and claustrophobic interiors; her struggle and will to survive despite an overwhelming sense of being uninvited and unwanted is encapsulated through the sheer vitality of her filmed body. Above all, Rosetta's restless movement is underscored by the haunting sound of her breathing escaping her body as if it were the beating of wings slowly faltering, weakened and imprinted partially in the air, a sound that keeps each moment alive in our minds.[67] The highly mobile cinematography might track Rosetta's relentless motion in a way that evokes the very conditions of her fraught existence, but the soundtrack also reveals an important state of bodily consciousness that should not be ignored. I will return later to the significance of digital technology to the foregrounding of breath in film, particularly in the cinema of von Trier, but it is also necessary to suggest how the sound of breathing is present in more conventional technologies of cinema.

Although such moments that take place in film excite interest in breathing and prompt further discussion, what is generated through each foregrounding of breath in the films I have discussed ultimately offers limited scope for reflection. This is to say that one cannot discuss films such as *Scream*, *Wings of Desire* and *The Silence of the Lambs* as thoroughly evocative of breath throughout: they offer concrete, diegetic examples of breathing in film, but they do not position it consistently, integrally, within their visual and aural economy. My interest is in films that articulate breathing through both their form and content, as a filmic condition that amplifies as well as transcends the narrative level of discourse. Furthermore, it would seem that breathing is connected to a form of filmic subjectivity that requires a theoretical model with which to analyse it. In order to take this discussion further and begin to construct a model of thought, it is necessary to focus more closely on the issues of subjectivity, thought and consciousness that have arisen through my analysis of film and the way in which these issues are also vital to Irigaray's philosophy of breath and her particular emphasis on the gendered, breathing body.

Irigaray's 'Le temps du souffle'

A number of questions that were raised in the previous section concerned the role of breath as an aspect of human subjectivity or interior consciousness, as well as the particular space of air as a fundamental aspect of being. Irigaray's philosophy of breath provides a highly appropriate context in which to explore such questions further. This section offers an overview of the phenomenological concepts and theoretical contexts that will be crucial to the way in which I engage with Irigaray's *Le temps du souffle* (*The Age of the Breath*) and its framing of human subjectivity.[68] While I trace the origins of Irigaray's thoughts on breathing, this section's introduction to Irigaray's *Le temps du souffle* will lead me to examine questions of the sexed body, gendered subjectivity and embodied thought that are newly established through Irigaray's conceptualisation of breathing. Finally, this section will engage with existing scholarly work on Irigaray's philosophy of sexual difference in film theory and the life-affirming, positive reflections on Irigaray's thinking through of sexed subjectivity which I intend to build upon during my theorisation of the place of breath in cinema.

In her 1983 volume *The Forgetting of Air*, Irigaray develops an important stage in her overarching project of sexual difference where the elemental nature of air, a different kind of invisible presence, also corresponds with a particularly feminine form of being.[69] Following *The Forgetting of Air* – Irigaray's phenomenological engagement with air – she develops several subsequent and distinct philosophical enquiries into breathing that are explored in her texts 'The Way of Breath', *Being Two: How Many Eyes Have We?*, *A Breath that Touches in Words*, *Everyday Prayers* and, most importantly, *The Age of the Breath*.[70] In these particular texts, Irigaray is concerned not only with the significance of air as a metaphysical construct, but with the way in which air has been absented and overlooked in Western culture and this leads her to re-examine her notion of subjectivity as one that is always already constituted by its relationship with air and breathing. Irigaray's deconstructive criticism of Heidegger relates forgetting not to an assumed psychological amnesia, but to a phenomenological and thus 'bodily' forgetting that her work aims to counter. Breathing, for Irigaray, thus evokes a kind of 'embodied thought' which recalls our autonomous existence in the world we live in.

Irigaray's philosophy of breath inherits much from her earlier phenomenological engagements with the thinking of Merleau-Ponty and Levinas in which she invokes a strategy of poetic mimicry in order to mirror the formal characteristics of the philosophical text brought into question. Indeed, Irigaray inhabits the 'breath' of philosophers she questions and undermines their linguistic integrity through her deconstruction of their syntax, pauses and tonality. Although these texts were written before Irigaray developed her philosophy of breath, her critiques of Merleau-Ponty and Levinas implicitly inform key concerns which will be the focus of *The Place of Breath in Cinema*. Irigaray's critique of Merleau-Ponty establishes a 'tangible intimacy', emphasising touch as a feminine form of contact that is felt without reference to the visible, while her dialogue with Levinas draws on a different phenomenological implication of touch through her work on the concept of the 'caress'.[71] It is through such earlier texts that Irigaray begins to affirm breath, taking her concept of the 'caress' to its fullest conclusion; she offers a valuable way in which to theorise both a 'tangible invisible' space and 'caress' that, as Vasseleu remarks, is 'not so much a touch as it is the gesture of touch'.[72] Indeed, several of Irigaray's texts directly relate breathing to a kind of caress, a 'touching upon in words',[73] in speech that presents many new possibilities for the discussion of sound and image and the weaving of breath as an 'aural texture' in the cinema. Yet breathing is not the same as touching, it is involved in embodied sensation, and to only speak of a caress when contemplating breathing limits our understanding of respiration. Therefore a new vocabulary is required in order to articulate the tactile or sensual nature of air. While my terms (in)visible and (im)material help me to specify the different contexts of embodied vision that breathing is implicated in, I also adopt the term 'breathing corporeality' in order to reflect Irigaray's specific theorisation of the breathing body.

Irigaray's philosophy of breath sharply contrasts with the modern French thought of Gaston Bachelard in his book *Air and Dreams* and Jean-François Lyotard's essay 'Scapeland' from his 1992 book *The Inhuman*.[74] While both

Bachelard and Lyotard develop theoretical approaches to breathing that are suggestive of anxieties and bear negative implications, Irigaray's *Le temps du souffle* is an enlightened contemplation of breathing. Although Irigaray's philosophical treatment of breathing might be criticised for its utopian ideology, her concern with the issue of preserving selfhood and restoring one's autonomy through breathing offers a vital way in which to re-view questions of identity, selfhood and the embodied and sensory nature of existence that are key to current critical discourses in the humanities.

For Irigaray, breathing is not sensuous *per se*, but part of an embodied subjectivity that flows between the senses of the body. Breath also comes to embody a natural temporality of the body as well as a silent interiority that is particularly pertinent to my exploration of breath in the cinema. Furthermore, Irigaray's contemplation of breathing as a spiritual dimension of being also presents questions about the immaterial and the transcendental in the cinema, with respect to an immaterial presence that has resonances with belief. Irigaray's most significant work on breathing other than *The Forgetting of Air* is her later text *The Age of the Breath*, a work that explicitly addresses a futurity made possible through an especially spiritual cultivation of breath. Although framed and contextualised by Irigaray's principal concerns with sexual difference as set out in the early work of *Speculum*, this 'age' or culture of breathing in many ways stages a phenomenological encounter that moves towards a new culture of difference still informed by the sexed body, but also inclusive of a third space: air as a fundamental mode of being for both the masculine and feminine subject.[75] Air thus fulfils a mediatory role between the sexes; in simpler terms, it engenders a positive space within which to live. Indeed, Irigaray's philosophy contends that the sharing of breath between men and women is more fundamental than the idea of exchangeable words, developing thought on the philosophical concept of breath as well as a practical way in which to address real, lived, subjective experience. Furthermore, Irigaray's thought draws attention to the shared breath between mother and child, an intrauterine sharing of oxygen that occurs even before birth. This Irigarayan sharing of breath will lead me to question the subject of the child in the films I discuss and the relationship between breathing subjects on screen, as well as the viewer's breathing body, especially where the foregrounding of breath relates to more than one body in the film. As we shall see, the figuring of the child will be important to my treatment of Egoyan, Cronenberg and von Trier's cinema and the role childhood plays in questioning key issues such as loss and the subjective notion of mortality.

Many existing film analyses engaging with the thinking of Irigaray focus specifically on filmic representations of women made by female filmmakers. Although such treatments of both Irigaray's work and the films themselves offer stimulating models of thought, they also tend to seal off possibilities that might have otherwise been open for thinking about the male subject.[76] This book not only theorises the male subject in the cinema, but also suggests, through breath, a form of embodiment that might relate to both sexes in separate ways. In exploring the relationship between the sexes in the films I examine, I work towards the notion of sharing breath as it is suggested on screen and also through viewing relations which underscore a kinship between the breathing body of the viewer and the locus of breath in the filmic diegesis.

One notable exception of an Irigarayan critic whose filmic analysis explicitly involves reflection on both sexes is found in the recent work of Lucy Bolton. Although Bolton's reading of female consciousness in her article 'The Camera as Speculum: Examining Female Consciousness in *Lost in Translation*, Using the Thought of Luce Irigaray'[77] concludes with an emphasis on the female subject, Charlotte (Scarlett Johansson), it is most striking that Bolton also affirms the male subject of the film, Bob (Bill Murray), whose friendship has a positive effect on the female's renewed selfhood. Bolton writes: 'The final exchange between Charlotte and Bob is inaudible to the viewer. This constitutes a marked "space between", which enables a meditation on Charlotte's future ... the emphasis rests on what and how Charlotte can become.'[78] Bolton outlines a theory which will bring men and women together rather than separating them as incompatible beings: an Irigarayan reflection on Eros that inspires new beginnings. This gesture towards the renewal and enlightenment of a new age is felt implicitly in my own work and, while I acknowledge its limits, I tend to share with Bolton an investment in the utopian thinking that Irigaray's more recent philosophy has encouraged.

While Irigaray's thought on the relations between masculine and feminine breathing subjects will inform my examination of issues such as personal identity, selfhood and mortality that are suggested through the locus of breath in film, I am also interested in the ways in which Irigaray's positive reflection on breathing and embodied subjectivity resonates with the restorative and contemplative aims of Marks's and Sobchack's sensuous models of thought. Indeed, Irigaray's theorisation of the gendered, breathing body introduces a new series of questions to the embodied viewing relations and particular modes of visuality that Marks attends to in her work on haptics. Above all, Irigaray's thoughts on the gendered, breathing body lead me to re-examine not only the gendering of bodies that are represented on screen, but the formal attributes of the film itself which come to stand for a physicality that might also be theorised according to a form of gendered perception. While my consideration of the specificity of the filmic medium, its form and 'physicality', builds on the theoretical models of Marks and Sobchack, it is Irigaray's thought which allows me to rethink such aspects of the film experience in terms that relate specifically to the gendered, breathing body. Thus the next section will closely examine the resonant connections between Irigaray's, Marks's and Sobchack's theoretical discourse, focusing on the key questions of embodied subjectivity and haptic discourse on which the main argument of this book is based – to think through the various ramifications, and specificity, of the locus of breathing in the embodied film experience.

Thinking with Irigaray, Sobchack and Marks

In the previous section I suggested how Irigaray's philosophy of breathing introduces a subtle tangibility of the body that is aural, as well as suggestive of a different kind of tactile perception. While the previous section developed thought on the sensuous possibilities of hearing and perceiving breath, the importance of the sexed body in Irigaray's discourse and the particular kind of consciousness of the mind and body that breathing evokes, these facets of Irigaray's thinking are re-examined in the context of the embodied film theories of Marks and Sobchack. Firstly, I consider how Irigaray's conceptualisation of breathing as a form of consciousness differs from Sobchack's interpretation of the breathing body in her analysis of the filmic apparatus; this leads me to re-view the implications Irigaray's thought on breathing bears for the sensuous film theory of Marks, especially in view of her own engagement with Irigaray's concept of the caress which she draws on in order to specify her interest in haptics. Marks's model of haptic visuality might be seen to be organised by the representation of proximity and touch that film's formal attributes call into play, but I suggest how breathing informs a visuality that might be more ordered by embodied thought and consciousness as it is evoked in the filmic diegesis, building on the spiritual dimensions of Irigaray's philosophy of breath. While a large proportion of this section is dedicated to fleshing out the theoretical crux of my argument which shows how Irigaray's thought enables me to take Marks's and Sobchack's embodied film theory further, the final part of this section will lay out the structure of each chapter of this book and the overarching argument that is central to my examination of the locus of breath in the films of Egoyan, Cronenberg and von Trier.

As we have already seen, Sobchack's theorisation of the filmic apparatus as a breathing body provides a vital discussion of breath from the perspective of film theory, but it is Irigaray's philosophy that enables me to question the rhythmic and repetitive nature of breathing that is central to Sobchack's argument. In several ways, Irigaray's theorisation of breath is also concerned with its rhythmic properties, but, unlike Sobchack's analysis, Irigaray argues that breathing is never repetitive since its expression through our bodies follows and moves in cycles that can never be repeated in the same way. According to Irigaray, breath attunes the body to a natural rhythm, a regulation, fundamental to all human existence. In this sense, breathing accords with a temporality of the human body that is also uniquely suggested through Irigaray's philosophy. Irigaray's reflection on breathing focuses on the bodily sense of time; furthermore, Irigaray's thought not only prompts a way of rethinking breath as a rhythmic form, but also suggests a path through breath that is always already open for change, moving forwards and progressing towards a new stage in her thinking.

Following her theorisation of the 'film's body', the model of the cinesthetic subject in Sobchack's later discourses foregrounds the importance of the senses as they work in synthesis (synaesthesia) to inform 'embodied sight'. In contrast, Irigaray's interest in positing breath amongst such a sensorium reconfigures the very ground in which Sobchack's model operates. Building upon Sobchack's model of thought, I speculate on the ways in which the senses are contingent to breathing.

While Irigaray's thought on breath offers a way of raising questions about the filmic subject within the film's diegesis, her work also informs my discussion of the filmic apparatus, enabling my argument to develop the theoretical model of haptics suggested by Marks. Marks's consideration of Irigaray's philosophical concept of the 'caress' enables her to clarify her position on haptics and, importantly, the ethics it implies. On Irigaray's critique of Merleau-Ponty and her proposal of the 'caress', Marks points out her continuation of mimetic structures (of looking and perceiving) which ultimately emphasise a shared ethics between the two philosophers:

> Irigaray's question, 'how to preserve the memory of the caress?' rests on a fundamental sense of loss: of a world of tactility experienced by the foetus and the infant, before language and vision organise its sensorium. Despite Irigaray's critique, I find that Merleau-Ponty shares her ethical insistence on defining a relationship between self and world that is symbiotic, indeed mimetic. They both emphasise that in embodied perception the perceiver relinquishes power over the perceived. The proximal senses are more capable of such a mimetic relationship than vision is, for while looking tends to be unidirectional, one cannot touch without being touched. Yet vision too, in so far as it is embodied, is able to relinquish some of the power of the perceived.[79]

The Irigarayan concept of the 'caress' thus offers for Marks a way in which to introduce the sense of touch to the field of vision that film has long been theorised in relation to. However, Marks cannot fully agree with Irigaray's assertion of touch as a feminine mode of perception and prefers to see 'haptics as a feminist strategy rather than a feminine quality'.[80] Marks does, though, suggest that her work is informed by a similar eroticism that the caress implies – what she describes as a proximity to the image which evokes 'an intensified relation with an other that cannot be possessed'[81] – but Irigaray's thoughts on breathing complicate such proximal relations. As the previous section suggested, Irigaray's philosophy of breath emphasises a different kind of proximity that can be engendered between two subjects, as well as within our own bodies. While Irigaray describes breath as a way in which we can return to ourselves, an interiority constituted through the flow of breath that is also comparable to what she terms a partial 'touching upon', it also represents the space of air that exists between two bodies.

While Marks develops a haptics that functions according to the viewer's proximity and closeness to the image, breath reconfigures these issues in a way that, as Irigaray suggests, 'weaves a proximity', an invisible passage between the subject and the exterior world, between viewer and film.[82] As we have seen during my brief analyses of films which have evoked breath in this introduction, a *visuality* that corresponds with the foregrounding of breathing in film tends to depend more on the role of sound and the ways in which the diegesis represents embodied consciousness on screen. The viewing relations that might be theorised according to the role of breath in film tend to relate to the viewer's perception of breathing in film and this involves thinking about the viewer's *breathing* body and their response to the diegetic bodies of the film.

While I share with Marks a theoretical investment in Irigaray's concept of the 'caress', her increasing, though largely implicit, interest in the spiritual genealogy of haptics is useful for thinking through the role of consciousness in Irigaray's philosophy of breath, its resonance with spirituality and its potential to inform a new kind of haptic discourse. In recent years, Marks has turned attention to the genealogy of the haptic form, a route of enquiry that has led her to examine the relationship between haptic perception and the role of belief and transcendence in the perception and creation of Islamic art.[83] While Marks has not written directly on the role of calligraphy in Islamic art, I am particularly drawn to the ways in which this ancient practice invigorates '*spiritual geometry fashioned by a material instrument*'.[84] A spiritual dimension of breathing is cultivated through concentration and clarity of thought, a kind of embodied consciousness that is actively sought by the calligrapher as their own breathing and the flow of the pen they move become implicated in each other through rhythms of thought and the practice of art. Thus, bearing Marks's assertion of the haptic resonances of Islamic art in mind, the calligraphic practice of Islamic artists suggests an example of a haptic aesthetic that might be informed by the spiritual implications of breathing precisely emphasised by Irigaray, albeit in the context of a religion that is entirely separate from the Buddhist traditions which inform her thought. Above all, the question of how the spiritual dimensions of breathing might be recreated and refigured in haptic terms according to the foregrounding of breath in film will be important to my engagement with Marks's model of haptic visuality. Haptic perception, for Marks, requires such an intense contemplation of the image that we lose ourselves to it; 'it dissolves the boundaries between the beholder and the thing beheld'.[85] However, the very gesture of contemplating breath, according to Irigaray, tends toward the spiritual and autonomous preservation of the self. Thus the foregrounding of breath in film suggests a contemplation or thoughtfulness towards the film that may preserve our subjectivity as viewers, rather than inviting us to lose ourselves entirely to it. In each of the films that I shall look at throughout the course of this book, various questions relating to the stabilisation, as well as destabilisation, of the subjectivity of the film viewer will be posed in order to establish the distinct order of embodied perception with which breathing corresponds.

My evaluation of Marks's and Sobchack's thinking in the light of Irigaray's philosophy of breath has led me to envisage the parameters of my theoretical investigation of the place of breath in cinema – the various 'bodies' I intend to analyse and the ways in which embodied subjectivity might be differently determined according to the role of breathing in film. My interest in the locus of breath in film engages with the thought of Irigaray in order to build on Marks's and Sobchack's analyses in relation to four areas of concern: the representation of bodies within the filmic diegesis, the film's body, which I accord with the formal attributes of film, the significance of gender to the 'bodies' I theorise, and the positioning of the viewer's body in the film experience that the locus of breathing suggests. The films of Egoyan, Cronenberg and von Trier will each suggest various ways in which to examine the implications of the formal, representational and thematic role of breathing which, in turn, enables me to reconsider the embodied nature of the film experience.

Egoyan, Cronenberg and von Trier are all contemporary auteurs whose work has slowly embedded itself within mainstream cinema while effectively remaining somewhat outside of the Hollywood system. Less constrained by studio demands, von Trier, Egoyan and Cronenberg maintain creative and ideological values that, in some way, tend to produce a cinema that is highly personal and subjective. Though one can argue that this inscription of the personal in the cinema of Egoyan, Cronenberg and von Trier can also be found in a number of other auteurs' work, it is nevertheless their distinct engagement with issues of selfhood and the fracturing of personal identity which lead to their unique foregrounding of breath.

The first chapter of this book re-views the organisation of on-screen space and its sensorial implications in the 'elemental topographies' of Egoyan's *The Sweet Hereafter*, *Felicia's Journey* and *Exotica*, drawing on Irigaray's thought on the proximal space of air and the gendered, breathing bodies which inhabit such environments in the diegesis and are expressed through the film's form. While the issue of spatial proximity leads the first chapter's investigation into the place of breath in Egoyan's films, the human body becomes the site of a different proximity that is measured in relation to other bodies, rather than in the context of the space it inhabits, in Cronenberg's *Spider* and *Videodrome*. The second chapter of this book explores the question of what it means to be a breathing body and the role of gender in determining the way in which such bodies are created on screen, in the film's form and through the viewing positions of each film. In Cronenberg's films, breathing suggests a point of bodily contact which differs from the sense of touch; the final chapter of this book develops thought on the centrality of the sound of breathing and its specific engendering of a point of contact, or kinship, between the viewer's body and the breathing bodies of the diegesis in von Trier's 'Gold Heart' trilogy.

Above all, it is the filming and organisation of space that orients our perception of breathing. The first chapter of this book begins to analyse the very conditions of inhabiting, perceiving and attuning to various modes of spatiality which shape the place of breath in cinema.

NOTES

1. See Steven Shaviro, 'Untimely Bodies: Towards a Comparative Film Theory of Human Figures, Temporalities and Visibilities', available at <http://ftp.shaviro.com/Othertexts/SCMS08Response.pdf> (accessed 1 February 2009).
2. See H. G. Wells, 'In Drury Lane', *The Invisible Man* (London: Penguin, 2005), p. 114.
3. See Claude Lévi-Strauss, *A World on the Wane* (New York: Athenaeum, 1975); Eng. trans. by John and Doreen Weightman from the French *Tristes Tropiques* (Paris: Plon, 1955), p. 210.
4. See Mulvey, 'Visual Pleasure and Narrative Cinema', *Screen*, 16:3 (Autumn 1975), pp. 6–18.
5. See Creed, 'Woman as Monstrous Womb: *The Brood*', in *The Monstrous Feminine: Film, Feminism and Psychoanalysis* (London: Routledge, 1993), pp. 43–58.
6. See, for example, Creed's analysis of *Alien* in 'Horror and the Archaic Mother: *Alien*', in *The Monstrous Feminine*, pp. 16–30.
7. See Chion, 'Immobile Growth', 2nd edition, *David Lynch* (London: BFI, 2006); Eng. trans. by Robert Julian from the French *David Lynch* (Paris: Cahiers du Cinéma, 1992), pp. 45–77 (p. 49).
8. See Chion's preface to his book *Audio-Vision: Sound on Screen* (New York: Columbia University Press, 1993); Eng. trans. by Claudia Gorbman from the French *L'Audio-vision (son et image au cinéma)* (Paris: Armand-Colin, 1991), p. xxvi.
9. See Brooks, 'The Sound of Knocking: Jacques Becker's *Le Trou*', *Screening the Past*, 12 (2001), available at <http://www.latrobe.edu.au/screeningthepast/firstrelease/fr0301/jbfr12a.htm> (accessed 7 December 2011).
10. For further reflection on the cultural significance of *Star Wars*, it might be useful to consult my recently compiled bibliography (co-edited with Will Brooker) at <http://www.oxfordbibliographiesonline.com/view/document/obo-9780199791286/obo-9780199791286-0059.xml> (accessed 29 October 2011).
11. For example, the online retailer Amazon lists at least three types of voice-changers: the Hasbro '*Star Wars* Darth Vader Voice Changer Mask' at <http://tinyurl.com/ckan9a> (accessed 20 November 2008); Rubies 'Darth Vader Sound Module' at <http://tinyurl.com/atceqp > (accessed 29 November 2011); and the Hasbro '*Star Wars*: The Clone Wars Voice Changer Helmet' at <http://tinyurl.com/amyqvq> (accessed 20 November 2010).
12. The closing moment of *Star Wars Episode III: The Revenge of the Sith* (Lucas, 2005) shows the mask being lowered on to the disfigured face of Darth Vader (then, Anakin Skywalker). Further details of Vader's injuries are available at <http://www.theforce.net/swtc/injuries.html#breath> (accessed 12 November 2010).
13. The feminist theorist bell hooks has argued that such feelings of threat are codified as racial, owing to the director's choice to cast a black actor (James Earl Jones) and the overall menacing representation of the dark villain's deep voice. See, in particular, hooks's discussion of white supremacist capitalist patriarchy in her video 'Cultural Criticism and Transformation' (1996, Media Education Foundation). Clips of hooks's video are available to view online at <http://www.youtube.com/watch?v=OQ-XVTzBMvQ> (accessed 3 April 2009).
14. See Gray, *Anatomy of the Human Body* (Philadelphia: Lea and Febriger, 1918).
15. Indeed, the earliest experiments with the moving image were undertaken for the purposes of physiology. For example, Eadweard Muybridge's pioneering efforts captured equine physiology in motion. One of the most compelling engagements with Muybridge's work and the relationship between cinema and science can be found in the writings of D. N. Rodowick. See, for example, Rodowick's *The*

Virtual Life of Film (Cambridge, MA: Harvard University Press, 2007). For further insight into the history of cinematographic experiments involving the human body, I strongly recommend Lisa Cartwright's *Screening the Body: Tracing Medicine's Visual Culture* (Minneapolis: Minnesota University Press, 1995).

16. See Bernard J. F. Lonergan et al. (eds), *The Collected Works of Bernard Lonergan: Philosophical and Theological Papers 1958–1964* (Toronto: University of Toronto Press, 1996), p. 245.
17. For a detailed introduction to the concept of *prāṇāyāma* or 'life force' and the practice of yoga, see in particular Oliver Leaman, *Key Concepts in Eastern Philosophy* (London: Routledge, 1999), p. 133.
18. See Émile Durkheim, *The Elementary Forms of Religious Life*, 2nd edition (Guildford: George Allen and Unwin, 1976), p. 243.
19. See Irigaray, *Speculum of the Other Woman* (Ithaca: Cornell University Press, 1985); Eng. trans. by Gillian C. Gill from the French *Speculum de l'autre femme* (Paris: Les Éditions de Minuit, 1974).
20. See Whitford (ed.), *The Irigaray Reader: Luce Irigaray* (London: Blackwell Publishing, 1991), p. 18.
21. See, for example, 'Spirituality and Religion', in *Luce Irigaray: Key Writings* (New York: Continuum, 2004), pp. 145–86.
22. See, for example, 'The Way of Breath', in *Between East and West: From Singularity to Community*, European Perspectives Series (New York: Columbia University Press, 2002), pp. 73–92; Eng. trans. by Stephen Pluháĉek from the French *Entre Orient et Occident: De la singularité à la communauté* (Paris: Grasset, 1999).
23. For example, Irigaray's engagement with Buddhism is implicitly felt throughout her critique of continental philosopher Martin Heidegger in *Being Two: How Many Eyes Have We?* (Rüsselsheim: Christel Göttert Verlag, 2000); Eng. trans. by Luce Irigaray with Catherine Busson and Jim Mooney from the French *À deux, nous avons combien d'yeux?*
24. See Merleau-Ponty, *The Phenomenology of Perception* (London: Continuum, 2002); Eng. trans. by Colin Smith from the French *Phénoménologie de la perception* (Paris: Gallimard, 1945).
25. See Sobchack, *The Address of the Eye: A Phenomenology of Film Experience* (Princeton: Princeton University Press, 1992).
26. See Irigaray, *Being Two: How Many Eyes Have We?*, p. 23.
27. See Marks, *The Skin of the Film: Intercultural Cinema, Embodiment and the Senses* (Durham, NC: Duke University Press, 1999) and *Touch: Sensuous Theory and Multisensory Media* (Minneapolis: University of Minnesota Press, 2002); see also Sobchack, *The Address of the Eye* and *Carnal Thoughts: Embodiment and Moving Image Culture* (Berkeley: University of California Press, 2004).
28. To quote Vasseleu's point in full in *Textures of Light: Vision and Touch in Irigaray, Levinas and Merleau-Ponty* (New York: Routledge, 1998), p. 67: 'Irigaray argues that "two lips" express a tangible intimacy without reference to the visible. This is not a pro-vision-al partitioning of flesh, but an interiorly constituted dimension of a different order.'
29. For Connor's discussion of art and air see, for example, 'Next-to-Nothing', *Tate Etc*, 12 (Spring 2008), available at <http://www.tate.org.uk/tateetc/issue12/air.htm> (accessed 12 September 2009); see also Connor, *The Matter of Air: Science and Art of the Ethereal* (London: Reaktion Books, 2010) and Mike Lloyd, 'Life in the Slow Lane: Rethinking Spectacular Body Modification', *Journal of Media and Cultural Studies*, 18:4 (2004), pp. 555–64.
30. I thank David Pinder, Department of Geography, Queen Mary (University of London), for suggesting Connor's work to me.
31. See, for example, Connor's essays 'Oxygen Debt: *Little Dorrit*'s Pneumatics', available at <http://www.bbk.ac.uk/english/skc/dorrit> (accessed 11 December

2009), and 'The Vapours', available at <http:www.bbk.ac.uk/english/skc/vapours> (accessed 11 December 2009).
32. See, in particular, Connor's paper 'Inebriate of Air: Gas, Magic and Omnipotence of Thought in the Nineteenth Century' given at the 'Magical Thinking' conference, Institute of English Studies, University of London, 11 May 2007. An extended version of the paper is available at <http://www.bbk.ac.uk/english/skc/inebriate/inebriate.pdf> (accessed 11 December 2010).
33. Connor's transcript of his broadcast at 21.30 on BBC Radio 3 on 13 June 2004 entitled 'On the Air' is available at <http://www.bbk.ac.uk/english/skc/onair> (accessed 23 February 2008). Connor's interview with Mark Morris, recorded on 27 June 2006 and distributed as part of the podcast interview series 'Architecture on Air', organised by the School of Architecture of the University of North Carolina at Charlotte, is available at <http://www.bbk.ac.uk/english/skc/atmospheres.htm> (accessed 20 May 2007). See also Connor's book on ventriloquism *Dumbstruck: A Ventriloquistory: A Cultural History of Ventriloquism* (Oxford: Oxford University Press, 2000).
34. See Connor's 'Windbags and Skinsongs', available at <http://www.bbk.ac.uk/english/skc/windbags> (accessed 14 June 2010).
35. See Lloyd, 'Life in the Slow Lane', p. 555.
36. Further details of Kimsooja's installation are available at <http://www.kimsooja.com/projects/breathe.html> (accessed 2 July 2011). I have written at greater length on Kimsooja's installation in a book chapter entitled 'The Breathing Body in Movement' in C. Nigianni, F. Söderbäck and H. Gunkel (eds), *Critical Lines, Feminist Flights* (Basingstoke: Palgrave, forthcoming).
37. See Kimsooja's website <http://www.kimsooja.com/projects/breathe.html> (accessed 2 July 2011).
38. See Sobchack, '"Suzy Scribbles": On Technology, Techne, and Writing Incarnate', in *Carnal Thoughts: Embodiment and Moving Image Culture* (Berkeley: University of California Press, 2004), pp. 109–34 (p. 134).
39. See Barthes, 'The Grain of the Voice', in *Image, Music, Text* (London: Fontana, 1997); Eng. trans. by Stephen Heath from the French *Le Grain de la voix* (Paris: Éditions de Seuil, 1981), pp. 179–89 (pp. 182–3).
40. Reiterer's work was presented at the Pompidou Centre, Paris, in 2006.
41. Film duration: 30 min, 16 mm projection, 3000 x 4000 mm overall display dimensions, variable installation, purchased 2005 by the Tate Modern, London. My thanks to Laura U. Marks for pointing out this particular film to me.
42. See Sobchack, *The Address of the Eye*, p. 207.
43. See Sobchack, 'Embodying Transcendence: On the Literal, the Material and the Filmic Sublime', *Material Religion*, 4:2 (July 2007), pp. 194–203.
44. See Sobchack's explanation of this term in her article 'What My Fingers Knew: The Cinesthetic Subject, or Vision in the Flesh', *Senses of Cinema*, 5 (2000), footnote 46, available at < http://www.sensesofcinema.com/2000/5/fingers> (accessed 7 December 2011).
45. See Sobchack, *The Address of the Eye*, p. 207.
46. Ibid. p. 207.
47. Ibid. p. 207. Such intensities, flows and shifts might also call to mind Deleuze and Guattari's concept of 'bodies without organs', if one were to adopt a Deleuzoguattarian perspective. See, in particular, Deleuze and Guattari, 'November 28, 1947: How Do You Make Yourself a Body Without Organs?', in *A Thousand Plateaus* (London: Continuum, 2004), pp. 165–84.
48. See Sobchack, 'Embodying Transcendence', p. 202.
49. Ibid. p. 202.
50. Ibid. p. 202.
51. See Sobchack's clarification of the cinesthetic subject in 'What My Fingers Knew'.

52. See Merleau-Ponty, *The Phenomenology of Perception*, pp. 245–6.
53. Forming an intimate engagement with film, for Don Anderson, is a key characteristic of studies benefiting from a Deleuzian school of thought. While reviewing Anna Powell's book *Deleuze and Horror Film*, Anderson claims: 'It would appear that an intimate involvement with film in place of the clinical distance performed by more psychoanalytically trained theorists is required to perceive the molecular becomings ... the corporeal responses as our senses stimulate the neuronal networks linked to organs like the heart (pace, pulse-rate) ... and the lungs (depth and rapidity of breathing).' In view of Anderson's comments, my investment in forms of intimacy, especially bodily intimacy and even, to a certain degree, the viewer's noted changes in breathing such as those suggested above, would thus be consistent with his thoughts on the effectiveness of Deleuze when involved with a personal engagement with film. However, while I acknowledge the Deleuzian resonances I implicitly share with Marks, I do not wish to situate my research within a strictly Deleuzian framework. See Don Anderson's review of Anna Powell's book *Deleuze and Horror Film*, *Rhizomes*, 11/12 (Fall 2005/Spring 2006), available at <http://www.rhizomes.net/issue11/anderson/review.html> (accessed 3 December 2010).
54. See, in particular, Marks, 'Video Haptics and Erotics', in *Touch*, pp. 1–20 (p. 8).
55. Ibid. pp. 4–5.
56. See Marks, 'The Memory of Touch', in *The Skin of the Film*, pp. 127–93 (p. 162).
57. See Marks, 'Haptic Visuality: Touching with the Eyes', *Framework: The Finnish Art Review*, 2 (2004), available at <http://www.framework.fi/2_2004/visitor/artikkelit/marks2.html> (accessed 7 June 2009).
58. See Frampton, *Filmosophy* (London: Wallflower Press, 2006), p. 6.
59. *Seeing Is Believing*, dir. Shauna Beharry, Canada, 1991.
60. See Marks, 'The Memory of Touch', in *The Skin of the Film*, pp. 127–93 (p. 127).
61. Ibid. p. 129.
62. See Shaviro, 'Untimely Bodies'.
63. *Alien*, dir. Ridley Scott, UK, 1979; *Aliens*, dir. James Cameron, USA, 1986; *Alien 3*, dir. David Fincher, USA, 1992; and *Alien Resurrection*, dir. Jean-Pierre Jeunet, USA, 1997.
64. See Mulvey, 'Netherworlds and the Unconscious: Oedipus and *Blue Velvet*', in *Fetishism and Curiosity* (London: BFI, 1996), pp. 137–54. See also Michael Atkinson's view of Oedipal themes in the film *Blue Velvet*, BFI Modern Classics (London: BFI, 1997), p. 21.
65. According to Frampton, Lynch uses sound 'inside-out', and in this sense it may be argued that the sounds of breath in *Blue Velvet* are more psychical than physical, or rather the sonification of Frank's perverse mind. Indeed, commenting on the particular creation of a vacuum effect, an 'absence' in *Lost Highway* (USA, 1977) is felt 'loudly', an aural motif of silence which comes to stand for the 'pure intention' of the protagonist. See Frampton, *Filmosophy*, pp. 121–2.
66. See, in particular, Martine Beugnet and Elizabeth Ezra's brief thoughts on Zidane's breathing body in 'A Portrait of the Twenty-First Century', *Screen*, 50:1 (Spring 2009), pp. 77–85.
67. I am extremely grateful to Philip Brophy for his correspondence with me on the matter of hearing the breathing body in film. See, in particular, Brophy's fascinating discussion of *Rosetta* in *100 Modern Soundtracks* (London: BFI, 2004), p. 195. Sarah Cooper also observes the significance of breath in *Rosetta*: 'As testimony to her almost ceaseless movement, the sound of her breathing accompanies her activities throughout' in 'Mortal Ethics: Reading Levinas with the Dardenne Brothers', *Film-Philosophy*, 11:2 (2007), available at <http://www.film-philosophy.com/2007v11n2/cooper.pdf> (accessed 7 December 2010).
68. See Irigaray, 'The Age of the Breath', in *Luce Irigaray: Key Writings* (New York: Continuum, 2004), pp. 165–70.

69. See Irigaray, *The Forgetting of Air in Martin Heidegger* (Austin: University of Texas Press, 1999); Eng. trans. by Mary Beth Mader from the French *L'Oubli de l'air chez Martin Heidegger* (Paris: Les Éditions de Minuit,1983). Breath is also tentatively gestured towards in Irigaray's *Elemental Passions* (London: Continuum, 1992); Eng. trans. by Joanne Collie and Judith Still from the French *Passions élémentaires* (Paris: Les Éditions de Minuit, 1982).
70. See Irigaray, 'The Way of Breath', in *Between East and West*; 'A Breath that Touches in Words', in *I Love to You: Sketch for a Felicity Within History* (New York: Routledge, 1996); Eng. trans. by Alison Martin from the French *J'aime à toi. Esquisse d'une félicité dans l'histoire* (Paris: Grasset, 1992), pp. 121–8; and 'The Age of the Breath', in *Luce Irigaray: Key Writings*. Irigaray's poetry also contains frequent references to breathing in *Everyday Prayers* (Nottingham: Nottingham University Press, 2004).
71. See Irigaray, 'The Invisible of the Flesh: A Reading of Merleau-Ponty, *The Visible and the Invisible*, "The Intertwining – the Chiasm"', in *An Ethics of Sexual Difference*, Continuum Impacts Series (London: Continuum, 2004), pp. 127–53; Eng. trans. by Carolyn Burke and Gillian C. Gill from the French *Éthique de la différence sexuelle* (Paris: Les Éditions de Minuit, 1984); and 'The Fecundity of the Caress: A Reading of Levinas, *Totality and Infinity*, Phenomenology of Eros', in *An Ethics of Sexual Difference*, pp. 154–79.
72. See Vasseleu, 'Illuminating Passion', in *Textures of Light*, pp. 109–122 (p. 114).
73. See Irigaray, 'A Breath that Touches in Words', in *I Love to You*, p. 124.
74. See Lyotard, 'Scapeland', in *The Inhuman: Reflections on Time* (Stanford: Stanford University Press, 1992), pp. 182–90; Eng. trans. by Geoffrey Bennington and Rachel Bowlby from the French *L'Inhumain. Causeries sur le temps* (Paris: Galilée, 1988). Lyotard's text opens with the lines: 'Cast down the walls. Breach and breath. Inhalation. BREATH. Inside and outside. This concerns the thorax. The muscular walls of the rib-cage, of the defences of the thorax, exposed to the winds. Your breath has been set free, not taken away' (p. 182); see Gaston Bachelard, *Air and Dreams: An Essay on the Imagination of Movement* (Dallas: Dallas Institute of Humanities and Culture, 1988); Eng. trans. by Edith R. Farrell and C. Frederick Farrell from the French *L'Air et les songes* (Paris: José Corti, 1987).
75. Daria Rogers, a philosophy PhD candidate at SUNY Stony Brook University, New York, is developing a study dedicated to Irigaray's philosophy of breath. Rogers's paper 'Cultivating Two Breaths' was presented at the annual Luce Irigaray Conference and Seminar, University of Liverpool, June 2007.
76. See, for example, Caroline Bainbridge's reading of the feminist filmmaker Marleen Gorris's *Antonia's Line* in 'Feminine Enunciation in the Cinema', *Paragraph: A Journal of Modern Critical Theory*, 25:3 (2002), pp. 129–43; Kaja Silverman's reading of Sally Potter's *Golddiggers*, 'Disembodying the Female Voice: Irigaray, Experimental Feminist Cinema and Femininity', in *The Acoustic Mirror: The Female Voice in Psychoanalysis and Cinema* (Bloomington: Indiana University Press, 1988), pp. 141–86; Liz Watkins's analysis of Jane Campion's *Portrait of a Lady*, 'Light, Colour and Sound in Cinema', *Paragraph: A Journal of Modern Critical Theory*, 25:3 (2002), pp. 117–28.
77. See Bolton's article 'The Camera as Speculum: Examining Female Consciousness in *Lost in Translation*, Using the Thought of Luce Irigaray', in Barbara Gabriella Renzi and Stephen Rainey (eds), *From Plato's Cave to the Multiplex: Contemporary Philosophy and Film* (Newcastle: Cambridge Scholars Press, 2006), pp. 87–97. See also Bolton's monograph *Film and Female Consciousness: Irigaray, Cinema and Thinking Women* (Basingstoke: Palgrave Macmillan, 2011).
78. Ibid. p. 95.
79. See Marks, 'The Memory of Touch', in *The Skin of the Film*, p. 149.
80. See Marks, 'Video Haptics and Erotics', in *Touch*, p. 7.

81. See Marks, 'The Memory of Touch', in *The Skin of the Film*, pp. 127–93 (p. 184).
82. See Irigaray, 'Rebuilding the World', in *The Way of Love* (London: Continuum, 2004), pp. 137–65 (p. 150); Eng. trans. by Heidi Bostic and Stephen Pluháček from the French *La Voie de l'amour*.
83. See Marks's paper 'The Haptic Transfer and the Travels of the Abstract Line: Embodied Perception from Classical Islam to Modern Europe', in Christina Lammer and Kim Sawchuck (eds), *Verkörperungen/Embodiment* (Vienna: Löcker Verlag, 2007), pp. 269–84. See also Marks, *Enfoldment and Infinity: An Islamic Genealogy of New Media Art* (Cambridge, MA: MIT Press, 2010).
84. To quote Soraya Syed's comments on the practice of calligraphy in Islamic culture, 'The Art of the Pen', available at <http://www.artofthepen.com/home.html> (accessed 10 October 2010).
85. See Marks, 'Haptic Visuality: Touching with the Eyes'.

1. THE HAPTIC LOGIC OF A BREATHING BODY: ELEMENTAL TOPOGRAPHIES OF MEMORY AND LOSS

Atom Egoyan's 1995 short film *A Portrait of Arshile*[1] combines images of the filmmaker's newly born son with stills taken from the Armenian painter Arshile Gorky's self-portrait. These images are assembled in order to create a video-letter to the child explaining the origins of his name, the two contrasting shots connected by a voice-over narrated by Egoyan and his wife Arsinée, informing us of the Armenian heritage and its history of genocide from which both 'portraits' implicitly inherit. Moving between the two Arshiles in the film, our attention is drawn to the textural differences between the extremely close and grainy images of the child and the photographed shots of the painting which appear increasingly silent and smooth. While it is clear that the pictures of Arshile Egoyan are less static than those of the painting, Egoyan's camera does not interrogate his human subject. Rather, it is the child that probes the presence of the equipment, bringing his face close to the lens and, at one point, breathing on it, briefly filling the frame with a cloud of vapour (reminiscent of the mimetic exchange of object and subject at work in Reiterer's installation *Breath* that was discussed in my introduction to this book). This vivid patch of moisture on the lens – breath – turns an ordinary home video into a rather more extraordinary filming and framing of human subjectivity. Most suggestively, the images of the child convey a proximity which calls to mind Marks's discussion of Beharry's *Seeing Is Believing* where grainy close-ups of the mourned mother's clothing foreground a relationship with the image that is on the threshold of physical experience, exemplifying Marks's concept of haptic visuality. Indeed, as Marie-Aude Baronian writes of Egoyan's film: 'Arshile's body is nearly caressed, nearly embraced',[2] but the act of breathing that we witness in Egoyan's video footage of his infant son disturbs the very conditions for which any form of sensuous engagement with the film may take place. While Baronian's use of the term 'nearly' reveals the ultimate failure of the image to possess the child, the nebulous imprint of mist on the lens may be seen to (inadvertently) compensate for such loss: it offers an alternative touch, not of skin to skin, but of breath to camera. In other words, if these images do, as Baronian suggests, communicate a desire to touch, then we must consider the question of how breathing might refigure such a proximity, especially when intimate relations formed through our conception of the visual field are re-oriented by the presence of breath within the diegesis. To put this question of proximity more simply, the patch of breath in *A Portrait of Arshile* can be seen to posit a different dimension of physicality in the three-dimensional space of Egoyan's film.

While I am principally concerned with the locus of breathing in feature films, *A Portrait of Arshile* must be acknowledged for its striking coalescence of themes and imagery which resonate with the concerns of this chapter: the diegetic evocation of breath, proximity, spatiality and, at its centre, the intertwined subjects of loss and childhood.

The theoretical framework adopted in this chapter consists of an engagement with Irigaray's discussion of the interweaving of air and breath in order to consider the filmic depiction of space in Egoyan's films. I will be focusing here on the ways in which Egoyan's filming of landscapes, interiors and their abstraction resonates with Irigaray's thought on the connections between the space of air and the breathing body, as well as the importance of proximity in serving this relation. I think through, and with, the logic of Irigaray's philosophy which places emphasis on breath as a point of mediation between the inside and the outside of the human body in order to map the relations between space and the breathing bodies inhabiting the screened environments in Egoyan's films. My enquiry into Egoyan's filmic spaces will primarily involve tracing significant gestures of formal and diegetic movement, especially transitory motifs which, I argue, come to stand for the constant mediation between body and world which breathing affords, according to Irigaray's philosophy. My exploration of the connections between the filmic depiction of movement, the space of air and the breathing body also leads me to examine the role of place in configuring 'textures' of image and sound in Egoyan's narratives, or what I term 'elemental topographies': filmic spaces which are shaped precisely through their elemental depiction of air and breathing. Central to my reading of Egoyan is the examination of spatiality configured in his loose trilogy of films which I approach in the order of *The Sweet Hereafter*, *Felicia's Journey* and *Exotica*.

While this chapter is much less concerned with the actual image of breathing that we are able to view in *A Portrait of Arshile*, the breathing child does, importantly, reappear both literally and symbolically in *The Sweet Hereafter*, the first and most substantial focal point of this chapter. The recurrent image of the breathing child is the very locus of trauma and loss at the centre of *The*

Sweet Hereafter's narrative trajectory, recalled as part of a potent memory that flows through the film's diegesis as well as its formal aesthetic. This diegetic representation of breathing also bears particular implications for the viewing experience of the film, orienting the viewer towards thinking about, and being sensitive to, the place of breath. However, the figuring of the breathing child in *The Sweet Hereafter* is the only point of interest in this book that is led by an explicit reference to breathing in the film's narrative. My theoretical approach to *The Sweet Hereafter*'s foregrounding of breath within its narrative will begin to move, importantly, towards the formal attributes of Egoyan's films and the viewing relations which suggest a film experience shaped by the locus of breath in film.

The Sweet Hereafter's particular envisaging of points of intersection between loss, memory and breathing will be further explored in *Felicia's Journey*, where I contemplate the notion of the breathing mouth as a place on the threshold between interior and exterior boundaries of the body, corresponding with a filmic spatiality which, I argue, is inhabited by both the viewer and the protagonists of the film. By contrast, the bodily and psychical experience of loss depicted in *Exotica* prompts reflection on a different filmic spatiality which might be seen to represent an asphyxiating and suffocating environment, both for the filmed subject and for the viewer. While the formal attributes of Egoyan's films are important to my conceptualisation of elemental topographies, the subject matter of each film will lead me to consider the ways in which breathing sheds new light on the thematic treatment of trauma, memory, loss and grief in the filmmaker's *oeuvre*.

Existing Criticism of Egoyan

Egoyan's corpus of work is considerable, to date consisting of thirteen feature films, a documentary and eleven short films. When I first embarked upon research for this book in 2006 a small number of substantial treatments of Egoyan had recently become available, including Jonathan Romney's invaluable 2004 overview of the director's work, and, shortly after, Monique Tschofen and Jennifer Burwell's edited volume of articles became available in 2007 entitled *Image and Territory: Essays on Atom Egoyan*.[3] Also in 2007, a major retrospective of Egoyan's fictional narratives, short pieces and documentary films was organised at the Pompidou Centre, Paris.[4] Yet despite the fact that it has been almost three decades since the release of Egoyan's first feature *Next of Kin* (1984), it seems his work is only now starting to gather the critical recognition it deserves – much later than initially anticipated by Carole Desbarat, Jacinto Lageira, Danièle Rivière and Paul Virilio in the first book-length study of the filmmaker in 1993.[5] The most recent scholarly publication on Egoyan has been offered by Emma Wilson as part of the University of Illinois's prestigious Contemporary Film Directors Series.[6]

While it is impossible to entirely account for the reasons why Egoyan has, until now, been the subject of few book-length analyses, it is likely that his tendency to explore, unflinchingly, deeply troubling aspects of the human condition, especially social and moral taboos such as incest and abuse, presents the critic with questions that cannot easily be answered, or elided.

The issue of coming to terms with the difficult subject matter of Egoyan's films is elegantly addressed by Wilson as she concludes her sensitive treatment of *Exotica*.[7] She writes: 'I have to ask myself what brought me to this point. What have I seen that has channelled me here? Is it something hidden I still have to find?'[8] Indeed, Egoyan has remarked on the importance of allowing audiences to develop their own subjective interpretation of his films. In interview, Egoyan admits: 'To me, the highest aim of any film is to enter so completely into the subconscious of the viewer that there are moments and scenes and gestures which can be generated by the spectator's imagination. That becomes part of the film they're playing in their mind.'[9] My engagement with *The Sweet Hereafter*, *Felicia's Journey* and *Exotica* further probes the boundaries between film and imagination that are called into question by Egoyan, but my particular focus is on the way in which such parameters of meaning and experience might be thrown into relief by the locus of breathing in each film. Above all, breathing plays an important role in the way *The Sweet Hereafter*, *Felicia's Journey* and *Exotica* are not only sculpted in the mind of the viewer, but experienced as embodied images.

My readings of *The Sweet Hereafter*, *Felicia's Journey* and *Exotica* suggest how Egoyan's films can be seen to *breathe* through their geographies of loss: breathing suggests a 'place' in which gestures of spatiality articulate such loss, as well as inscribing it in the film experience. While my investment in the particular theme of loss in this chapter offers new ways in which to come to terms with some of the most troubling aspects of Egoyan's work, my analysis also opens up a space in which to envisage a new treatment of the theme of catharsis in each of the films I discuss. These new narratives of recovery, which I locate in Egoyan's filmic 'climates', suggest the prospect of some kind of acknowledgement and mediation of loss specifically enabled by the role that breathing plays in each film; my engagement with Irigaray's positive reflection on breathing and the element of air will be crucial to the way in which such spaces of recovery can be found in Egoyan's films.

While the analysis of filmic space examined in this chapter draws attention to Egoyan's elemental topographies of air and the breath, existing treatments of space in his films tend to address broader, geographical and cultural contexts in order to reflect on the filmmaker's thematic concern with issues of cultural identity and nationhood.[10] As *A Portrait of Arshile* suggests, questions of heritage and culture persist to haunt the filmmaker's work and lead to some of the most challenging examinations of identity, cultural memory and public and private loss. However, the question of cultural identity in Egoyan's work will be viewed more generally in this chapter, particularly in the context of his filmed environments and their evocation of strangeness, both for the character on screen and for the viewer. Existing criticism has sought to situate Egoyan's films within a context of diasporic filmmaking, but my interest in breath reflects primarily on broader questions of foreignness in terms that relate more to embodied experiences beyond the frame of cultural difference.[11]

In my introduction to this book I argued that Marks's model of thought emphasises haptics as a form of spatial navigation of the field of vision, 'coming into contact' with film's perceptual space. In contrast, Irigaray's philosophical thought on the spatial and, to a certain degree, temporal dimensions of breathing enables me to develop a haptic theory according to the spatiality of air and breath found in Egoyan's work. In this respect, I consider air according to mobility, fluidity and the defining of space within Egoyan's films, while breath evokes the *interiority* of such spaces, the tone, emotion and voices at play in the diegesis of the film. According to Irigaray, contemplating breath also involves thinking about the air that surrounds us: 'We still live our lives in a universe which is composed of and is described in terms of natural elements, we are made of them and we live in them, they determine our attractions, our affects, our passion, our limits, our aspirations.'[12] Irigaray's interest in the elements, especially the element of air, represents a concern with the carnality and materiality of the earth we occupy as human beings. My reflection on the representation of the element of wind, in particular, will shape my treatment of filmic space in Egoyan's films. My approach to haptic theory might also be seen to build upon what Giuliana Bruno has described as a way of 'understanding habitation as a component of a notion of the haptic'.[13] If air, according to Irigaray, is the most fundamental space in which to live, the logic of Bruno's thinking suggests that a haptic enquiry into the space of air is especially apt. This chapter shows how such an 'airy' mode of 'habitation' and its visual concordances are sensitive to both the intimate and isolating properties of air and its creation of 'emptiness', a viewing relation that will be foregrounded in my analyses of on-screen whiteness and snow in *The Sweet Hereafter*, the network of videoed 'absences' of *Felicia's Journey* and the poetic, elliptical images of the wind in the grass in *Exotica*. While Irigaray's thinking will lead me to re-examine the ways in which haptic theory requires the image to be thought of in terms of proximal relations, it will also offer ways of introducing a hapticity oriented towards the study of sound, especially the sound of silence and filmic soundscapes of wind, an element that I argue is particularly important to Egoyan's articulation of memory and loss.

The Breathing Child: *The Sweet Hereafter*

Watching the misty appearance of breath in *A Portrait of Arshile*, I am struck by this imprint of the child which suggests poignantly to the viewer, more than any other aspect of the image, the words 'I am here, I am real, but one day I will be no longer'. A child's breath is memorialised as a treasured moment in *A Portrait of Arshile* and thus it seems memory and loss both become embodied through breath. Such a signification of loss is (quite literally in the case of *A Portrait of Arshile*) part of a process of materialisation. However, this is not to say that breathing becomes equated with any definite or absolute materiality since it belongs to a system of invisible acts (internal and external: inhalation, exhalation, sighs, gasps). Indeed, my interest, as I have underlined in my introduction to this book, is in the interval between the material and the immaterial that breath suggests: the place of the (im)materiality of breath that I shall begin to flesh out in this chapter. As my introduction to this book suggests, this (im) materiality of breath poses questions that relate precisely to the hapticity of a breathing body as one that is always already in a state of flux or disappearance from, and appearance in, a plane of reality.

Following Barthes's thought on the photographic image, Marks views haptic perception as essentially a form of melancholia which destabilises the viewer through their experience of fleeting or 'disappearing' materiality.[14] However, the melancholic narrative of *The Sweet Hereafter* and its traumatic representation of breathing offers a different perspective on loss. Above all, my engagement with Irigaray's philosophy will enable me to explore the cathartic possibilities of breathing. In *The Sweet Hereafter*, a traumatic event is emblematised by a breathing body, represented explicitly in the film's narrative; my treatment of the film will show how breathing troubles the central depiction of loss and mortality, ultimately opening up a new discourse of life reawakened and affirmed.

The Sweet Hereafter is adapted from the Russell Banks novel of the same name.[15] The literary origins of the film are important in so far as the novel provides the subject matter for Egoyan, but the film's structure differs from Banks's novel. Indeed, Egoyan emphasises the narrative of *The Sweet Hereafter* as a medieval allegory through his use of the Robert Browning poem *The Pied Piper of Hamelin*, a meta-narrative within the film.

The narrative of *The Sweet Hereafter* is set in the fictional British Columbian town of Sam Dent whose small community dwells amongst a glacial landscape of snow-capped mountains and sparse, open terrain. A school bus accident has resulted in the deaths of all but one of Sam Dent's children and a lawyer arrives to help the mourning community seek damages against the company responsible for the design of the bus which crashed. The lawyer, Mitchell Stephens (Ian Holm), is plagued by phone calls from his heroin addict daughter Zoe (Caerthan Banks) which reveal that she is HIV positive as a result of sharing needles with other addicts. Stephens visits the parents of the deceased children as well as the bus driver Dolores (Gabrielle Rose) and her disabled husband Abbott (David Hemblen), convincing some that there are grounds for a case, but is also rejected by others. Nicole (Sarah Polley), the only surviving victim of the crash apart from Dolores, has had an incestuous relationship with her father Sam (Tom McCamus), but after the accident their relationship ends. Stephens persuades Nicole to testify, but she is compelled to lie, claiming Dolores was speeding and thereby destroying Stephens's case. Nicole's decision to lie is a refusal to exchange the lives of her classmates for any financial compensation, setting a path towards healing for the community.

The moment in the novel that bears a greater significance in the film is one that evokes the threat of losing a child precisely through their inability to breathe. The scene unfolds as the middle-aged and embittered protagonist Stephens describes an event from his earlier life as a young father faced with a deeply troubling and terrifying dilemma, an event that has haunted him ever since it happened. Stephens describes in meticulous detail how his infant daughter Zoe had stopped breathing after being bitten by spiders nesting in the mattress of an old bed, detailing the unbearably long journey to the hospital and the experience of dealing with the very real prospect of having to perform an emergency tracheotomy on her. During his recall of the event, Stephens breaks his composure and his inner turmoil is revealed through his lengthy, traumatic soliloquy:

> I was awakened by the sound of her breathing, it was laboured. I looked across and noticed she was sweating and all swollen. I grabbed her and rushed to the kitchen and splashed some water on her face . . . the nearest hospital was forty miles away . . . the doctor explained how to perform an emergency tracheotomy. How to cut into her throat, the windpipe, without causing her to bleed to death – he said there would be a lot of blood, I said I didn't think I could do it, and he said, he said, 'Mr Stephens, if her throat closes up and her breathing stops, you're gonna have to.'[16]

The clinical is here fused with the deeply personal through this threat of losing the child and her precious last breaths. The narrative's emphasis on paternal responsibility, in particular, has led critics of the film to comment on the scene's representation of male anxieties and the repressed fantasies of fatherhood.[17] However, such existing analyses of the film tend to obscure the significance of the child's breath, for it is that bodily gesture that risks being lost. Not only does this point in the narrative serve as a diegetic representation which draws attention to the breathing body, but its precise positioning within the structure of the film implies an importance that transcends its function within the plot: most strikingly, the images of this richly symbolic memory are juxtaposed, exactly halfway through the film, with the recollection of the bus accident. In this sense, we bear witness to the unfolding of two traumatic events which seem to be implicated in each other not only through their figuring of children, but through their formal suggestion of two intercut, embodied images of loss.

Initially, Stephens's voice can be heard as we view an evenly lit close-up of the breathing child's face, a knife positioned inches away from her neck. This troubling image of the child is the pressure point in the sequence twinned with the horrified face of Billy Ansell, played by Bruce Greenwood, who witnesses the bus carrying his children plunging, irretrievably, into the icy depths of a

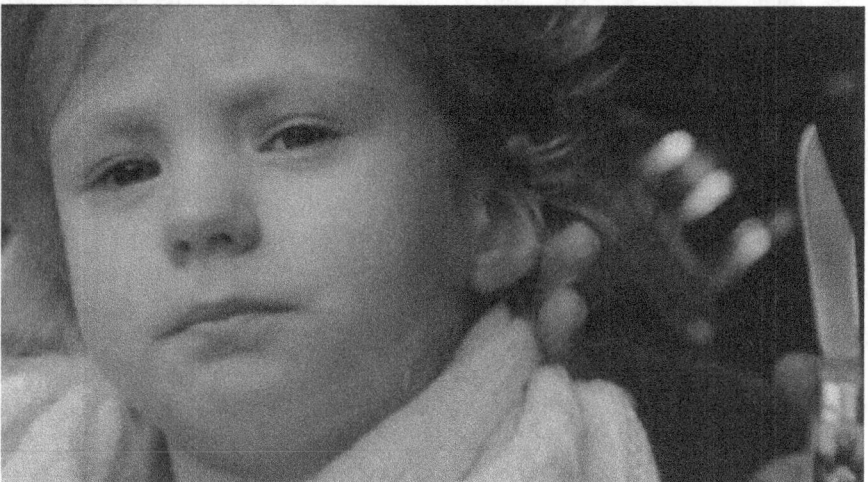

Figures 1.1 and 1.2 A sleeping family and Zoe. (Images courtesy of Atom Egoyan, © Ego Film Arts.)

lake. While Stephens admits at the end of his story that he did not have to perform the emergency tracheotomy on his daughter, since he reached the hospital in time to save her life, Zoe's unwillingness to recover from drug addiction in adulthood renders her 'already dead' to him, and thus separate perspectives on the loss of a child converge, both formally and contextually. Both traumatic events are alluded to from the very beginning, as my discussion of the opening titles will suggest, but their stalled presence and embodiment of entwined conscious states raise questions about the extent to which we experience the film as a corporeal, 'breathing' encounter, between the viewer and film, as well as between those represented in the film's diegesis.

The opening sequence of the film serves to establish the importance of breathing through Egoyan's densely atmospheric use of cinematography, colour and shot composition. We encounter an overhead shot of three naked bodies sleeping on a bed, a small child between its mother and father amongst folds of white linen. Contrary to the view held by Katherine Weese and Crissa-Jean Chappell that this opening image is an implied memory or 'flashback', I want to suggest that it represents a mode of embodied consciousness beyond Stephens's that is neither his implied memory nor his imagined perception of that moment, since his point-of-view shots are filmed in a very different way.[18] Indeed, the convergence of real and imaginary realms of the film call to mind the Deleuzian concept of the crystal image in which the real and virtual become entangled within each other.[19] Furthermore, the fact that this image of the mother, father and child appears for a few moments just as the bus accident is recalled and precedes Stephens's testimony of the event in which he nearly lost his daughter is pertinent, since it leads us out of the trauma of the bus crash and into other psychical terrain.

Egoyan has remarked on the image of the sleeping family in *The Sweet Hereafter* as one that encourages us 'to suddenly think of heaven, so that we're suddenly transposed into this other world',[20] and indeed, as I shall later suggest, the transcendental resonances of the scene reflect an Irigarayan, meditative kind of breathing which accords with some other, (im)material world. In this sense, the 'cut' away from the bus accident embodies an incision into the 'body' of the film which prefigures the possibility of the diegetic cut into Zoe's breathing throat. The risk of cutting into the film at this moment, like the risk attached to performing the tracheotomy, seems not to draw attention away from breathing, but to heighten its presence in the film experience. Such contradictions in the film's form raise questions about the gaps between seeing, feeling and viewing and how we interpret or 'sense' images.

I will stage various returns to these questions of viewing breathing bodies on screen throughout this book, but here I want to begin by sketching out the connections between the human bodies on screen and their involvement in awakening the viewer to a *breathing filmic corpus* – an embodied dimension of the film that comes alive through the formal heightening of the diegesis.

Initially, the three bodies, unified in their pale, fleshy radiance, are remarkably still, and the balanced lines of the white sheets against the muted background of the ochre wooden flooring emphasise a hushed equilibrium of calmness. However, Egoyan's frequent collaborator, the cinematographer Paul Sarossy, employs an aerial shot of the bed in order to close this sequence, producing an unusual sense of perspective, especially since it places the viewer in a very unnatural position. Thus the intimate scenario of the sleeping family is undermined by the formal attributes of the image. Furthermore, the fact that it is also a tracking shot that Sarossy employs and we pass, if very slowly, over the bed suggests that this moment is fleeting, layering upon the image a vulnerability that exceeds the nakedness of the sleeping subjects within the frame.

The aerial shot tends to distance the viewer from the image, emphasising the young family as a united 'continent'; the topos of the skin becomes landscape territory that is observed not through a totalising view but from a perspective that is, to borrow from Bruno, 'nowhere' and 'now here'.[21] Although Bruno's thinking refers more to aerial images of cities, her reflection on overhead images and their sense of being 'nowhere' and 'now here' is particularly apt since the image of the sleeping family reappears during Stephens's recollection of the experience detailing the trauma of the tracheotomy and is also juxtaposed with the moment in which the school bus accident takes place, sealed between the two events of the film which serve to represent its particular 'geography'. In this respect, the image of the family pinpoints a particular 'place' in the formal structure and trajectory of the film.

The film theorist Steven Dillon has commented on Egoyan's particular attendance to the gesture of place offered by the film's title, and has described the filmmaker's allusion to 'an authentically re-imagined space'.[22] Thus following Dillon's view, the image of the family re-imagines and accentuates a position of always being 'between': a mobilised here/after that the film's title also explicitly alludes to, the naked bodies of the image echoing a greater breathing filmic corpus that is neither inside nor outside the tragic events of the film.

While watching these opening images from *The Sweet Hereafter* we encounter not only the breathing bodies in the diegesis but begin to respond to the film as embodied viewers whose breaths are involved in the film experience. Most interestingly, our awareness of breath does not begin through the stifled gasps of the child on screen, but in these first few moments which we also return to after the tragic accident is represented: the impact of the scene in which we view the accident compels us to 'draw breath'. In this respect, our viewing process is consistent with the mimetic model of Marks's spectatorial theory in which mimesis presumes a continuum between the actuality of the world and the production of signs about that world.[23]

While Marks's mimetic model of spectatorship offers an appropriate methodology with which to examine the viewer's awareness of breathing in *The Sweet Hereafter*, psychoanalytic discourse deepens an appreciation of the sense of loss and its intertwinement with breathing in the film. In her essay 'The Expanded Gaze in Contracted Space: Happenstance, Hazard and the Flesh of the World', Sobchack refers to the dark image of the bus falling into the white ice of the lake as 'a slow spread of a grey stain'.[24] Sobchack suggests that the shape and colour of the bus in the filmic image corresponds with a kind of Lacanian anamorphosis that is, according to a symbolic field of visuality and meaning that immediately, infinitely exceeds us and reminds us of our own finitude and death, something akin to an indelible mark or stain.[25] While I do not wish to pursue further the psychoanalytic framework Sobchack proposes, her thoughts are useful in clarifying the concordances between the viewer's physical and subconscious reaction to the spectacle of the accident, especially since these moments in the film are coupled with the prolonged tension of

Mitchell's story in a way that can be described as causing us to gasp, literally holding our breath. The images of the accident, or rather its experience, not only remind us of our own mortality, as Sobchack's thoughts suggest, but encourage us to experience this thought in the flesh, precisely through our drawing of breath. In this sense, the moment of (symbolic) exhalation, of relief and, in many ways, closure, remains unfulfilled until much later in the film when we are left with the closing images of Nicole and her resolutely dignified voice, speaking of her new town 'with its own special rules' and content to be living in the 'sweet hereafter'.

This breathing dimension of the film is brought to life in the mind and body of the viewer precisely through the way in which the images invite us to consider relations between sight and the unseen; breathing comes to stand for this aspect of the film which tends to gesture towards an (im)material realm: a space which conjoins the living and the dead, the visible and the absent. Breath comes to represent a place between the seen and absent, especially through the images of the family which open the film and its complex iconography. When the image of the sleeping family is shown for the second time in the film, straight after the images which recall the bus accident, we become acutely aware of a tension between presence and absence, between what is visible and absent, or rather the inability to place this moment on the bed as before or immediately after the child has been bitten by the poisonous spiders responsible for the swelling of her throat, since we cannot 'see' the difference. In this sense, we have been betrayed by our eyes and we are prompted to contemplate what lies beyond vision. Egoyan poses here an important question about the ambivalence of sight or, rather, knowledge and truth. Thus from the very outset of the film, not only is attention drawn to the way in which knowledge is communicated, but the foregrounding of silent bodies in the opening sequence also encourages us to think about what we cannot see and this is symbolised through the notion of breathing.

The opening titles of films, for Marks, often contain haptic images, especially those which are predicated on uncertain knowledge: 'It seems appropriate to begin them with haptic images that make viewers unsure of their relationship to the image and the knowledge it implies.'[26] While the opening images from *The Sweet Hereafter* are not formally suggestive of the 'thicket of barely legible images'[27] that Marks's concept of haptic visuality tends to deal with, Egoyan's combined use of camera movement, sound and the haptic imagery of skin produces a similar tone of uncertainty that resonates with Marks's thought. Most importantly, Egoyan points towards the importance of our senses, particularly hearing, and the subtle noise of breathing. Indeed, in this context, what the image of the family provokes is an attendance to breath that is also resonant with the spiritual, foregrounded by stillness and silence, the focal point that the camera moves towards and flows out from as if touching upon the fragility of a moment.

Closing on this aerial height, I am reminded, in particular, of the 'altitude' of breath that Irigaray alludes to in her book of poetry *Everyday Prayers*. Irigaray encourages the contemplation of unity and creation through an attention to breath, promoting a state of soaring, higher being surging through the veins as breath enters the lungs and nourishes the soul.[28] This Irigarayan higher being is closer to rebirth in the light of a shared subjectivity:

With you breathing is becoming different,	*Avec toi le respirer est autre,*
Fresher,	*Plus frais,*
Higher,	*Plus haut,*
Altitude,	*Altitude,*
That gathers us together,	*Qui nous rassemble,*
Making each of us one,	*Nous faisant uns,*
Creating the we.	*Créant le nous'.*[29]

Thus Sarossy's high-angle shot stimulates a hapticity, an embodied, breathing sensation that occurs not from a literal proximity to the image, but from its emphasis on proximity to an interior consciousness, both mind and flesh. Similarly, Egoyan's frequent use of multiple aerial shots of panoramic views over the film's dramatic landscape of ice and rugged terrain represents the notion of a third subjectivity or an inter-subjective position. In this, one might take the children of the film to be symbolically reborn through a mobilised gaze of higher altitude, recalling an ethereal wandering of disembodied observers. This mobile view 'gathers us together', to reiterate Irigaray's poetic voice, from a 'heavenly' height of transcendence, as Egoyan puts it in interview.[30] Thus Sarossy's framing of the family in the film's opening sequence evokes an embodied consciousness which may also be seen to reflect the perspective of the children in the film and their positioning as celestial observers. In sum, our awareness of breath in the opening sequence is tied to the lost children in the film, breath becoming symbolic of their presence which lives on in the formal properties of the image.

While it is the formal use of camera movement in the opening sequence which evokes breath, it is the film's content and its representation of snow which not only fleshes out a new dimension of the relation between the absent children of the film, the spaces of the film and its formal attributes, but raises questions about the filming of air and its implications for discussion of haptics. The snow in *The Sweet Hereafter* represents an 'elemental topography' suggestive of both the transcendental nature of the film and its elemental qualities. The transcendental is often referred to by Irigaray as a coming into being through 'whiteness',[31] a welcoming colouring of the divine that is also earthbound; above all, white is the translucence of breath, the condition for reflection and the positive space of silence, according to Irigaray. Thus it is particularly apt that the aerial shots of the snow-bound landscape should evoke the presence of the lost children, as if conjuring a realm of immortality in the space of the film. Yet shots from the film which present a view of the snow from a more 'earthbound' perspective, rather than an aerial height, do not emphasise the contours of the mountains or the shape of the land; these shots are almost entirely white and, in this respect, they place special emphasis on colour and light in the film which bear implications for the way in which air, breath and especially sound are configured in the film. These images of the brilliant white snow in *The Sweet Hereafter* also evoke the presence of the children in the film, but unlike the aerial shots of the landscape, they introduce an auditory dimension to our perception of their implied presence.

The colour white, for the filmmaker and artist Derek Jarman, bears negative connotations: it is a dark omen, a clinical tone associated with the unwelcome, the unfamiliar and the unseen within. In an extract from Jarman's *Blue* (1993), a narrator's emotive, yet measured voice muses: 'In the first white light of dawn I turn white as a sheet, as I swallow the white pills to keep me alive ... attacking the virus which is destroying my white blood cells.' Counter to the clinical sense of white that Jarman evokes, the dominance of white in *The Sweet Hereafter*, specifically through its elemental presence as snow and frozen water, emphasises a prevailing territory that prompts an Irigarayan reflection on the auditory possibilities of whiteness, a syntax of silence that I shall now theorise in the next section as a haptic 'sensory refrain'. My development of an Irigarayan haptics focuses on Egoyan's use of sound and the depiction of white spaces in the film as a sensory environment; an 'elemental topography' suggested through the on-screen representation of a real, lived environment.

Escaping Haptic Logic and the Sensory Refrain

What do our breathing bodies make of the elemental realities we bump up against – the textures of rock, the tastes of wind and water?[32]

David Abram

At first there is whiteness.[33]

Luce Irigaray

If colour is organised light, must it not have a meaning as different combinations of air have theirs?[34]

Maurice Merleau-Ponty

In my introduction to this book, my discussion of the particles of air key to the installation art of McCall enabled me to show how the space of air can become foregrounded as a visible presence. While the shaft of light in McCall's installation highlighted particles of air, it is Egoyan's focus on the whiteness of snow in *The Sweet Hereafter* which emphasises the space of air and, importantly, breathing. *The Sweet Hereafter*'s filmed geography of snow and its focus on human movement through that terrain leads to a different breathing, 'elemental topography' embedded in the very image of an environment.

The previous section showed how the cinematography of *The Sweet Hereafter*'s opening sequence symbolised a kind of movement and composition within the film which comes to represent a form of interior consciousness resonant with Irigaray's thoughts on the cultivation of breath. This section rethinks the diegetic representation of movement prompted by the particular filming of snow which features prominently during a scene in which we view the protagonist Stephens as he treks through the wintry vistas of Sam Dent.

In the previous section, the filming of the silent, sleeping figures in the opening sequence was discussed according to the way in which it encourages an attentiveness to the mind and flesh, but this section shows how the static shots of Stephens's body in motion tend to elicit a different bodily response from the viewer. It is not Stephens's body *per se* which prompts an embodied perception of the image or rather a bodily identification with the character's presence. Rather, it is the image's representation of snow which invites an embodied response and thus we respond more to the environment than to the image of Stephens. This environment is, importantly, one which foregrounds the elemental properties of air.

The mode of viewing suggested by Marks's model of haptic visuality might be characterised as a way in which to respond to different filmic environments. For example, Marks's discussion of the figure of the tourist, prompted by Bill Viola's meditation on the experience of the Tunisian Sahara in *Chott El-Jehrid (A Portrait of Light and Heat,* 1979) and Mauro Giuntini's Brasilia in *Brasiconoscopio* (1995), serves to show how the filming of vistas bears haptic implications.[35] Yet the folds of cloth described by Marks during her analysis of Beharry's *Seeing Is Believing* are, in my view, suggestive of oceanic waves, rippling shapes which evoke aerial shots of the sea – a sensuous connotation that prompts a different view of the film's sensory appeal.[36] It may be argued, then, that Marks's 'haptic logic' of film involves movement across a sensuous terrain, territory traversed by the body of the viewer.

I want to examine what happens when a filmic terrain is suggested by the elemental space of air.[37] According to Irigaray, air is certainly not 'nothing'. Irigaray's thinking reminds us that air is not a vacuum of emptiness which alienates us from each other. For Irigaray, air serves to create a bridge that allows openness between us. Indeed, as Irigaray's thoughts imply in her critique of Heidegger's philosophy, air is a place unlike any other:

> No other element can for him [the human being] take the place of place. No other element carries with it – or lets itself be passed through by – light and shadow, voice or silence ... No other element is in this way space prior to all localisation, and a substratum both immobile and mobile, permanent and flowing.[38]

During one particular scene in *The Sweet Hereafter* which I will now discuss, Egoyan's filmic rendering of 'light', a radiant whiteness cultivated from the colour of snow in the diegesis, and 'silence' suggestively calls to mind Irigaray's reflection on air as an important environment. I will term this 'place' in Egoyan's film a 'sensory refrain': an alternative logic of embodied space. This 'sensory refrain' allows light and silence to pass through it, to echo Irigaray's reflection on air. Importantly, the filming of snow in *The Sweet Hereafter* permits a flow of light and silence which opens up a space of breath for the viewer.

At first, as Irigaray remarks in *Elemental Passions*, 'there is whiteness'.[39] Early on in *The Sweet Hereafter*, Stephens is observed through a silent set of long and medium shots in a white landscape of snow. He treads uneasily through the image, journeying in order to convince the Ottos, parents of one of the accident's victims, that they must prepare for a lawsuit against whoever must be to blame.

Whiteness consumes Stephens's small, darkly clothed body, a figure pacing laboriously from the right side of the screen to the left, a gash of white surrounding him. As we view this image Stephens appears to be the focus of the scene, but upon closer consideration it becomes apparent that Egoyan firmly situates him at the margins of the picture. Indeed, positioning Stephens at the margins of the image reinforces the film's narrative since he is continually represented as an outsider from the perspective of the community, as well as in reference to his detached relationship with his daughter. However, the way in which we view this scene does not echo Stephens's bodily movement slipping from one corner to another, it invites a caress of the screen, of its 'smooth space'. Thus our identification is not with Stephens, but with the film image itself. What it is we are caressing exactly will be part of my later discussion on how Irigaray posits a theory about breathing as a kind of tactile gesture and the way in which *The Sweet Hereafter* proposes a filmic enactment of touch sensitive to the 'thickness' and tangibility of breathing. Before going further to suggest how this tangibility of breath is evoked in the film, it is useful to look more closely at the use of silence and its imbrication in the snowscapes of the film.

While whiteness plays a part in creating an impression of expansive spatiality, lightness and air, it is the sonic quality of the film, or rather its suggestion of silence, which returns us to an interior consciousness, a contemplative 'sigh' or, more precisely, refrain. The geography of snow tends to enhance the foregrounding of silence in film, but while the figuring of such an icy geography in films such as the experimental video *True North* (Isaac Julien, 2004) conveys the constant seeping inertia of dripping ice through a soundscape, *The Sweet Hereafter* presents its frozen territory as a specifically silent rather than 'fluid' space.[40] This silence affords contemplation of breath, prompting us to think about its presence. Such a contemplation of breath tends to evoke a bodily presence that is differentiated from the body in the frame of the film (the figure of Stephens). This bodily presence which we identify with may come to represent the missing children of the film, an imprint of their existence that lives on beyond the earthbound realm of the film's diegesis.

The loss of the children in the film is thus articulated through the film's formal and diegetic evocation of snow's silent, white spatiality and the way in which it affords a contemplative space for breath. In order to understand further the relations between loss, silence and breathing it is useful to turn to the analysis of breathing offered by the film theorist Reni Celeste in her fascinating article 'The Sound of Silence: Film Music and Lament'.[41] Engaging with the thought of Lyotard and his claim that loss occupies a silent domain in which 'the breath is a wind of terror',[42] Celeste argues that silence conveys a terrible anguish, a sign of our inevitable extinction: breathing. As I have argued in my introduction to this book, Lyotard's post-modern thoughts on breathing as a wholly disturbing act in his philosophical text *The Inhuman* sharply contrast with the positive view Irigaray supports in her text *The Age of the Breath*. Celeste finds Lyotard's thoughts on breathing particularly useful in shedding new light on the relations between the post-modern subject in film and the tragedy of silence evoked through soundtracks and the diegesis of the films themselves. Celeste concludes with the view that breathing makes silence possible and its role within the cinema is to make manifest something beyond both sound and vision: primordial loss, or what Lyotard has called 'the breathing of lament – what enters through the body, sensations, aesthesis, is not just the form of an object, it's the anguish of being full of holes'.[43] While Celeste's thought on the melancholic nature of breath and foregrounding of silence seems particularly resonant with the way in which the loss of the children is articulated through silence in *The Sweet Hereafter*, it is the thought of Irigaray which proposes a rather more affirmative perspective on silence. Importantly, Irigaray's theorisation of the relationship between silence and breathing informs a mode of viewing that is not only attuned to the sensorial and tangible qualities of breath, but enables reflection on the cathartic possibilities of *The Sweet Hereafter*.

Irigaray's concern with breathing is not attached to loss but rather to preserving and restoring an interior life, a silence that is made fecund. When I view the image of Stephens in the snow in *The Sweet Hereafter*, my perception of stillness and silence seems to heighten an awareness of what Irigaray might describe as a 'serene spatiality'[44] which evokes the intersecting and intermingling place of air and breath. The sensuous qualities of hearing silence and of being enveloped by whiteness that are generated by the images of snow in *The Sweet Hereafter* come to suggest what can only be described as a *sensory refrain*, a logic of viewing experience that encourages the awakening and the attentiveness of a 'different flesh': an embodied experience that is sensitive to the space of air.[45] Later, in my chapter on the films of von Trier, I will show how the viewer's breathing body becomes more crucially implicated in the filming of air and breath, but my aim here is to first emphasise the haptic possibilities of air which introduce a different kind of sensory dimension to the film experience. In Egoyan's *A Portrait of Arshile*, the viewer's attention is drawn to the air that the child exhales, a wispy cloud reminding us of the place of air that exists in the diegesis, as well as between subject and viewer. While the air in *A Portrait of Arshile* seems to open up the three-dimensional space of the image, positing a further depth and relation contained within the frame, air is emphasised through a different diegetic environment and bodily relation with the image in *The Sweet Hereafter*.

There is a gesture of tactility suggested through the figuring of Stephens in the dense whiteness of the snow, a touch cultivated though silence. However, Irigaray's theorisation of breathing as a tactile gesture tests the concept of tactile perception in the film and, more specifically, enables my conceptual development of a haptic theory which brings into play the breathing body of Irigaray's philosophical model of thought.

An invaluable reading of tactile perception, as it is more generally understood, in Egoyan's *Felicia's Journey* has already been developed by Marks in *Touch*. Marks calls upon the amplified graininess in Egoyan's *mise en abîme* of video within film in *Felicia's Journey* in order to show how 'a kind of haptical sensation' takes place, encouraging the viewer to respond to the texture of the image as if it were a bodily force.[46] Marks's model owes much to the theorisation of 'local' and 'smooth space' in the work of Gilles Deleuze and Félix Guattari and it is this context of spatial navigation and orientation that is most important to my analysis of *The Sweet Hereafter*. Indeed, my particular engagement with the thought of Deleuze and Guattari is implied through my use of their term 'refrain' in this section's title, a term which reflects their investment in modes of territorial navigation and 'assemblage' pertinent to their reflection on haptic modes of seeing.[47]

The definition of haptics that is proposed by Deleuze and Guattari in their book *A Thousand Plateaus* requires the eye to fulfil the function of the hands, a negotiation of a 'smooth space' in which the proximal (touching, feeling) is privileged over the distant (optical vision) and whose orientations, landmarks and linkages are in continuous variation. For example, the conditions expected by the traveller in the desert, steppe, ice and sea are considered to be 'local spaces of pure connection'.[48] Deleuze and Guattari's thought on the conditions of the open terrain, the bracing wilderness experienced by the traveller, calls to mind the rugged landscapes of *The Sweet Hereafter*.

While Egoyan's framing of the protagonist Stephens evokes Deleuze and Guattari's figure of the 'traveller' whose body encounters unfamiliar, rural geographies (indeed, Stephens is originally from New York and thus may be described as a foreigner), the snow-capped mountains and white expanses of ice that dominate *The Sweet Hereafter* certainly arouse an interest in relation to 'smooth spaces' and the forces of nature which implicitly compel 'pure connection'.[49] However, it is in Egoyan's precise framing of these environs and their representation of air, whiteness and silence that I am most interested. Thinking through such spatialities leads me to ask what kind of 'air' a traveller might meet with in the desert or at sea, for these local 'spaces' are determined by their relationship to the elements where air becomes embodied as a source of energy and movement. Indeed, as a consequence of such forces, the traveller might also meet with the sand storm and the gale. All of these 'airy' conditions are especially illuminated by Irigaray's thought on air as 'the only available "there is" – a place before and beyond any other'.[50]

Irigaray is interested in the intermediary space of air, its inter-subjective nature as an element which flows through all things but which does not conceal the presence of other human beings in its currents and invisible networks of exchange. Indeed, when writing on the desert as a space best understood locally, Marks also underlines the importance of wind and the breeze: 'The desert is not empty, but it can only be navigated through close attention to the wind, the dunes, oases and plant life.'[51] However, for Marks, the desert is never only smooth; as Deleuze and Guattari have also observed, it 'lives only with the disciplining concept of interchange with the striated'.[52] Yet air can also be viewed from a distance, as Egoyan's film shows us, communicating vastness and visual detachment, as well as simultaneously evoking the tactility of snow, its coolness enveloping us as whiteness. In this respect, the filming of air represents a simultaneous movement between the near and the distant, a proximal relation that also is key to Marks's concept of haptic visuality: 'a dialectical movement from far to near'.[53]

The place of air is at the interchange between smooth and striated. While the term 'striated' can be used to refer to a space that is delimited, Deleuze and Guattari's conception of the term is useful in order to develop thought on its potential to generate new ways of thinking about the spatiality of air. In their discussion of visual space that is more optical than tactile, it could be argued that air is objectless, ungraspable, and in this sense the striated is fleeting and unobtainable. Furthermore, since breathing is silent and the striated refers to the non-proximal senses, which include hearing, this would also imply that a 'breathing space' is less 'smooth' than it is 'striated'. However, breath can also be 'touched'; as Irigaray suggests, it can become a 'different kind of flesh'.[54] This Irigarayan formulation of a fleshly encounter suggested through breathing refers not to a concrete physicality, but to the perception of a space or interval that exists between ourselves and our environment: 'a look of the flesh living in and of the air'.[55]

If breathing were to be conceived of further as a kind of 'touching' as Irigaray implies in 'A Breath That Touches in Words', then it becomes more associated with a smooth space. Thus Irigaray's phenomenological approach to language and sound is particularly useful in thinking through the haptic implications of breathing. While Irigaray's aim is to introduce a corporeal textuality to words in order to speak of the body as well as the mind, she also opens up a space in which to consider the sensuousness of breath: 'an attentiveness to the sensible qualities of speech, to voice tone, to the modulation and rhythm of discourse, to the semantic and phonic choice of words. There is nature and spirit, breath, sensibility, body and speech.'[56] Unlike Marks's reference to the grain of the image which compels 'tactile visuality', a caress of air, in the case of *The Sweet*

Hereafter, is not anchored in the texture of the film, but the diegetic force of air itself. Just as Marks suggests that 'looking at hands would seem to invoke the sense of touch through identification',[57] looking at air, that is, its foregrounding through images of whiteness and silence, invokes a sense of the flow of air, of breathing.

In the context of the film and its themes of mortality and loss, Irigaray's thoughts on the way in which breathing can evoke a 'look of the flesh living in and of the air'[58] bear implications for the figuring of the lost children in *The Sweet Hereafter* and the viewer's experience of such loss; our identification with the film is ordered by the filming of air which, as we have seen, foregrounds a sensuous rhythm or 'sensory refrain' evocative of breath. Thus the film elicits a filmic and spectatorial space of contact between the viewer and the 'unseen' children – an embodied relation is made possible through breathing.

While silence is suggested as an aspect of haptic viewing as we watch Stephens cross the plain of white snow, the use of sound effects and music during the opening titles of the film draws attention to a different kind of haptics related to the filming of objects, the sound of wind and its involvement in the creation of a sonic 'elemental topography' of breathing sounds present on the soundtrack of *The Sweet Hereafter*. This concern with the music used in the film and its evocation of a breathing 'space' will be the focus of the next section of this chapter. The previous section considered the ways in which the filming of snow served to suggest a spatiality that prompted reflection on the nature of hearing silence, a gesture that, for Irigaray, tends to correspond with a contemplation of breathing. The next section is concerned not with the notion of hearing silence, but rather with the particular use of instruments and their evocation of breathing, namely the use of the flute. This instrument not only serves to emphasise the centrality of breath in the film, but re-orients the viewer towards a different perspective of the film's representation of embodied difference, loss and mortality. Furthermore, the use of the flute, as we shall see, also offers a new way in which to reflect on the issues of cultural difference and exilic contexts which are key to Egoyan's *oeuvre*.

'Whispering on the Threshold of the Body': Breathing Sounds

At first there are shadows. The camera tracks in close up across beams of wood; we are near enough to observe the grain of the timber. Shadows play across the wood in gentle flickering movements. Very slowly, light begins to filter through and the rich texture of the wood emerges from the darkness. The sound of a lone flute accompanied by birdsong can be heard on the soundtrack, but this birdsong, an evident dawning, is briefly interrupted by the sound of harsh winds, a blizzard. These first few moments from the film tacitly emphasise an Irigarayan representation of the elements, namely air and earth.

Firstly, we do not perceive the wood according to a pre-given objectivity, we focus upon its natural texture and colour without associating it with any man-made forms. This way of 'seeing' is described by Irigaray as an opening up of a 'third ground', a free reserve of energy which gives us back our vision by seeing through the eyes of an irreducible being, that is to say that such vision cannot be reduced to terms we already know and understand as our own.[59] Importantly, this 'third ground' is also described by Irigaray as breath and thus Egoyan's use of the flute foregrounds this relation. Certainly, the flute is a woodwind instrument that is most dependent upon a regulation of air through breath in order to produce a sound, its rising and falling harmony rhyming with the natural cadence of a breathing body. As we enter this Irigarayan 'vision', the birdsong and the ambient gusts of wind are also evocative of a communion with the elements and nature, introducing the viewer to a contemplation of difference that restores a spiritual and autonomous sight. This combination of sound and image connotes an 'elemental topography' which reflects the transcendental yet also earthbound realm of the film, heightening the viewer's sensitivity to the natural world that is evoked throughout *The Sweet Hereafter*.

For Dillon, Egoyan's film is located within a tradition of filmic poetry that also includes the works of Derek Jarman and Andrei Tarkovsky.[60] But, in addressing those spaces that are made fecund by a poetic syntax, *The Sweet Hereafter* does not merely embody a lyrical discourse, it cultivates an exchange between the viewer and the viewed, the heard and the silent, a kind of refrain in which, as Irigaray suggests, 'breath touches in words'.[61] While Irigaray's thought on breath and words implies a linguistic context, her thinking is applicable to the embodied nature of music, especially the flute playing which relies on the breath control of the player. Thus it is apt to describe the use of flute playing in *The Sweet Hereafter* as a kind of breath that 'touches' in music, to echo Irigaray's thinking. Unlike my previous analysis of whiteness and the filming of snow, the kind of tactility suggested during the title sequence is between the breaths exhaled by the flute player heard on the soundtrack and the silent viewer whose breathing might come to represent a different body inhabiting the cinematic space of the film.

The presence of the flute on the soundtrack of *The Sweet Hereafter* is hypnotic, yet also strange and cryptic. However, existing critical analyses of the soundtrack offer limited reflection on Mychael Danna's choice of music.[62] Egoyan has suggested that the breathing body had indeed been a conscious consideration in the filmmaking process, specifically evoked through the flute playing of Danna's score and its deliberate embodiment of *The Pied Piper* fable, pointing out that 'the Persian flute player was asked to emphasise the breathy extremes of his instrument'.[63] Egoyan's remarks on the 'breathy' sounds of the flute reflect, then, an interest in attuning the viewer not only to the music but, more precisely, to the sound of a particular 'body' that plays each note. Essentially, Egoyan attunes the viewer to the rhythm of breath enabled by the musician's embouchure (the particular shaping of the lips and facial muscles as part of the performance technique required to play wind instruments). However, while the sound of the flute and the medieval theme it articulates foreshadows the centrality of Robert Browning's *The Pied Piper of Hamelin* in one of the film's key sequences featuring Nicole reading the tale to Billy Ansell's beloved children, the particular style of playing reworks the tale as one that dwells on the tragedy of the exiled. It is here, in this writing of an aural language and framed geography specific to the film, that another motif of difference emerges, relevant to Egoyan's reflections on cultural difference throughout his *oeuvre*.

Before I further trace the diasporic implications of Egoyan's choice of instrument during the opening sequence of the film, it is important to consider how we might associate the flute with the emblematic loss of children within the film. The loss of a child especially corresponds with the sound of the flute in Wilson's essay on the work of a different director, 'Kieślowski's Lost Daughter: *Three Colours: Blue*'.[64] For Wilson, the flute is an instrument of lament and its haunting whisper deeply associated with the death of the female protagonist's (Julie, played by Juliette Binoche) only child.[65] The significance of the flute in *The Sweet Hereafter* might accord with Wilson's perspective on the loss of children whose absence is most acutely recalled by the gentle timbre of the flute. However, the flute is also a significant mediator. If we consider the sound of the flute in Browning's poem to act as the embodiment of the join between two worlds, the land from which the children were taken and the land they are about to enter, it is not the signifier of the tragic that Wilson describes but rather the mediator of the tragic, the threshold of the exile. Indeed, Browning's poem has been described as a reference to immigration in the Middle Ages and the colonisation of Eastern Europe in which whole families disappeared to foreign lands:

> And I must not omit to say,
> That in Transylvania there's a tribe,
> Of alien people who ascribe,
> The outlandish ways and dress,
> On which their neighbours lay such stress,
> To their fathers and mothers having risen,
> Out of some subterraneous prison.[66]

Another reference to the exilic occurs during the film's opening theme in which the flute solo enters into dialogue with a ney flute, an Armenian folk instrument which is also one of the oldest forms of the flute. The choice of instrument is particularly apt since the ney flute emphasises an ancient nostalgia; it also evokes Egoyan's more frequent use of the Armenian duduk.[67] Indeed, in interview, Danna has also suggested that the ney flute symbolises the foreignness of the piper in the myth whose ethnicity is embodied by music.[68]

Yet Egoyan's particular inscription of the personal through his choice of the ney flute also articulates cultural difference in terms of the tragic events of the film, generating a strong sense of momentum which also closely connects the present with the past. Earlier, I suggested that the place of breath in *The Sweet Hereafter* was closely related to its representation of the loss of children in the film and their mortality (specifically the children involved in the bus accident, but also Stephens's child Zoe), and it is here in the 'breathy' sounds of the flute playing that this tenuous boundary between life and death is fully brought to light – it may be seen to represent the infant's shallow breathing recalled by Stephens, as well as the symbolic breath of the mourned children who breathe no longer in the diegesis of the film.[69] Furthermore, the momentum of the rhythmic breathing sounds of the flute player evokes the continuous passing of the lived body from one place to the next, marking out the place of the here/ after that is alluded to in the film's title. Ultimately, if breath can afford the possibility of touch, as Irigaray's thoughts suggest, then the flute playing serves as a gesture of proximity which circulates between the film's main themes of life and death, loss and mortality, and its central subjects. As Irigaray writes of the nature of breathing, it weaves a proximity, *between*.[70]

The Place of Stillness

We do not see the breathing body of the ney flute player in the opening titles of *The Sweet Hereafter*. Rather, the sound of the flute playing opens up a space in which to enter the film, orienting the viewer towards a particular kind of thinking and seeing necessary in order to begin making sense of its experience. By contrast, the closing moments of the film are led by the on-screen presence of Nicole, whose breathing is emphasised through her visible stillness and composure. Importantly, it is the situating of Nicole's body within a particular place which also prompts a sensitivity to her breathing, in relation to both the way in which she is positioned in the mise en scène and the formal positioning of the sequence within the film's non-linear narrative.

While previous sections have suggested how the locus of breath in *The Sweet Hereafter* relates to the children of the bus accident, this section will show how Nicole is also suggestive of another breathing subject in the film. Indeed, Nicole's presence contrasts with the diegetic absence of the lost children and Zoe, whose whereabouts cannot be traced by Stephens or the film's viewer. In this respect, unlike the children of the film, Nicole represents a living survivor, like Zoe, who survived the poisonous spider bites as a child. Yet the adult Zoe features in the film only during scenes which represent phone conversations between her and her father, Stephens, framed tightly so as to register only the immediate environment surrounding the various telephone booths she uses to contact him. Thus Nicole's breathing body holds our attention at the end of the film as a poignant reminder of the way in which she serves as a sentient, breathing body, a survivor, who is also a guardian of a particularly special 'place' where the townspeople are content to be living on in the 'sweet hereafter'. The final images of the film foreground Nicole's breathing body as a restorative and recuperative presence which signifies a positive shift away from grief.

One of the final and most enigmatic scenes in Egoyan's *The Sweet Hereafter* rests on Nicole, the lone surviving child of the film's central tragedy, who inhabits a silence that is only broken by the sound of her own voice. We view Nicole standing before a luminous, out-of-focus Ferris wheel; the combination of her static body and the moving object behind her creates a tension between foreground and background that is further emphasised by the wheel's illumination, a series of dancing lights moving throughout the film's space and depth.

In interview, Sarah Polley, who plays Nicole in *The Sweet Hereafter*, has commented on the ways in which Egoyan allows 'characters to have the stillness that people have in real life'.[71] However, I would add also that he captures the transcendental in this gesture; significantly beyond a naturalistic aesthetic, the motionless, silent figure of Nicole in the above image authenticates a sublime affirmation that resists the objectification of the female body within the frame. In her book *Fetishism and Curiosity*, Mulvey argues that the stilled image of the female form removes the viewer from the diegetic space in order to remind them of the pleasure of looking at an objectified apparition.[72] But the sense of stillness suggested by Egoyan, rather than the actual use of the stilled image, in the above scene does not expel the viewer from the diegesis in order to satisfy a fetishistic desire. Egoyan uses stillness to draw our attention to small gestures and, in this respect, I am reminded particularly of the exquisite formalist style of Sergei Paradjanov's *The Colour of Pomegranates*,[73] a film that Egoyan has remarked upon as 'endlessly mysterious'.[74] A considerable contribution to the mysterious quality of Paradjanov's film, and thus its transcendental style, is generated through immensely meditative imagery such as water flowing, pages of books fanning outwards, hats flapping in the wind and statuesque heads turning subtly away from us. The artifice of an elliptical turning or a slow sequential movement, like the abstract motion of the Ferris wheel in *The Sweet Hereafter*, gives the impression of a 'still-life', a stillness that is emphasised by movement. My analysis of this image is prompted by a two-fold interest in Egoyan's portrayal of a still and silent filmic landscape and the way in which it foregrounds the relationship between the outer space of air and the interiority of the breathing body.

The last few lines of dialogue which accompany the final images of Nicole are crucial to my understanding of this scene in relation to breathing. On the soundtrack, we hear Nicole read the last lines from Browning's *The Pied Piper of Hamelin*:

> For he led us, he said, to a joyous land,
> Joining the town and just at hand,
> Where waters gushed and fruit trees grew,
> And flowers put forth a fairer hue,
> And everything was strange and new.

In the context of the film, Nicole's repetition of the last line ('And everything was strange and new') refers to the legacy of the tragic event. However, this parting line may also be explored usefully from an Irigarayan perspective. In her book *Being Two: How Many Eyes Have We?* Irigaray develops thought on Heidegger's notion of the 'face' which explores the notion of being only in relation to already known concepts and structures created by man; Irigaray suggests that to put a 'face' on to anything is to narrow our vision, to condemn ourselves to a limited knowledge of the world. Similar to my earlier discussion of the wood during the film's opening titles, the final scene of the film marks a return to the issue of an 'interior' sight. For Irigaray, we must 'look with the other', that is, perceive other human beings without any preconceived notions and respect their difference. The kind of contemplation and perception of looking that is conveyed in the closing moments of *The Sweet Hereafter* preserves a similar space for reflection whilst sight remains intact. Indeed, Nicole's glance towards the camera during the closing sequence is especially suggestive not only of *her* vision, that is, her perspective which makes it possible for the community to mourn their losses without the intervention of Stephens, but of her relationship to others including those which are no longer visible – to the children she once knew and loved. Importantly, Irigaray's thought suggests that it is breathing which most helps us to contemplate beyond the visible:

> breath remains invisible ... To contemplate the invisibility of the other, gives or gives us again life, including the life of sight ... We are nourished by an energy emanating from him, or from her, which touches us in a mysteriously luminous manner.[75]

Nicole's composure suggests that her breathing is also likely to be calm and meditative and thus, in the light of Irigaray's thinking, she might be seen to be contemplating the invisibility of the other subjects of the film – the children. Furthermore, for Irigaray, breathing comes to represent an invisible relation between subjects; when this relation is contemplated, its energy is luminous: a symbolic light embodying the relationship between two subjects. If we consider the mise en scène of the film, the Ferris wheel lights articulate a cycle of movement within the image which recalls a generation of light, of energy. This light is directly associated with Nicole, and her voice and gaze both emphasise an interior consciousness which suggests that we witness, indirectly, a generation of an inner light marking not only a point of renewal in the narrative but the possibility of the return, the 'return to self' which is the safeguarding of (Nicole's) feminine autonomy. With these thoughts in mind, the land that Nicole speaks of in which 'everything is strange and new' can be read usefully as an Irigarayan contemplation of the other which does not attempt to put a 'face' on being but to respect difference, the difference that the tragic event engenders which also posits a unique understanding of being for the viewer. According to the diegetic content of the film, the deceased children represent the absented 'other' of the community, but it is specifically Nicole's realisation and respect for the 'other' that allows the people of Sam Dent to embrace a path towards healing. At this point, it becomes clear that we must think of Nicole, too, as another breathing child at the centre of the film, paralleling Zoe's position, whose image seems to represent the warning of death in both childhood and adulthood.

Nicole's guardian-like presence sets a path for recovery. This healing is emphasised through both the spatial and temporal dimensions of the image, as well as Nicole's dominant position within the diegetic space of the film. These aspects of the film imply a pattern of returning reinforced by the reappearance of the Ferris wheel, first viewed when the children are alive, and the cyclical movement it embodies – a return which is absolutely evocative of the position breathing affords us. That is, we touch upon ourselves without repetition, and become flesh illuminated with, as well as beyond, the visible parameters of sight.

Felicia's Journey: The Orality of the Place

As we have seen in my analysis of *The Sweet Hereafter*, Egoyan's evocation of breathing through the film's various elemental topographies demonstrates the ways in which filmic space might be theorised according to its relationship with the breathing bodies that are represented on screen. Thus the boundaries between body and space become unsettled through the presence of breath. While my analysis of the flute playing in *The Sweet Hereafter* draws attention to the breathy sounds of the music and its register of the particular 'place' of the breathing body in the filmic diegesis, my reading of *Felicia's Journey* will re-orient discussion towards the notion of the breathing mouth and the significance of orality in shaping filmic spaces. I want to show how the gesture of the breathing mouth and Egoyan's formal address of space are implicated in each other, prompting a different reading of the passage between body and space with which breathing corresponds.

In *The Sweet Hereafter*, breathing attunes the viewer to a particular consciousness, of the mind and flesh, and my analysis of *Felicia's Journey* will think through the particular formal and diegetic motif of journeying and the various suggestions of voyaging in the film in order to shed light on a different consciousness motivated by the film's foregrounding of breathing. As the film's title suggests, *Felicia's Journey* is about making transitions, physical and psychical, real and imagined: the film's title reflects a consciousness of journeying pertinent to human experience. This particular consciousness of journeying that is evoked through *Felicia's Journey* informs a filmic 'breathing space' – the representation of a spatiality which refers not only to the formal style of the film, but also to the way in which I rethink Egoyan's investment in issues of selfhood and loss, themes which are also important to *The Sweet Hereafter* but which re-emerge differently in *Felicia's Journey*. My analysis of the locus of breath in *Felicia's Journey* shows how issues of loss and memory are especially framed by questions of autonomy and self-possession, as well as the twinned themes of obsession and control.

In his book *Subtitles: On the Foreignness of Film*, co-edited with Ian Balfour, Egoyan describes cinema's visual economy as one that 'makes us feel both inside and outside of ourselves at the same time'.[76] Egoyan's thought seems to underline, above all, the significance of interior and exterior boundaries that are brought into question by the cinematic apparatus whose liberating visual mechanics stimulate our perception and knowledge of the world. Importantly, Egoyan's notion of the cinema as both an 'interior' and 'exterior' viewing experience can be elaborated upon when considered in relation to Irigaray's thoughts on breathing – a movement specifically between the outer world and the invisible dwelling of the body: 'Air is that in which we dwell and which dwells in us, in varied ways without doubt, but providing for passages between – in ourselves, between us.'[77] The 'passage', according to Irigaray, permits movement and, furthermore, the site of entry and exit of breath is marked by a 'blank, white mouth',[78] an incandescent becoming or ascension, arrival. For Irigaray, the 'mouth' and the 'passage' represent two significant stages in her conceptual approach to breathing and, most importantly, they fulfil a vital connection between the outside and the interior space of the body: breath between lips that embarks upon a voyage around and between the folds of the outside world and the centre of our bodies. Indeed, as Irigaray insists of air: 'The sky isn't up there, it's between us.'[79]

Irigaray's particular thoughts on orality and the notion of the voyage allow me now to examine the spatial topographies of Egoyan's film *Felicia's Journey*. I want to examine the ways in which bodily and sexual difference may be radically engendered through the figuring of the passage and its evocation of a breathing mouth. Thus the notion of the breathing mouth itself is figured according to a spatial logic in my reading of the film. Furthermore, my analysis will consider what is exactly asked of, or equally demanded by, an open mouth. Indeed, the consumption of food and its related activities, especially cooking, are important to *Felicia's Journey*, but the rituals involved in preparing, eating and digesting food prompt questions about the nature of orality and its wider implications when thought through in the context of the locus of breath in the film. Furthermore, my reflection on the ways in which the filmic, spatial economy of *Felicia's Journey* evokes the Irigarayan notion of the passage of breath leads me to re-view the role orality plays in shaping our perception of mourning and subjective memory in the film. While much of my analysis of *Felicia's Journey* will focus on the ways in which the locus of breathing introduces a new dimension to the theme of loss and its especially ritualistic recollection in the film, I will also demonstrate how breathing deepens the representation of recovery beyond the consumptive pleasures and perversions that the role of food suggests – positing breath as a different kind of nourishment of the body and soul.

Felicia (Elaine Cassidy) is a young Irish girl who travels to England in search of Johnnie Lysaght (Peter MacDonald) with the intention of telling him that she is carrying his child. Journeying across the industrial landscape of Birmingham, Felicia encounters Joseph Hilditch (Bob Hoskins), a reclusive catering supervisor obsessed by his late mother Gala (Arsinée Khanjian), a TV chef. Hilditch offers to assist Felicia in finding Johnnie but his good intentions conceal a hidden threat: it is implied that Hilditch has already befriended and killed many young delinquent girls and videotaped their conversations with him, compelled to possess them in the same way he possesses his mother's body through videotapes of her shows. Felicia is offered a room at an evangelical sanctuary run by Miss Calligary (Claire Benedict), but when she informs her that her money has been stolen – which Hilditch had taken earlier as a guarantee that she would need his help again – she is soon forced to leave. Felicia arrives at Hilditch's home and is immediately welcomed. Upon learning that Felicia is expecting a child, Hilditch realises that he cannot go through with her murder unless the child is aborted, making an appointment at a clinic for Felicia before convincing her that it is the right thing to do. After visiting the clinic, Felicia is drugged by Hilditch. Whilst digging a grave in the garden, Hilditch is confronted by Miss Calligary. Hilditch begins to break down, allowing Felicia to leave before he commits suicide. Finally, we view Felicia tending to a communal garden and reciting the names of Hilditch's victims, a naming that in some way reclaims their right to an identity that had been denied in death.

The film opens with two scenes which are, in essence, passages that are suggestive of interior and exterior crossings or boundaries that map spatial territory in two very different ways: firstly a continuous tracking shot through Hilditch's house from the living room to the kitchen, and secondly the voyage Felicia makes across the water, travelling from Northern Ireland to Birmingham. I will explore these sequences in more detail along with their broader resonance and reference within the context of the film in order to show how breathing is signified through various forms of passaging or journeying, diegetically and formally. My exploration of the notion of the passage in *Felicia's Journey* will show how Egoyan introduces a relationship between the filming of locations and his filmed, on-screen breathing bodies.

The film opens inside Hilditch's house. The camera rests upon an image of a doorway and it tracks, at a stately pace, through to a kitchen where we encounter Hilditch for the first time as well as his mother Gala, whose voice and image can be seen and heard emanating from a small portable television.

I want to go back again to this moment in which we glimpse the doorway, its subtle positing of a shift from one interior space to another and, more specifically, Egoyan's staging of vision as a mediated practice. Here, the screen is divided into three sections, or rather it is split by three horizontal lines suggested by the shape of the doorway that, in turn, dissects the image into distinct, formal spaces; on the left and right side of the screen there are two glass panels and at their centre we view the cream interior of the kitchen. At

Figure 1.3 A televisual presence: Gala (Arsinée Khanjian). (Image courtesy of Atom Egoyan, © Icon Productions.)

first, the interior feels warm and homely, but this is offset by Egoyan's use of Malcolm Vaughan's 'The Heart of a Child', a deeply nostalgic song which seems to prompt an increasingly nauseous tone, its sugary sentiments and lush orchestral score echoing loudly in the space of the film. The lyrics of Vaughan's song take us deep into Hilditch's inner psyche, aptly introducing a man we will come to know more as a child, whose heart is torn between the love and hate of his mother. Importantly, the sickly nausea of the music is prescient of the images we later view of Hilditch as a boy being force-fed bits of liver by Gala, and thus it can also be seen to emphasise the role of orality in the film. However, the spatiality that is suggested in the opening of the film also gestures towards the importance of the breathing mouth.

As Vaughan's music seems to fill the empty rooms we move through, the camera begins to close in on the kitchen, framing its space in a way that blocks out the foreground of the image, since the lower part of the image is obscured, saturated in darkness. Crucially, something occurs here that signals a shift in the film's spatiality. The heavily darkened, lower part of the image serves to suspend the kitchen in a position of floating detachment, in effect severing it from the rest of the house and the 'real-space' that it connotes. Therefore,

Egoyan's composition of the sequence proposes a 'disembodied' reality in which the kitchen signifies an interior that exists both inside and outside of the film's spatial topography; it anticipates the disjunction in reality that the kitchen embodies. Furthermore, the kitchen is a radical displacement of domestic space, no longer the realm of the feminine but an (in)visible dwelling – a breathing liminal space for the monstrous male psyche and its own imagined reality. This 'disembodied' vision and its association with the feminine is also illuminated when considered in relation to Egoyan's many references to both the film and opera *Salomé* and its female protagonist who desires her lover's head on a gilded plate, a key context which I shall later return to in more detail.

The frame of the doorway also forms the shape of an open 'mouth' and the kitchen is thus situated *inside* this mouth; the domestic space most associated with consumption is emphasised by Egoyan's framing of it by a doorway which we pass through in order to meet with Hilditch. In her writings on the films of Peter Greenaway, Bruno theorises the filmic apparatus as an embodiment of orality. Earlier, I showed how Bruno's concept of a filmic 'topos' was useful to my analysis of the aerial shots of bodies in the opening moments of *The Sweet Hereafter*, but it is her reflection on the resonances between looking and eating which raise questions about the cinematography of *Felicia's Journey*. She writes: 'The cannibalistic delight of inward transformation moulds space and, eventually, digests it with its eye-mouth.'[80] While eating is an important ritual for Hilditch, Egoyan's use of cinematography when filming inside Hilditch's house does not represent Bruno's concept of the 'eye-mouth'; rather, the way in which he promotes a mobilised gaze during the above sequence serves to suggest that the camera embodies a breathing mouth. Here, Egoyan suggests we are not the objects passing through into this passage or 'mouth', as Bruno's concept implies, but rather breath itself. In response to the eye-mouth or *occhia-bocca* that Bruno describes, I would like to term this movement in Egoyan's film an invocation of a *bocca di respirazione*, to echo Bruno's adoption of the Italian language which is also her mother-tongue. This 'breathing mouth' constitutes a position that dwells on both the inside and the outside of visible space and subjectivity in *Felicia's Journey*.[81] Earlier in this chapter I suggested how the space of breath in *The Sweet Hereafter* occupied a level of consciousness that was also twinned with the positioning of the viewer, but in *Felicia's Journey* the notion of the passage comes into play in order to suggest a different breathing spatiality.

The passage that Egoyan suggests in this sequence, both in the prolonged dolly track up to the kitchen and in his literal framing of the doorway, invokes a kind of corporeality '*in absentia*'. If we consider the filmed objects of the first few seconds of the film, it becomes clear that Egoyan is fleshing out a character that has no desire to touch yet is haunted by a displaced corporeality. For all of Hilditch's collections of rare eggs (recalling the precious blue hyacinth macaw eggs smuggled by Thomas in *Exotica*), toys and other ephemera that we observe in their display cases, the nature of bodily contact is limited to the caress of his detached gaze. Emphasising the space of a curator's gallery, Egoyan gestures towards the pregnant emptiness that haunts public spaces. This particular mediation of the private and personal through the public domain epitomises Hilditch's perception of his mother as a public figure whose persona irrevocably mediated his own personal experience of motherhood. Therefore the body of the mother and her breath, an embodiment of speech and love, can never be fully possessed by Hilditch since it must be mediated through the visual network that the screen produces. This suggested duality between the outside and the inside, the public and the private, the interior psyche and the outer material world of objects, affirms a particularity of 'place' that is founded upon the absented body of the mother, a passage towards her that is forever stifled by her loss.

The second passage we view in the film's opening sequence is Felicia's departure from Northern Ireland on board a ferry, a journey through exterior space that directly contrasts with the film's opening shots of interior space within Hilditch's home. The camera offers a fleeting glimpse of the mainland before we encounter the sea and eventually Felicia with her back turned from us, gazing at her homeland from the decks of the ferry. After a few moments, Felicia moves away from us and our view of her is blocked as she passes under the metal framework of the ferry's upper deck. We view Felicia climbing a set of stairs and then, again, she comes into view in full profile, quietly absorbing the moment of departure.

Unlike the previous sequence from Hilditch's house, these introductory images of Felicia produce a sense of space that specifically defines her relationship with land and her place within the outside world. Felicia is, in a sense, outside of everything; she is moving beyond familiar territory and even her last glimpse of home is fresh to her since she has most certainly never left Northern Ireland and thus never viewed it in this way before; to her it is just a line of rugged land on the horizon. Therefore what we observe here is a 'look' – the entire sequence is concerned with Felicia's gaze, positing her as a viewer within the diegesis.

Felicia is introduced to us through focus on her diegetic gaze, mirroring our first impression of Hilditch as we watch his eyes trained on the television image of his mother. However, while Hilditch's body is introduced as relatively immobile, Felicia's body can be seen constantly moving within the screen, emphasising her youthfulness, as well as her physical relationship with the immediate environment she inhabits. Furthermore, Felicia's gaze is unmediated and therefore, within the terms set up by Egoyan in his staging of the film, pure.

Unlike Hilditch's static composure in the previous sequence, Felicia moves freely within the frame and we come to know her through her physical presence within the geographical space of the film, often walking into and out of our field of vision. Egoyan also tracks Felicia through a dominant use of aerial shots which, firstly, has the effect of locating her firmly within a particular place or environment and, secondly, acts to distinguish our view from Hilditch's objectifying clasp. Felicia's sensible corporeality is also emphasised through many later images in which we view her touching or being touched by others, including the hands of her lover, her father and her grandmother, and her own hands on the railings of the ferry or pressed against the glass windowpane of a house that refuses her access, or her fingertips running along the labels on the videotapes that Hilditch has made of his 'lost girls'.

A sense of touch in the film has been explored by Patricia Gruben in her essay 'Look but Don't Touch: Visual and Tactile Desire in *Exotica*, *The Sweet Hereafter*, and *Felicia's Journey*' but her reflection on the notion of the tactile as a kind of possession can be complicated if we return to my conceptualisation of breathing in the film.[82] As we have seen, Hilditch's videotapes of his mother might represent his attempt to resurrect his mother's breathing body. While breathing sheds new light on the theme of possession in *Felicia's Journey*, an argument I will develop later in this chapter, it is the thought of Irigaray which enables a syntax of 'duality' to take place through breath, a relation that is less ordered by possession and more suggestive of Felicia's cultivation of breathing. In order to flesh out the paradigms of duality at work through the foregrounding of breath in *Felicia's Journey*, we must first pay closer attention to Felicia's role in the film as a presence which moves within a breathing spatiality.

With reference to the exact location of the above scene, the public space of the ferry is the setting for a contemplative moment for Felicia, thus turning that which is outside inside. One of the most important ways in which the interior corresponds with the site of breath is through Egoyan's use of sound. Accompanying the above image we hear an ancient Gaelic song 'Coinleach Glas an Fhómhair' ('The Green Stubble-Field of Autumn') sung by a lone woman's voice. The melancholic lyrics of 'Coinleach Glas an Fhómhair' recall a young man's brief affair with a woman soon to be wed to another man, mirroring Felicia's short-lived affair which led to her fleeing Northern Ireland in search of her lover. While Felicia's story might be seen to echo the lyrics of 'Coinleach Glas an Fhómhair' and its theme of betrayal and departure from Northern Ireland, I am more interested in Egoyan's auditory evocation of a 'nourishing' physicality, familiarity and comfort which calls to mind a mouth opening up in song. Unlike Gala's videotaped, staged performance of hospitality and warmth which we hear towards the end of the opening sequence introducing us to Hilditch's strange 'comfort zone', the sound of the music underscores a kind of breathy presence reflective of Felicia's more natural and elemental relationship with the world.

The flow of rich vocality and breath embodied by the sound of the song to me presents an image of a solitary, female mouth opening in song. Unlike Gala's frozen-in-time, static and superficial voice, the orality of this scene which introduces Felicia is most suggestive of an openness and fluidity, the crossing of interior/exterior borders, as well as the didactic tradition in which Felicia's personal history has been passed on to her from other generations and, most pertinently, her great-grandmother (Marie Stafford), whose maternal familiarity is evoked through the gentle voice of the female singer. While the voice of Gala emanating from the portable TV set in the film's opening scene also embodies a personal history for Hilditch, his is one that is, crucially, compromised by her television persona and her rehearsed performances. Felicia is denied the image of the mother in this scene, but the non-diegetic voice on the soundtrack emanates from a space of authenticity, unlike the memory of Gala.

Above all, 'Coinleach Glas an Fhómhair' is played over images of the ocean which comes to stand for an 'elemental topography' of water. While the television screen is the object of Hilditch's gaze in the preceding scene, the site of Felicia's gaze is the ocean, an elemental force of nature rather than technology. The ocean is a particularly important aspect of Irigaray's critique of patriarchy, but while air and water are hardly thought about together in her writing, *Felicia's Journey* provides new ways in which to question the relation between breath, air and the fluidity of feminine consciousness.[83]

First of all, the voice we hear on the soundtrack of the film establishes a feminine subjectivity that the sea comes to stand for in Irigaray's work. According to Margaret Whitford, the ocean exemplifies, in Irigaray's thought, an inversion of the mirror, the 'realm of semblance' that is privileged throughout patriarchal discourse as an emblem of order, knowledge and control.[84] This inversion of patriarchy glistens with the fluid textures of water, but it holds no risk of drowning: it is a place where one can breathe underwater:

> I would rather live in a seaweed hollow than in your gleaming palaces. And roll in the grass than in your ice fields. And drench myself over and over again in sea and shower, rather than be clean and polished so that I can shine in your sun's brilliance.[85]

The 'gleaming palace' that Irigaray refers to in the above passage bears particular resonance with our first meeting with Hilditch inside his home, or what I consider to be a site of attractions, 'polished' for his own visual pleasure. Similarly, the barren 'ice fields' of Irigaray's prose also evoke Hilditch's symbolic infertility, his incapacity to love and his refusal to accept Felicia's pregnancy. On the other hand, Felicia is immediately associated with the sea, exiled from her domestic home and thus sheltered by the outside world and the wide open spaces that must be navigated more through the sensations of her body than through vision alone. Yet she is not swallowed up by the spaces she inhabits; she 'breathes' inside of this fluidity.

However, although she can breathe within such a climate, Felicia still yearns for another freedom, obtained within the familial bonds of her lover and child. In a dream that takes place later in the film, Felicia imagines her child sitting on the shoulders of his father, Johnnie, as they walk amongst the ruins and fields of her homeland. The ruins, in particular, recall the ancient relics of Egoyan's earlier film *Calendar* (1993), whose crumbling walls emblematise the fragile possibility of reconciliation with the past. In this respect, Felicia bears comparison with the image of Arsinée Khanjian, who played the wife of Egoyan's Canadian-Armenian protagonist (credited as The Translator), photographing his homeland. But unlike Khanjian, she is less self-assured and still journeying towards selfhood and self-possession.

Indeed, Felicia cannot seem to escape the image and sensation of the clasp of others, unlike Khanjian, whose directness, signified through her confident gaze towards the camera, mediates the proposition of being known and objectified. Another moment from *Felicia's Journey* further probes Felicia's desire for autonomy that is specifically aligned with the sense of touch. During scenes which show her attending an abortion clinic with Hilditch, Felicia is seen to be anaesthetised before the film cuts to a close-up of her imagined child reaching over Johnnie's eyes. As though blindfolding Johnnie, the child's hands mediate a way out of the hands of others, reversing this gesture of control. In this, Felicia dreams of countering a patriarchal vision, a desire for her future generation to inherit a different legacy, to walk amongst the unknown and the new without the burden of history that has marked her own life. Indeed, it would seem that in order to fulfil such a desire, Felicia yearns to share the air with the ruins and feel it move through her as it whispers between the stones and the shivering blades of grass beneath her feet. In this sense, Felicia cultivates her breath. It is especially apt to recall here Irigaray's assertion that 'by cultivating breathing, we can gain an access to our autonomy, open a way for a new becoming and for sharing with other traditions'.[86] This cultivation of breathing is made manifest through the environ Egoyan composes – the sweeping blades of grass and the open expanse of sky which dominates the images of Felicia's dream. I will return again to the pastoral imagery of grass and wind during my reading of Egoyan's *Exotica*, but their presence in *Felicia's Journey* differs from this earlier film precisely since such exteriors permit the possibility of being able to breathe or, in Irigarayan terms, have access to air which provides a 'lofty freshness . . . now a source of hope and of greater perfection'.[87]

Lost Breaths: Archival Spaces and Absent Bodies

The interior and exterior passages that I have discussed in this section foreground Egoyan's representation of spatiality and orality in a way that articulates a specific 'breathing space', a filmic spatiality which surfaces through the filming of locations in *Felicia's Journey*. What I have addressed so far in my reading of *Felicia's Journey* is my concern with the physical geography of the film and its representation of real space, the rooms and environments which situate the central characters within a spatial context. Yet the film also generates a fourth dimension, a pivotal hyper-reality that emerges from the screen of technology, synthetic video footage and frames within the frame of the film, constituting an 'other' realm in which the film inhabits. Earlier, my discussion of *A Portrait of Arshile* demonstrated how breathing can posit a different dimension of physicality in the diegetic space of the film, but this section will show how Egoyan's use of video footage in *Felicia's Journey* comes to represent a realm of absence or archival space which corresponds with the silenced, breathing bodies of the 'lost girls' captured on Hilditch's tapes. This realm of videoed encounters in *Felicia's Journey* configures an archive of suffocated bodies.

The self-reflexive appearance of a TV screen within the frame of the film has been declared by Egoyan as a thematic obsession, one that is indeed present in *Felicia's Journey* since its narrative centres on the repetition of viewing that the video recording device offers; in this sense, the film recalls some of Egoyan's earlier work such as *Next of Kin* (1984), *Family Viewing* (1987) and *Speaking Parts* (1989), as well as the more recent *Adoration* (2009), in which the theme of personal disintegration through access to video technology is fully explored.[88]

In her essay 'The Body as Foundation of the Screen: Allegories of Technology in Atom Egoyan's *Speaking Parts*' Elena del Rio argues that it is the reconfiguration of the human body itself that has 'a structuring role in the production and reception of images', but I want to consider how breathing is involved in such reconfigurations of screened corporeality.[89] In this chapter I have argued that *Felicia's Journey* manifests a kind of corporeality *in absentia*, thus the actual *presence* of the body cannot be assumed. During the next chapter I draw attention to the filmic representation of breathing videotapes, objects in the mise en scène of Cronenberg's *Videodrome*, in order to explore the way in which breathing troubles the relation between objects and subjects, but the following analysis of the video footage of Hilditch's 'lost girls' first enables a space in which to begin fleshing out the connections between the materiality of technology and the human, breathing body. In this respect, I trace the 'screen environments' of *Felicia's Journey* and their orality as observed through the editing of various shots of the girls as 'talking heads'.

There are two distinct types of video present in *Felicia's Journey*: the archival footage that Hilditch has acquired of his mother's television programme, and the surveillance tapes he has made himself of the numerous girls he has invited into his car and subsequently murdered (at least, we are led to believe he has murdered the girls according to the evidence the videos offer us). Earlier, I suggested that Hilditch's repetitive viewings of his mother's television programme reflect his desire to resurrect her breathing body, 'embalmed'[90] by the television medium. The video archive of his 'lost girls' containing fly-on-the-wall footage of the murders represents a different viewing ritual which appears to collectively fetishise the breathing bodies of unloved young women on the fringes of society. However, we are introduced to the role of video within the film not via its visual presence, but rather through Gala's voice. Importantly, the young girls are also introduced to the viewer through the sound of their voices on surveillance tapes, and thus Hilditch appears to 'access' not only the bodies of the women he has on tape, but their animated bodies – their 'talking heads'. It is my argument that their breathing mouths, rather than their voices alone, are what Hilditch most desires to possess.

Egoyan's focus on the television monitor further emphasises the potency of screens in producing alternative memories and their involvement in shaping our imagination, themes echoed throughout Egoyan's *oeuvre*. Rather than focusing on the castrating implications of *Salomé*'s central moment in which the female protagonist demands the head of John the Baptist, I want to observe the fixation that is alluded to here, one that also demands the 'head', and thus Hilditch's identification with a feminine subjectivity. Although such an identification with a female subjectivity leads ultimately, in the film, to murderous intentions, which appears to contrast with an Irigarayan conception of the feminine, Hilditch's fixation enables a reading of male subjectivity propelled towards gaining (symbolic) access to air, to breath. The act of violence carried out by Hilditch when he strikes at them is directed at the girls' mouths, suffocating them with a cloth as he forces his hands over their faces. Certainly, the mouth is also the point of entry for the poison Hilditch prepares for Felicia disguised in a glass of milk.[91]

Drawing on the surveillance footage, I want to focus on the formal qualities of these images which have also been played collectively as part of a video art installation entitled 'Evidence' for the Oxford MOMA exhibition 'Notorious: Alfred Hitchcock and Contemporary Art'.[92] The surveillance tapes consist of images of three girls framed very closely, the camera placed as if in the position of the rear-view mirror of the car. Furthermore, the high angles of the shots tend to suggest that the camera presses against the foreheads of the girls' faces, the images cut off just a few inches below their chins. This framing emphasises the mouths of the girls, and thus Hilditch's videos might be seen to represent an objectification of the voice that also captures an essence of their physical presence through their breath. According to Irigaray's reflection on the spiritual dimensions of breathing, Hilditch's images seem, then, to capture the soul. Indeed, the prominence of the girls' voices, as well as the image of their mouths, on the tapes also recalls the claim made by Barthes during his discussion of various vocal techniques adopted by opera singers that 'breath is the soul'.[93] Thus it would seem that Hilditch's focus on the breathing mouths and voices of the girls represents a desire to capture not only their bodies but, more importantly, their souls. In this way, Hilditch's actions might be seen to reflect his desire to save their 'lost souls'. Hilditch is also a 'lost soul', unloved like the girls, and therefore he identifies with them.

Hilditch's omission from the edited tapes also reflects his desire to identify with the girls; indeed, his very presence in the videos would threaten to disrupt identification with them. Hilditch's presence is only implied as the girls address someone outside of the shot, their breathing voices constantly gesturing and responding to another voice that has been edited out of the footage. Hilditch's

Figure 1.4 Video excerpt from *Evidence* (1999) as exhibited at Oxford's MOMA. (Image courtesy of Atom Egoyan, © Ego Film Arts.)

absence suggests a deliberate erasure of his own subjectivity, focusing on the girls and the archival space that the videos represent.

Certainly, the voices and breathing mouths of Hilditch's young, female victims collectively represent a specific place in the film or 'media environment',[94] which Geoff Pevere has described as an inherent feature of Egoyan's films. The roughly defined and flickering 'video-faces' of the girls thus flesh out a media space made of recorded bodies and multiple screens which allow us to inhabit the psychical world of Hilditch. In this chapter, I have argued that the media environment in *Felicia's Journey* serves to preserve the breaths of the dead victims as prominent silences felt only by Hilditch (the observer), but they are also designed to enable a very particular kind of mourning to take place. These silences or, rather, breaths taken by the girls, technologically manipulated through Hilditch's editing, also serve to invoke the relationship Hilditch possesses with his mother, perpetually mediated by her 'screen' presence. The (artificial) erasure of Hilditch's subjectivity from the site of memory completes his ritualistic staging of trauma propelled by an abusive relationship with Gala. Here, Hilditch engages in his own kind of 'family viewing', to recall the title of Egoyan's 1987 film, assembling a genealogy of the unloved.

Yet, while Hilditch's archival spaces may be seen to preserve the breathing bodies of his victims, his decision to hang himself at the end of the film might reflect a desire to finally come to terms with his crimes. In this respect, Hilditch's suicide accords with a desire to sever the flow of breath needed to survive, finally cutting himself off from breath in a way that echoes the suffocation of his 'lost girls'. Unlike the videos of the girls and Gala, no one will resurrect Hilditch via a network of video images; certainly, his death will also mean that the videotapes are likely never to be played again. Thus the videotapes will gather dust and be allowed to decay, their materiality eroding in a manner that suggests a kind of release of the girls and their souls. Hilditch's self-destruction is crucial in order to grant the girls and his mother a peaceful end, no longer restless breaths haunting the materiality of his video images; his choked breaths at the end of the film embody a vital moment of catharsis, of recognition of his crimes and realisation of the end of breathing, of what it truly means to be mortal.

While the videotapes of the girls might naturally erode over time after Hilditch's death, marking the end of their video existence, the closing images of the film also emphasise the way in which Hilditch's death enables the possibility of mourning for their loss, a ritual that is specifically enacted by Felicia. This mourning takes place within the enclosure of a communal garden in an urban environment, the names of the girls called out by Felicia as she is filmed at work tending to the plot of land. The garden, then, marks a kind of funereal space, a final place of rest for the girls whose names are ritually recalled by Felicia in memory of their passing, a gesture that also aptly serves to emphasise the importance of Felicia's relationship with nature which I have underlined throughout my reading of the film. Above all, Felicia's soothing recitation of the lost girls' names contrasts with the words of anguish and pain that were last spoken by the girls, her slow, measured calling out of their names foregrounding her control over her body and the flow of breath between her lips: a sign of her autonomy at last granted in this final act of catharsis.

Exotica: Asphyxiating Geographies

'*He wants to believe that Lisa's still there.*'
'*Why would somebody want to do something like that?*'

While the collection of video images in *Felicia's Journey* suggests an archival space in which the breathing bodies of Hilditch's victims are embalmed and preserved rather than mourned, the spaces of Egoyan's *Exotica* are precisely constructed in order to assemble an asphyxiating place of mourning. These spaces of mourning in *Exotica* bear implications for their inhabitants, foregrounding breath through their representation of enclosure and claustrophobia.

In my reading of *Felicia's Journey*, my engagement with Irigaray's thought on the passages and flow of breath enabled me to rethink the filming of space and our navigation through such environments as suggested through the formal properties of the film. This investigation into what I described as the particular 'orality' of *Felicia's Journey* led me to examine the way in which the image of the breathing mouth became a vital aspect of the archival spaces that the videos collectively embodied. My treatment of *Exotica*'s filmic climates engages with Irigaray's thoughts on the spatio-temporal nature of air and breathing in order to reflect on the representation of mourning. Above all, my analysis will demonstrate how the spaces of *Exotica* work to emphasise a suffocating realm in which mourning can take place. Longing is expressed not only in the mise en scène but through the formal attributes of the film and, thus, the space of suffocation in *Exotica* transcends the narrative and diegetic space of the film. My analysis shows how the locus of breath draws attention to a different kind of viewing experience which situates the viewer within what I describe as a claustrophobic spatiality. Importantly, my theorisation of a mode of viewing ordered by *Exotica*'s restricted and limited spaces for air and breath develops thought on a more risky and vulnerable form of embodied visuality that differs from the viewing relations of *The Sweet Hereafter* and *Felicia's Journey*.

In *Exotica* we are drawn into the world of a group of people whose lives revolve around a strip club, 'a very particular place', as its owner Zoe (Khanjian) describes it, which serves the very special desires of its inhabitants. We watch the tax inspector Francis Brown (Greenwood) wait for Christina (Mia Kirshner) to dance for him, her schoolgirl outfit resurrecting the memory of his dead daughter Lisa, whom Christina also knew and took care of as her babysitter. Eric (Elias Koteas), the strip club's emcee, also watches Christina, for reasons not unconnected to Francis's loss. Behind the scenes of the club, Zoe watches everything through two-way mirrors. Fated to be propelled towards the secrets of the club, Thomas (Don McKellar), a pet shop owner, conceals a smuggling trade which imports exotic species and is first filmed meeting with various men in an opera house to have sex, yet he refuses to openly acknowledge his own homosexuality. When Francis is brought in to inspect Thomas's accounts, all of *Exotica*'s characters begin to refract a prismatic range of perspectives which tightly intersect, enmeshed in each other's desires and unspeakable losses. The club stills the heart and the breath of those who enter, remapping desire as an 'asphyxiating' compulsion.[95]

Mourning is central to *Exotica*. We bear witness to Francis's desperate attempts to deal with the loss of his daughter, a perspective twinned with Eric's coming to terms with the knowledge that he discovered her body at the same time as meeting Christina, his former lover, while assisting police in their search for the lost girl. Interwoven through the principal narrative of loss in *Exotica* are references to other lost loved ones such as Thomas's recently deceased father and Zoe's mother, from whom she inherited the club. Wilson and bell hooks have underlined the place of suffering in *Exotica*, carefully marking out the stages of violation, fantasy and sublime yearning which appear to 'soothe'

the wounds of such incredibly intense trauma. Yet, as Wilson has noted, this mourning is 'faulty'.[96] Thus Francis's behaviour, his particular rituals of mourning, might be seen to be, on the surface, cathartic, but ultimately such behaviour only serves to increase his pain. This is to say that instead of relieving the pain of loss, the film consistently shows how the repetitive loop of behaviour which each character gravitates towards only enhances their suffering. Wilson writes: 'The search to deny the loss of the child in erotic pleasure and re-enactment is seen by the end of the film to be asphyxiating, a trap of traumatic repetition.'[97] Indeed, my treatment of the film will explore further the meaning behind such 'asphyxiation', especially in the context of the interior and exterior settings of the film. If the 'lost girls' of *Felicia's Journey* can be described as suffocated victims, then the spaces of *Exotica* bring to light a different reading of asphyxiated bodies in the films of Egoyan.

Intimate Dwellings

The 'Exotica' club is the place most associated with the unfolding of loss in the film and its mise en scène constructs a space of claustrophobia and tension that is a suffocating environment which facilitates both the real and imaginary conditions for mourning.

When we first enter the club, we are immersed in its dazzling blue light and patches of shadowy enclosure casting beams of cobalt intensity over waxy ferns and flowers arranged throughout the club. The blue tint in the darkness first creates the impression of a midnight sky, turning the inside outside, with its evergreen foliage tricking us into believing we are walking amongst the moonlight. In her analysis of the club's aesthetic sensibility, Wilson emphasises Egoyan's interest in evoking the iconography and colour palette of Henri Rousseau's paintings which are also, for her, felt in the opening titles of the film as 'a shot moving along the walls of the set, across lush tropical plants, creating a three-dimensional Rousseau image'.[98] However, like all things in *Exotica*, nothing is fixed to any one time, place or form: the film is about transgressing these boundaries, and common experience is communicated, paradoxically, through difference. In this context, the exotic jungle of the club also mirrors a pool of fantasy, an Atlantis where all things lost reside. For Jeremy Taylor, the ancient myth of Atlantis comes to represent 'psycho-spiritual intuitions of our deepest selves',[99] a definition that resonates with the power of the nightclub to draw out hidden memories and emotions or, as the film critic Girish Shambu puts it, to 'cultivate' fantasy.[100] Certainly the film's set design, the light picking out details such as the scallop-shaped gold stage lights and stone facades, also calls to mind a sunken underworld. Furthermore, the azure strobe effects create a murky density which mirrors Thomas's fish tanks and their almost opaque waters. In this strange, hybridised environment, bodies sweat and writhe to the beats of contemporary Arabic songs, Western synthesised music and, most memorably, Leonard Cohen's 'Everybody Knows'. Voices seem distant and submerged: Eric's solicitous narration while Christina dances ripples across the stage like a silvery searchlight in the water and the inner sanctum of Zoe's boudoir almost shudders with reverberation, anchored to the heart of the club.

Voices and breaths emerge from the bodies of the club's inhabitants, but they are ultimately drowned inside its vibrant, pulsing interior. Eric's voice, amplified by a microphone, is the only breathing voice audible in the club, like a shaft of air penetrating the mist and the shadows, chilly against Christina's bare flesh. Here, the treasure of such an Atlantis is the recovery of Francis's daughter summoned through Christina's presence, once her babysitter and now the nymph-like guardian of her memory.

The watery depths of the club slowly suffocate its inhabitants. According to Irigaray, breathing constitutes a form of remembering, in contrast to the forgetting of being that she critiques in the writings of Heidegger. The slowing down of breath, then, amounts to a widening gap between past and present – a distortion of memory, as well as time. This sense of time, according with the flow and pace of breathing, resonates with the representation of the club itself, a realm which seems to be founded on a very different kind of temporal relation, namely one that is locked in the near past and an unchanging continuum of the present. As the inhabitants of the club appear to 'suffocate' inside, time slows down; it does not become still, but neither does it find any constancy; it follows the logic of the club's 'immemorial waters', as Irigaray might suggest.[101]

Interestingly, Shambu has also reflected on an acute sense of 'uneasy claustrophobia' associated with the scenes set inside Thomas's pet shop in *Exotica*, but the lack of air that Shambu observes is not the same as the breathless conditions that are implied through the images of the club.[102] The pet shop scenes evoke a strong sense of tension that might be described as claustrophobic, owing much to the cluttered and unevenly lit mise en scène as well as the narrative focus on the uneasy relationship between Francis and Thomas, but *Exotica*'s breathlessness is more bound up with the rituals of desire and pleasure that take place inside the club. Yet there is a further space of suffocation that Shambu's comment touches upon, but does not probe any further: the film's formal representation and its effects on the viewer.

Pastoral Visions and Suffocation

Not only is the strip club a space of symbolic, potentially 'pleasurable' suffocation or rather asphyxia, but the images of the film also gesture towards an overwhelming proximity which presses up against us, compelling us to pull away. During one particular scene just before we view low-angle images of Christina and Eric walking across the open stretch of land as they search for the body of the missing child, we are first offered extreme close-ups of the blades of grass, its dry, brittle streaks dragging us closer into the earth. Positioned so near to the roots of the grass, perhaps we crouch, tiger-like,

Figure 1.5 Christina in the club's exotic underworld. (Image courtesy of Atom Egoyan, © Ego Film Arts.)

recalling Rousseau's *Surprise!* (1891), dwelling amongst this dense texture. Yet if we are tigers then we must ask the question of what it is we are prey to or preying on, since to dive into such a place would suggest battle or anticipation of some kind of threat. While the lucid shape and texture of the grass bears strong comparison with Rousseau's imagery, the close-up also produces a considerable degree of unease, suffocating the viewer with its low-angled proximity, compounded through its implicit suggestion of the yet-to-be represented spot where the body of the lost child will eventually be found.

The softly swaying blades of grass and their collective, sweeping shiver which fills the wider, lingering shots of the search group as they appear on the horizon are also elemental, bearing traces of the wind and the air as filmed motion on screen.[103] This is, as Irigaray writes, 'the air we breathe, in which we live, speak, appear: the air in which everything "enters into presence and comes into being"'.[104] While the silent image of whiteness in *The Sweet Hereafter* created the conditions for a possible contemplation of air, spatiality and emptiness, which draws attention and encourages the breath of the viewer, the actual figuring of wind suggested through the shifting movement of the grass here in *Exotica* is filmed in such a way that it appears to be rather 'suffocating' for the viewer. Thus the filming of wind does not grant the viewer access to air, it tends to elicit the reverse. However, this is not to say that the device of the close-up is quintessentially responsible for creating such effects of suffocation, since this would presuppose that all formal qualities always produce the same affects, but rather that the combination of what is filmed and its formal representation leads us to feel discomforted and that this particular sequence might best be called 'suffocating'.

In contrast to the way in which I consider the images of grass in *Exotica*, their suggestion of breathlessness and anxiety, the philosopher Simon Critchley has observed the recurrent, unforgettable images of wind in the kunai grass in Terence Malick's *The Thin Red Line* (Malick, 1998) as shots which effect a calmness on screen, reflective of 'the beautiful indifference of nature'.[105] At first, the shots in *Exotica* featuring the pastoral imagery of the fields appear tranquil, unfolding in their own time, unhurried and patient, comparable with Malick's images of grass. However, the close-ups of the grass in the breeze, as well as its gentle ruffling of Christina's hair, remind us of the context of such images, suggesting we ought to be careful not to forget that a search is taking place for a missing child, whose body might be found at any moment. Indeed, Eric and Christina meet on the search, their increasing desire for each other dangerously burdened by the fact that they discover Lisa's body together, and therefore any sense of calm is undermined by what follows. Egoyan expresses such ambivalence formally in his close-ups of the grass which instantly diminishes any false sense of ease and startles the viewer with their dark foretelling of something 'hidden'. Indeed, the filming of grass encourages feelings of apprehension and ambivalence towards the images in a way that is also amplified through the non-linear structure of the film. It is a discomforting thought to know that the wind is 'indifferent', as Critchley might imagine, to yielding blades of grass or the human bodies which might walk or rest amongst it. In this respect, the image of the wind offers an uneasy truth which has a bodily effect upon the viewer as a constricting, suffocating experience.

While Critchley's reflection on the existential nature of the wind in film sheds light on the human relations in *Exotica* and the way in which they unfold against a backdrop of atmospheric, pastoral landscapes, Sobchack has also placed emphasis on the sensory appeal of wind and air.[106] Sobchack's enquiry into the filmic representation of wind and air is led by her interest in the locations of the film *Black Narcissus* (Michael Powell and Emeric Pressburger, 1947), especially its portrayal of a convent in the Himalayas, a place that endures the forces of nature at their most extreme and whose bells swing pendulum-like in a palace of winds. Above all, the wind aids theatricality and dramatic effect in Powell and Pressburger's film, but its subtle, delicate movement through the grass in the filmed spaces of *Exotica* is more evocative of naturalistic realism and a microcosm of sensation. In *Exotica*, the breeze which shakes the grass shows the presence of air, but the formal qualities of the image

Figures 1.6 and 1.7 Ambivalent thresholds: searching for Lisa. (Images courtesy of Atom Egoyan, © Ego Film Arts.)

take our breath away. While images of nature can overshadow the portrayal of human drama, according to Critchley's view of the film,[107] Egoyan never drifts from the questions of human nature which are at the centre of his film, and his filming of the grass in *Exotica* precisely underlines human experience.

Concluding Thoughts on Egoyan

Breathing creates an ambivalent sense of space in the films of Egoyan. Just as the images of the child's breath in *A Portrait of Arshile* refigure the three-dimensional space of the film, the grass in *Exotica* draws attention to a depth of space that air inhabits. In my discussion of Arshile's breath on the camera lens in *A Portrait of Arshile*, I underlined possibilities of proximal and haptic relations which are involved in the viewing experiences of Egoyan's films. However, my theoretical focus on breathing has not simply afforded a new line of haptic enquiry; rather, what is brought to light through my engagement with *The Sweet Hereafter*, *Felicia's Journey* and *Exotica* is the importance of breath as a development beyond tactile relations. For example, while the grass in *Exotica* might suggest a visible texture that invites a tactile response, these images communicate beyond a sense of touch, as I have argued, and it is the evocation of air and breath that constitutes precisely a bodily relation which cannot be analysed in terms of its 'tangibility' alone.

As should now be apparent, the concept of haptics needs to expand in order to take on board the significance of breath in Egoyan's films. My engagement with the spatial relations that are especially pertinent to haptic discourse and Irigaray's philosophy of breath has demonstrated how Egoyan's films flesh out a kind of filmic spatiality of breath, a mapping of filmic space which I have described as an exploration of Egoyan's 'elemental topography'. Furthermore, Irigaray's thinking also bears implications for the way in which issues of gender emerge in Egoyan's films, especially the representation of female autonomy that is negotiated through the foregrounding of breath. Male subjects, such as Hilditch in *Felicia's Journey*, are led by a desire to appropriate and possess the breath of others in order to compensate for their own loss of autonomy that breathing comes to represent.

As we have seen in Irigaray's theorisation of the way in which air and breath are implicated in each other, their representation of a specifically fluid, spatio-temporal realm prompts reflection on the articulation of 'place' in *The Sweet Hereafter*, a film whose spaces suggest a form of embodied consciousness which invites the viewer to think about breath, as well as encounter it as part of the film's sensory appeal. Since breath is bound up with the thematic loss of children in *The Sweet Hereafter*, Egoyan's foregrounding of breath in the film experience suggests a space of mortality, and indeed immortality, which deepens and enhances identification with the subjects of loss in the film. Vital to this mode of identification in *The Sweet Hereafter* is the film's use of sound and silences which promote a sensitivity to breath that is also visually aligned with what I have theorised as the filming of air. While the viewer's sensitivity to air and breathing in *The Sweet Hereafter* calls to mind Irigaray's transcendental thought on breath, and thus a rather more cathartic view of the film's narrative, the locus of breath and air in *Felicia's Journey* accords with a macabre space of the embalmed and 'undead' whose breaths live on, not in the form of the film, but as a resurrected or 'resuscitated' presence captured on video in the diegesis of the film. While the filmed space of air and breath in the videos of *Felicia's Journey* comes to stand for a form of mourning, this theme is reconfigured through an especially risky form of bodily identification prompted by the embodied spaces of *Exotica* and its 'asphyxiated' filmed bodies whose intense psychical pain provokes an acute bodily identification precisely articulated through feelings of suffocation. Importantly, this embodied sensation of suffocation raises questions about the more troubling aspects of thinking through the place of breath in film beyond the largely positive view offered by Irigaray. Indeed, what emerges as one of the most vital points of this chapter is the way in which breathing introduces an ambivalent form of bodily identification with the film.

While it is the acute, inner psychical pain of the protagonists of *Exotica* which elicits an embodied sensation of discomfort for the viewer through 'suffocating' effects, trauma is first and foremost registered on screen as a visible suffering in the flesh in my discussion of the films of Cronenberg in the next chapter. Irigaray's interest in the physicality and sensuousness of breath is explored in order to work through a different bodily identification which responds to the disturbing images of the intensely feeling and traumatised bodies most importantly suggested through two films: *Spider* and *Videodrome*. My theorisation of a mode of bodily identification relating to the very locus of breath in *Spider* and *Videodrome* involves not only the forms of physicality that are foregrounded formally and diegetically, but Cronenberg's particular fleshing out of another differentiated, breathing 'body' in the film experience which, I argue, his formal style comes to represent. My focus on physicality and its evocation of breathing in *Spider* and *Videodrome* will enable me to more closely investigate the viewing experience as it might be ordered by the filming of the sexed, breathing subject and the implications it bears for the theorisation of autonomy and selfhood that was pertinent to this chapter, but re-viewed according to the radical revisioning of sexuality and sexual difference in Cronenberg's films.

Notes

1. *A Portrait of Arshile*, dir. Atom Egoyan, Canada/UK, 1995.
2. See Baronian, 'History and Memory, Repetition and Epistolarity', in Monique Tschofen and Jennifer Burwell (eds), *Image and Territory: Essays on Atom Egoyan* (Waterloo, ON: Wilfrid Laurier Press, 2007), pp. 157–76 (p. 170).
3. See Tschofen and Burwell (eds), *Image and Territory: Essays on Atom Egoyan*, and Jonathan Romney, *Atom Egoyan*, World Directors Series (London: BFI, 2004).
4. The retrospective was entitled 'Atom Egoyan: le tableau et le cadre'. The programme of events is available at <http://tinyurl.com/cyo65f> (accessed 28 July 2009).
5. See Desbarat et al., *Atom Egoyan*, trans. Brian Holmes (Paris: Éditions Dis Voir, 1993).

6. See Wilson's *Atom Egoyan*, Contemporary Film Directors Series (Champaign: University of Illinois Press, 2009). Indeed, I am grateful to Wilson for generously sending me proofs of her work prior to publication.
7. See Wilson, 'The Female Adjuster: Arsinée Khanjian and the Films of Atom Egoyan', in *Cinema's Missing Children* (London: Wallflower Press, 2004), pp. 28–40.
8. Ibid. p. 40.
9. See Geoff Pevere, 'Difficult to Say: Atom Egoyan Interviewed by Geoff Pevere', in *Exotica* (Toronto: Coach House Press, 1995), pp. 43–67 (p. 50).
10. See, in particular, Svetlana Boym, 'Between the Borders of Cultural Identity: Atom Egoyan's *Calendar*', *CineAction*, 32 (Autumn 1993), pp. 30–4; and Jonathan Romney, 'This Green Unpleasant Land', *Sight and Sound*, 9:10 (October 1999), pp. 34–5.
11. For further insight into the diasporic nature of Egoyan's films see, in particular, Hamid Naficy, 'Close-up: Atom Egoyan's Accented Style', in *An Accented Cinema: Exilic and Diasporic Filmmaking* (Princeton: Princeton University Press, 2001), pp. 36–9.
12. See Luce Irigaray, *Sexes and Genealogies* (New York: Columbia University Press, 1987), p. 89; Eng. trans. by Gillian C. Gill from the French *Sexes et parentés* (Paris: Les Éditions de Minuit, 1978).
13. See Bruno, 'An Archive of Emotion Pictures', in *Atlas of Emotion: Journeys in Art, Architecture and Film* (London: Verso, 2002), pp. 247–79 (p. 250).
14. See Laura U. Marks, 'Loving a Disappearing Image', in *Touch: Sensuous Theory and Multisensory Media* (Minneapolis: University of Minnesota Press, 2002), pp. 91–110.
15. See Russell Banks, *The Sweet Hereafter* (London: Picador, 1992).
16. *The Sweet Hereafter* DVD, Momentum Pictures, World Cinema Collection 2001.
17. See, in particular, Katherine Weese, 'Family Stories: Gender and Discourse in Atom Egoyan's *The Sweet Hereafter*', *Narrative*, 10:1 (2002), pp. 131–51, and Austin Sarat, 'Imagining the Law of the Father: Loss, Dread and Mourning in *The Sweet Hereafter*', *Law and Society Review*, 34 (2000), pp. 5–46.
18. See Weese, 'Family Stories'; and Chappell, 'Alain Resnais and Atom Egoyan', *Cinetext* (2003), available at <http://cinetext.philo.at/magazine/chappell/resnais_egoyan.html> (accessed 10 September 2009).
19. See Gilles Deleuze, *Cinema 2: The Time Image* (London: Continuum, 2005), p. 79; Eng. trans. by Robert Galeta and Hugh Tomlinson from the French *Cinéma II: L'Image-temps* (Paris: Les Éditions de Minuit, 1985).
20. See David Johnson's interview with Egoyan, 'Writing and Directing *The Sweet Hereafter*: A Talk with Atom Egoyan', *Scenario: The Magazine of Screenwriting Art*, 3:4 (1997), pp. 42–6 (p. 42).
21. See Bruno, 'Haptic Routes: View Painting and Garden Narratives', in *Atlas of Emotion*, pp. 171–203 (p. 177).
22. See Dillon, *Derek Jarman and Lyric Film: The Mirror and the Sea* (Austin: University of Texas Press, 2004), p. 25.
23. See Marks, 'The Memory of Touch', in *The Skin of the Film: Intercultural Cinema, Embodiment and the Senses* (Durham, NC: Duke University Press, 1999), pp. 127–93 (p. 139).
24. See Vivian Sobchack, 'The Expanded Gaze in Contracted Space: Happenstance, Hazard and the Flesh of the World', in *Carnal Thoughts: Embodiment and Moving Image Culture* (Berkeley: University of California Press, 2004), p. 94.
25. Ibid. pp. 94–5.
26. See Marks, 'The Memory of Touch', in *The Skin of the Film*, pp. 127–93 (p. 177).
27. Ibid. p. 173.

28. See, in particular, Irigaray's text 'The Age of the Breath', in *Luce Irigaray: Key Writings* (New York: Continuum, 2004), pp. 165–70.
29. See Luce Irigaray, *Everyday Prayers* (Nottingham: Nottingham University Press, 2004), pp. 150–1.
30. See David Johnson's interview with Egoyan, 'Writing and Directing *The Sweet Hereafter*', *Scenario*, pp. 42–6 (p. 42).
31. See Irigaray, *Elemental Passions* (London: Continuum, 1992), p. 7.
32. See David Abram's abstract at <http://www.ethicsinplace.org/pages/paperabstracts.html> (accessed 2 September 2009).
33. Irigaray, *Elemental Passions*, p. 7.
34. Merleau-Ponty, *The Phenomenology of Perception* (London: Continuum, 2002), p. 375.
35. See Marks, 'The Memory of Touch', in *The Skin of the Film*, pp. 127–93 (p. 178).
36. See Marks, 'The Memory of Things', in *The Skin of the Film*, pp. 77–126 (p. 113).
37. See Marks, preface to *The Skin of the Film*, p. xi.
38. Irigaray, *The Forgetting of Air in Martin Heidegger* (Austin: University of Texas Press, 1999), p. 8.
39. See Irigaray, *Elemental Passions*, p. 7.
40. It is useful to note that snow and its implications for the theorisation of human geography in film is the subject of Claire Thomson's article 'It's All About Snow: Limning the Posthuman Body in Tarkovsky's *Solyaris* and Vinterberg's *It's All About Love*', *New Cinemas: Journal of Contemporary Cinema*, 5:1 (April 2007), pp. 3–22.
41. See Celeste, 'The Sound of Silence: Film Music and Lament', *Quarterly Review of Film and Video*, 22 (2005), pp. 113–23.
42. See Lyotard, quoted in Celeste, 'The Sound of Silence', p. 118.
43. Ibid. p. 119.
44. See Irigaray, *The Forgetting of Air in Martin Heidegger*, p. 167.
45. See Irigaray, *Everyday Prayers*, p. 79.
46. See Marks, 'Video Haptics and Erotics', in *Touch*, pp. 1–22 (pp. 8–9).
47. See Gilles Deleuze and Félix Guattari, '1837: Of the Refrain', in *A Thousand Plateaus* (London: Continuum, 2004), pp. 342–86 (p. 344).
48. See Deleuze and Guattari, '1440: The Smooth and the Striated', in *A Thousand Plateaus*, pp. 523–51 (p. 544).
49. Ibid. p. 544.
50. See Irigaray, *The Forgetting of Air in Martin Heidegger*, p. 8.
51. See Marks, 'Asphalt Nomadism: The New Desert in Arab Independent Cinema' (2006), available at <http://www.sfu.ca/~lmarks/writings/files/Asphalt%20Nomadism.pdf> (accessed 8 December 2011).
52. Ibid.
53. See Marks, 'The Memory of Touch', in *The Skin of the Film*, pp. 127–93 (p. 163).
54. See Irigaray, *Everyday Prayers*, pp. 150–1.
55. See Irigaray, *The Forgetting of Air in Martin Heidegger*, p. 116.
56. See Irigaray, 'A Breath that Touches in Words', in *I Love to You: Sketch for a Felicity Within History* (New York: Routledge, 1996), p. 125.
57. See Marks, 'The Memory of Touch', in *The Skin of the Film*, pp. 127–93 (p. 171).
58. See Irigaray, *The Forgetting of Air in Martin Heidegger*, p. 116.
59. See Irigaray, *Being Two: How Many Eyes Have We?* (Rüsselsheim: Christel Göttert Verlag, 2000), p. 21.
60. See Dillon, *Derek Jarman and Lyric Film: The Mirror and the Sea*, p. 25.
61. See Irigaray, 'A Breath that Touches in Words', in *I Love to You*, p. 121.
62. For example, see Gustavo Constantini, 'Leitmotif Revisited', available at <http://filmsound.org/gustavo/leitmotif-revisted.htm> (accessed 1 May 2009).
63. These comments are taken from Egoyan's correspondence with me via email,

dated February 2008. I am very grateful to Marcy Gerstein at Ego Film Arts for helping to make this correspondence with Egoyan possible.
64. See Wilson, 'Kieślowski's Lost Daughter: *Three Colours: Blue*', in *Cinema's Missing Children*, pp. 16–27; *Three Colours: Blue*, dir. Krzysztof Kieślowski, Poland, 1993.
65. Ibid. p. 21.
66. See lines 289–95, *The Pied Piper of Hamelin, Robert Browning Selected Poems* (New York: Penguin, 2004), pp. 30–8.
67. Egoyan's composer Mychael Danna more frequently employs the duduk, a similar-sounding instrument to the ney flute.
68. See Doug Adams, 'An Interview with Mychael Danna', *Film Score Monthly*, January 1998, available on Danna's personal website at <http://www.mychaeldanna.com/Interviewsframe.html> (accessed 10 April 2009).
69. It is useful to note that the name Zoe means 'life-giver'; this gives symbolic weight to its use in Egoyan's *The Sweet Hereafter* and *Exotica*.
70. See Irigaray, 'Rebuilding the World', in *The Way of Love* (London: Continuum, 2004), pp. 137–65 (p. 150).
71. See Laura Winters, 'A Gentle Interpreter of Human Fallibility', *The New York Times*, 23 November 1997, p. 17.
72. See Mulvey, 'Cosmetics and Abjection: Cindy Sherman 1977–87', in *Fetishism and Curiosity* (London: BFI, 1996), pp. 65–76. Mulvey has further explored the significance of the stilled image in her most recent book *Death 24x a Second: Stillness and the Moving Image* (London: Reaktion Books, 2006).
73. *The Colour of Pomegranates*, dir. Sergei Paradjanov, Armenia, 1968.
74. See Egoyan, quoted in Monika Maura's review '*The Colour of Pomegranates* (a.k.a. *Sayat Nova*)', available at <http://www.kamera.co.uk/reviews/pomegran.html> (accessed 8 December 2011).
75. See Irigaray, *Being Two: How Many Eyes Have We?*, p. 21.
76. See Egoyan, introduction to *Subtitles: On the Foreignness of Film* (Cambridge, MA: MIT Press, 2004), pp. 21–32 (p. 21).
77. See Irigaray, *The Way of Love*, p. 67.
78. See Irigaray, *Elemental Passions*, p. 7.
79. See Irigaray, 'When Our Lips Speak Together', in *This Sex Which Is Not One* (Ithaca: Cornell University Press, 1985), pp. 205–18 (p. 213); Eng. trans. by Catherine Porter from the French *Ce sexe qui n'en est pas un* (Paris: Les Éditions de Minuit, 1977).
80. See Bruno, 'M Is for Mapping: Art, Apparel, Architecture Is for Peter Greenaway', in *Atlas of Emotion*, pp. 283–329 (p. 295).
81. Bruno refers to the phrase *occhia-bocca* in the context of when it was first used by Pier Paolo Pasolini, 'Map Is for Mapping', in *Atlas of Emotion*, p. 294.
82. See Gruben, 'Look but Don't Touch: Visual and Tactile Desire in *Exotica*, *The Sweet Hereafter*, and *Felicia's Journey*', in *Image and Territory: Essays on Atom Egoyan*, pp. 249–74.
83. For Irigaray's thoughts on fluidity and female subjectivity, see in particular 'The "Mechanics" of Fluids', in *This Sex Which Is Not One*, pp. 106–18.
84. See Whitford, 'The Same, the Semblance and the Other', in *Luce Irigaray: Philosophy in the Feminine*, 2nd edition (London: Routledge, 1995), pp. 101–22 (p. 104).
85. See Irigaray, 'Speaking of Immemorial Waters', in *The Marine Lover of Friedrich Nietzsche* (New York: Columbia University Press, 1991), p. 59; Eng. trans. by Gillian C. Gill from the French *Amante marine* (Paris: Les Éditions de Minuit, 1991).
86. See Irigaray, 'Part IV: Introduction', in *Luce Irigaray: Key Writings*, pp. 145–9 (p. 146).

87. See Irigaray, *Everyday Prayers*, p. 49.
88. See Jonathan Romney, *Atom Egoyan*, World Directors Series (London: BFI, 2004), p. 2.
89. See del Rio, 'The Body as Foundation of the Screen: Allegories of Technology in Atom Egoyan's *Speaking Parts*', *Camera Obscura*, 38 (1996), pp. 94–115.
90. See Romney, '*Felicia's Journey*', *Sight and Sound*, 9:10 (October 1999), pp. 34–5, available at <http://www.bfi.org.uk/sightandsound/review/215> (accessed 7 May 2009).
91. For a detailed, contextual discussion of Egoyan's direction of Richard Strauss's opera *Salomé*, see Kay Armatage and Caryl Clark, 'Seeing and Hearing Atom Egoyan's *Salomé*', in *Image and Territory: Essays on Atom Egoyan*, pp. 307–30.
92. See Kerry Brougher, Michael Tarantino and Astrid Brown (eds), *Notorious: Alfred Hitchcock and Contemporary Art* (Oxford: Museum of Modern Art, 1999). I am very grateful to the public relations officer Sara Dewsbury at Oxford's Museum of Modern Art for helping me with my research on this exhibition and sending me a copy of the archived catalogue.
93. See Barthes, 'The Grain of the Voice', in *Image, Music, Text* (London: Fontana, 1997), pp. 179–89 (p. 182).
94. See Pevere, introduction to *Exotica*, p. 40.
95. Wilson uses this term to describe the unsuccessful acts of mourning at work in the film which only lead to more pain. See Wilson, 'The Female Adjuster', in *Cinema's Missing Children*, p. 40.
96. This term refers to a comment made by Egoyan in interview with Romney: 'There's a group of analysts in Toronto who have looked at all my films. They've told me that from their point of view, all my films deal with a process called "faulty mourning" – when a patient builds up a ritual of mourning which only accentuates and exaggerates the sense of loss which they think they're dealing with,' quoted in Wilson, *Atom Egoyan*, p. 79. See also bell hooks, '*Exotica*: Breaking Down to Break Through', in *Reel to Real: Race, Sex and Class at the Movies* (London: Routledge, 1996), pp. 27–33.
97. See Wilson, 'The Female Adjuster', in *Cinema's Missing Children*, p. 40.
98. See Wilson, *Atom Egoyan*, p. 73.
99. See Taylor, *The Living Labyrinth: Exploring Universal Themes in Myths, Dreams, and the Symbolisms of Waking Life* (Mahwah, NJ: Paulist Press, 1998), p. 54.
100. See Shambu, 'The Pleasure and Pain of "Watching": Atom Egoyan's *Exotica*', *Senses of Cinema*, 13 (2001), available at <http://www.sensesofcinema.com/2001/13/exotica> (accessed 8 December 2011).
101. See Irigaray, 'Speaking of Immemorial Waters', in *The Marine Lover of Friedrich Nietzsche*, p. 59.
102. See Shambu, 'The Pleasure and Pain of "Watching": Atom Egoyan's *Exotica*'.
103. For a more detailed discussion of the representation of the wind in film, it is useful to note the fascinating work of Christian Keathley in his book *Cinephilia and History, or The Wind in the Trees* (Indianapolis: Indiana University Press, 2006).
104. See Irigaray, *An Ethics of Sexual Difference*, p. 108.
105. See Critchley, 'Calm: On Terrence Malick's *The Thin Red Line*', *Film-Philosophy*, 6:48 (2002), available at <www.film-philosophy.com/vol6-2002/n48critchley> (accessed 20 March 2009).
106. Sobchack's paper was entitled 'Fleshing Out the Image: Phenomenology, Pedagogy and Derek Jarman's *Blue*' and was presented at the 'Film and Philosophy/Philosophy and Film' International Conference, 2008.
107. See Critchley, 'Calm: On Terrence Malick's *The Thin Red Line*'.

2. AN 'AIR IN FLESH':
AN ANATOMY OF BREATH, CARNALITY AND TRANSCENDENCE: THE BREATHING BODIES OF DAVID CRONENBERG

The truth of a body appears in its dismembering, in its tearing apart, when the blood bursts out of the skin: the skin, instead of an envelope, becomes a surface to break. The mutilated body reveals its interiority, its depth, the secret of its life. Unity is given only to be broken, releasing the infinitely fragile secret that the soul and the breath, the desire, the passion for the unique and the infinite are the same as the wrenching of the body from itself, the *membra disjecta* and their very disjection exposed in the raw. In every sense, the *soul blows* through the body.[1]

Jean-Luc Nancy

To forget being is to forget the air, this first fluid given us gratis and free of interest in the mother's blood, given us again when we are born, like a natural profusion that raises a cry of pain: the pain of a being who comes into the world and is abandoned, forced henceforth to live without the immediate assistance of another body.[2]

Luce Irigaray

In her essay 'The Inside-Out of Masculinity', Linda Ruth Williams describes Cronenberg as a 'surgeon' whose fascination with 'inner beauty', like that of the Mantle twins in *Dead Ringers*,[3] conceives of the 'opened body and the eye which sees as subjectively the same'.[4] Furthermore, according to Williams, the act of opening up the body is far more interesting to Cronenberg than that of viewing it.[5] This turning 'inside-out', then, as Williams puts it, characterises

Cronenberg's thematic undoing of bodies and flesh in films such as *Rabid* (1977) and *Crash* (1997), a kind of taxidermy of the subject (recalling György Pálfi's Cronenbergian debt in his 2006 feature debut *Taxidermia*). Yet such permeating of inner and outer boundaries, reversals and inversions also calls to mind the dualistic nature of breathing which unsettles boundaries between ourselves and the outer world we inhabit. The intertwined passages of air and breath suggest a unique locus of synthesis and interdependency key to the philosophy of Irigaray.[6] While Irigaray's thoughts on the passages of breathing have enabled me to shed light on the diegetic and non-diegetic representation of movement in Egoyan's filmed spaces, this chapter will show how breathing is involved in Cronenberg's unstitching and unfolding of human bodies.

Central to this analysis will be the discussion of Cronenberg's formal use of editing and composition, which will be thought through in relation to the particular logic of olfaction made manifest in *Spider* and the objectification of breathing in *Videodrome*. Such anatomic reworkings, of the body on screen and the formal aspects of the film – the 'film's body' – will come to stand for what Irigaray describes as 'an air in flesh': the breathing body and its debt to an interior carnality which illuminates sensation.[7] The film theorist Steven Shaviro has already referred to Cronenberg's work as 'unsparingly visceral, an aesthetics of the flesh'.[8] My engagement with the thought of Irigaray opens up a space in which to theorise a new aspect of Cronenberg's aesthetic through particular focus on *Spider* and *Videodrome*'s complex figuring of the relations between breathing, the senses and the way in which boundaries between humans and objects can be called into question through the presence of breath. Chronologically speaking, *Videodrome* and *Spider* represent two very different periods in Cronenberg's career with a gap of seventeen years between them. While *Spider* and *Videodrome* are comparable in the sense that they reflect themes in Cronenberg's *oeuvre*, my concern is with the locus of breath that draws these films together.

In the previous chapter I theorised the diegetic presence of breath according to the framing of, and interplay between, motion and space in Egoyan's films. This led me to reconsider the materiality of Egoyan's filmic representations and draw attention to breath as a different kind of texture or 'surface' experienced by the viewer, both aurally and visually. These 'surfaces' were theorised according to my use of the term 'elemental topography' which underscored my interest in the element of air and its sensory possibilities. However, it is the breaking and opening up of such 'surfaces' that is the focus of this chapter.

While Egoyan's films also offered ways in which to refigure the inner and outer trajectory of breath through body and environment, particularly in the context of 'foreignness' and cultural difference, Cronenberg's evocation of the breathing body's visceral and psychical interior raises new questions about bodily difference when it is internalised and deeply embedded in conceptions of the self in his cinema. A strong motif that was also questioned in the previous chapter was the real and symbolic figuring of the breathing child, drawing together the snap-shot of a child breathing on a camera lens in *A Portrait of Arshile* and the centrality of the suffocating child in *The Sweet Hereafter*. Egoyan's films might be seen to objectify the image of the breathing infant, but Cronenberg's *Spider* does not emphasise its child subject as a breathing body through the actual image of breathing. Rather, *Spider* situates us *inside* the subjective realm of the breathing child's experiences, and this perspective, I argue, is an especially *sensory* evocation of breathing.

The shift towards the inner, sensorial and experiential world of the child in *Spider*, rather than its recorded, captured and recalled image (as we have seen in *The Sweet Hereafter*, *Felicia's Journey* and *Exotica*), leads me to re-examine the way in which subjectivity is configured through breathing and the theorisation of autonomy that is viewed as 'feminine' in Irigaray's thought. The previous chapter showed how the female protagonists of Egoyan's films, especially Felicia and Nicole, embody a quest for selfhood and self-possession that accorded with a feminine cultivation of their breathing. In Cronenberg's films, it is not only the female protagonists whose breathing cultivates a particular gesture of autonomous selfhood; rather, his radical treatment of sexual difference complicates gender boundaries and thus breathing is aligned more with a feminine identity than a female body *per se*. Cronenberg's radical revisioning of sexual difference bears implications for the way in which viewers identify with the filmed bodies on screen; while *Spider* proposes a route of bodily identification that is based on a male character's identification with his mother, thus enabling a kind of male access to a female breathing body, a key moment in *Videodrome* depicts a process of metamorphosis in which the male body becomes feminised, and this foregrounds breathing as a vital aspect of the film's evocation of bodily trauma.

According to Irigaray, breathing engenders human subjectivity, and this has implications for the way in which Cronenberg's representation of embodied subjectivity can be interpreted. Re-viewing *Spider*, this chapter will show how acts of objectification in the film are further complicated when such objects also tend to 'breathe', presenting a troubling dimension of subjectivity that is also prefigured in *Videodrome*'s breathing video cassettes, where breathing also emphasises the bodily, and 'cyber-sexual', aspects of technology in the film.

Filmic 'Flesh', Filmed Bodies and Irigaray

There are bodies which flesh out the characters in films, those visible as diegetic bodies in the frame, and then there are bodies whose anatomies are made up of filmic 'flesh', as it were, the 'film's body' which, to quote Sobchack, 'serves the material existence of the film as functionally embodied and thus differentiated in existence from the filmmaker and spectator'.[9] However, Sobchack's use of the term 'material' cannot be entirely applied to the idea of breathing, as I have made clear in my introduction to this book. Thus the question is how to determine what the film's body is if breathing is a prerequisite of embodiment, as Irigaray argues. My interest in the breathing bodies of Cronenberg's cinema takes into consideration the bodies of the protagonists, the 'film's body' and the role breath plays in emphasising the issue of gender. While my reflection on Cronenberg's gendered bodies refers largely to the subjects on screen, I will also consider how the 'film's body' serves to position the viewer within a gendered form of spectatorship.

My interest in the 'film's body' leads me to explore the formal aspects of the films I discuss, contained within the non-diegetic space of *Spider* and *Videodrome*. Following Sobchack, much criticism has sought to emphasise the specificity of the filmic medium as a differentiated body in the film experience, most notably in the work of Marks, Nicole Brenez and Martine Beugnet.[10] In contrast, I want to show how a space for breath can be posited in the 'film's body'. In the introduction to this book I acknowledged Sobchack's important reference to the film's body as a 'breathing subject'[11] in which celluloid images functioned as the passage of air or 'breaths' spooling into and out of the body of the apparatus, but this chapter will envisage an approach to film form which develops from Sobchack's analysis.

Earlier, I called upon Marker's suggestive imagery in his film *La Jetée* in order to suggest how dissolves coupled with the sound of Ravel's heartbeat embody a blinking eye, evoking a kind of synthesis between sight and breath which comes to stand for a waking consciousness or hallucinatory state. The relationship between editing and breathing in film is also observed by Beugnet, but her views refer more to an intensity of visceral motion than hallucination. In her work on the dialogue between the French filmmaker Claire Denis and the French philosopher Jean-Luc Nancy, cultivated through Denis's 2004 adaptation of Nancy's 2000 text *L'Intrus* (*The Intruder*, 2004), Beugnet draws a striking comparison between the pace of the film's editing and the rhythm of the text:

> As the text unravels . . . its rhythm also recalls that of irregular breathing or a heartbeat: hurried passages, where a series of short interrogative sentences collide, are followed by clauses using elaborate phrasing and long sentences between parentheses that create suspended moments of reprieve.[12]

Beugnet's thought suggests that the rhythm of breath and the rhythm of a heartbeat are conjoined, unified, but breath can evoke a sense of pace that is differentiated from the pulse of a heartbeat. As we have seen, the thought of Irigaray suggests a syntax and rhythm of breath that can be heard through the sound of the voice. Irigaray's thinking implies that breathing can suggest the flow of language and thought that may be felt through the editing of a film. My analysis of the foregrounding of breath in Cronenberg's *Videodrome* and *Spider* will show how editing techniques not only accord with a sense of viscerality but, importantly, relate to each film's engendering of sexual difference, the sound of vocality and the way in which bodily trauma is articulated and experienced by the viewer. However, this is not to say that my contemplation of the film's breathing body in this chapter will be limited to the editing techniques employed by Cronenberg; my analysis will demonstrate how the formal representation of breathing both contradicts and complements the diegetic breathing bodies in the film. For example, my conception of the film's breathing 'body' includes Cronenberg's use of wide-angle lenses for close-ups in *Spider*, film colour, framing, depth of focus and composition. Throughout this discussion of Cronenberg's bodies, the thought of Irigaray structures my reading of breath, as it relates to what she describes as 'an air in flesh'.[13]

As I have suggested in the introduction to this book, Irigaray's writing must be located in the context of her criticism of phenomenology. In the text 'The Invisible of the Flesh: A Reading of Merleau-Ponty, *The Visible and the Invisible*, "The Intertwining – The Chiasm"', Irigaray offers a critique of Merleau-Ponty's envisioning of a language where subjective being is expressed not with but through the body – what he describes as the phenomenological or lived body.[14] Irigaray centres on Merleau-Ponty's persistent appropriation of the tactile or 'flesh' as metaphor for our outer, exterior relationship with the world as one that is joined together not by touch, but by vision alone. What Irigaray proposes in response to Merleau-Ponty's privileging of vision is an interior dimension to phenomenological discourse, a theory that reclaims the tactile in terms of an interior being and also claims such tangibility as distinctly feminine: the 'tangible invisible' as opposed to Merleau-Ponty's intertwining of the visible and the tangible.[15] Irigaray's claim that breath is 'the flesh of air' is a further articulation of the 'tangible invisible' where respiration corresponds not only with invisibility, but also with tactility. It is this 'tangible invisible' that is made manifest in my discussion of Cronenberg's films, especially in relation to his filmic representation of sexual difference. This tactile dimension to breathing considers the flow of breath itself and its passage from the outside to the inside of our bodies as a form of touching oneself as well as the air 'touching' us in a way that fleshes out our interior, corporeal subjectivity.

Breath Becoming Body in *Spider*

Cronenberg's cinema recurrently calls into question the often detached, repressed relationship we have with our bodies and my argument is that this concern is inclusive of breathing. It is logical to assume that breath is always already involved in any filmic allusion to the corporeal since the diegetic or non-diegetic representation of any human body constitutes the possible presence of breath. In my introduction to this book I suggested that viewers might be able to hear the actors breathe when they are close-miked, but Cronenberg's foregrounding of breath is much more explicit. For example, both the video cassettes of *Videodrome* and the typewriter of *Naked Lunch* (1991) are visibly breathing objects which invite further analysis, not only as objects that breathe, but as artefacts of a residual, human physicality that the locus of breath tends to imply. In *Spider* this residual physicality is displaced as gas which becomes equated with the presence of a human body – the body of the protagonist's (undead) mother. In a cinema that is so centred on revealing those processes of the body that we repress – the interior – Cronenberg compellingly shows us, metaphorically as well as literally, the body's unsung register: a precisely Cronenbergian breath.

In general, critics are drawn to Cronenberg's questioning of corporeality, his subjectivity and his thematic representation of a fantastic or spectacular transgression of cultural boundaries: accepted sociality, sexuality and identity.[16] Most notably, Creed's adoption of Julia Kristeva's psychoanalytic model of abjection as a method of deconstructing the representation of the woman's monstrous body in *The Brood* (1979) is the earliest and indeed one of the most frequently cited readings of Cronenberg from a psychoanalytic perspective.[17] Such an approach ultimately privileges the psychical over the somatic. However, it is my view that breathing is an activity that involves our minds *and* bodies and it is this relation that is most thoroughly foregrounded in Cronenberg's cinema.

Like Egoyan's *The Sweet Hereafter*, Cronenberg's adaptation of Patrick McGrath's *Spider* positions breathing at the heart of its narrative and it is this precise embedding of breath within the film that structures my analysis.[18] Spider, the central protagonist, is traumatised by an early childhood event in which he murdered his own mother. It is his recollection of this event, the pursuit of truth and the unravelling of a distant past which informs the trajectory of the entire film. Eventually, we learn that Spider poisoned his own mother whilst she was sleeping by exposing her to gas fumes. The role of breathing or, rather, the mother's breath in *Spider* bears comparison with my reading of Egoyan's *Felicia's Journey* and, on the surface, it is true to say that both films are concerned with memory and its material as well as immaterial, psychical effects upon the lived body when personal histories are displaced or distorted. Yet *Spider*'s reconfiguration of breath in relation to the particular body/bodies of the film is entirely different.

Previous readings of *Spider* have engaged with its notable representation of filmic time, in particular the way that its chronology is split between two parallel perspectives offered by the same subject, the child and the adult Spider,[19] but in my view this forms only part of the story offered by Cronenberg's film. *Spider*'s narrative serves to bring together two claims about breathing in relation to the film's portrayal of the maternal body and the olfactory sense. Unlike *Felicia's Journey*, the mother's vocality in *Spider* is subsumed by sensation, a prickling, smothering invisibility, air that is also signified by an olfactory presence: the inescapable *smell* of gas. Thus the presence of gas becomes an external manifestation of the mother's (undead) body. Yet, for the online film theorist K-Punk, 'the outside is already inside' for Spider, recalling Williams's thoughts on the 'inside-out' world of Cronenberg's films.[20]

The olfactory sense has a complex relationship with air. We breathe through our organ of smell: the nose. Yet it is breathing that facilitates this act simultaneously with another organ: our lungs.[21] It is most striking, then, that *Spider*'s central protagonist recalls his mother as a haunting presence of gas, emphasised by a gasworks and a gas fireplace, both permanent reminders of her loss. Moreover, this physicality has an overwhelming effect upon the protagonist, eliciting a collapse of bodily borders that recalls Cronenberg's thematic address of intoxication. However, for the first time in Cronenberg's entire *oeuvre*, the effects of transgression are not directly visible and are communicated in a different way from the infectious bodies of earlier films such as *The Fly* (1986), *The Brood* or *Shivers* (1975).

Upon release from a psychiatric hospital where he was being treated for acute schizophrenia, Dennis Clegg (Ralph Fiennes) – or Spider, as he is referred to by his mother (Miranda Richardson), due to his fascination with arachnids and making webs – takes shelter in a boarding house run by the tyrannical and unsympathetic Mrs Wilkinson (Lynn Redgrave). Coincidentally, the boarding house is located very near to Spider's old childhood home, and this proximity to the past forces him to try to recall a kind of personal history, attempting to make sense of the many real and possibly imagined memories that plague his thoughts. Very early on it becomes clear that Spider's mother is dead and that this is the most painful memory of all. We see the adult Spider as the spectator in the scenes that he is remembering/imagining, the young Spider (Bradley Hall) inhabiting the same space as his older self. It is revealed that Spider suspected his father, Bill (Gabriel Byrne), of having an affair with a woman named Yvonne Wilkinson (also Miranda Richardson). In an attempt to make a connection between the past and the present, the older Spider turns his attention to Mrs Wilkinson and concludes, given her surname, that she is Yvonne. Soon after, we learn that the young Spider heard his father conspiring with Yvonne to murder his mother and later Spider appears to watch them bludgeoning Mrs Clegg to death before burying her in a shallow grave. Unable to bear this horrifying truth, Spider plots to murder Yvonne, his new step-mother. Simultaneously, the older Spider repeats the actions of his younger self, attempting to murder Mrs Wilkinson, whom he mistakes for Yvonne. Using an elaborate network of string and rope, the young Spider connects this 'web' to the kitchen gas pipes, and as Yvonne sleeps he pulls on the device, releasing the gas. When the body is found it is not Yvonne's corpse but his mother's. Spider stands in Mrs Wilkinson's bedroom whilst she sleeps, clutching a hammer in his hand, but his intentions are never followed through. Closing the film, a car arrives to return Spider to the psychiatric hospital, and it is his peaceful acceptance of this that implies both an acknowledgement of and a deepening desire for recovery.

For Spider, past and present sharply intersect.[22] Spider's experiences of the world represent a collision of perspectives, interactions and thoughts which frequently invoke some form of remembering. To be caught in this cycle or, rather, web of distraction is also physical, every sensation tainted by loss and each step towards contact of any kind interwoven with grief. Yet this suffering of the flesh is only part of Spider's story of embodied trauma. At the centre of this pain is a more subtle articulation of loss and it is through the opening titles of the film that this is first introduced. The breathing body serves as a marker of mortality that gestures towards the burden of existence in spite of an unforgivable act of matricide.

Suffering

Spider's opening titles, animated by Cuppa Coffee Studios, begin with a series of highly detailed stains and markings. Although it would seem that these first glimpses of the film are most obviously evocative of Rorschach inkblot drawings – images used to interpret a subject's state of mind according to the meaning he or she attaches to them – it is the uncertain condition of physicality that is established here.[23] Furthermore, it is this particular representation of corporeality that builds towards an evocation of the *breathing* body.

At first there are five barely visible water marks that stain a wooden surface, an evident trace of something left behind. This image is followed by several others, all of which appear to have been subjected to a process of staining, in some shape or form. We view more images of burnished, peeling, etched, scratched and layered textures, thus giving a physicality to the Rorschach imagery in a way that emphasises a dimension that is not psychical, but primarily tactile. Indeed, these almost monochrome images, abstractions, function in a way that recalls the medium of painting as well as sculpture. The Rorschach images used by psychiatrists have little relationship with any textural medium, they are merely flat ink blots designed to provoke and penetrate the unconscious mind, the psyche. However, Cronenberg's sequence resonates with a fragmented 'presence' on screen, one that becomes increasingly tactile through its emerging shapes, indentations, markings and scratches.

In interview, Cronenberg's elaboration on the design of each interior setting of the film (the boarding house, in particular) makes explicit reference to the importance of the wallpaper's tactile nature:

> The wallpapers that we imported from England were all vintage, brown, mouldy, and decayed – all those English things that you feel in your bones if you ever were in England in the 1960s. So once again, very tactile, and the tactility controlled the visual aspects of the film.[24]

This tactility is prefigured in the title sequence and echoes the skin of the wallpapers used. Yet, while the sequence evokes a material presence, it also gestures towards the immaterial. In a sense, there is no image, only the unveiling of presence itself, the unfolding of a metamorphosing state of being that is suggestive of Cronenberg's thematic portrait of suffering and recovery, not only of the mind, but of the flesh.[25]

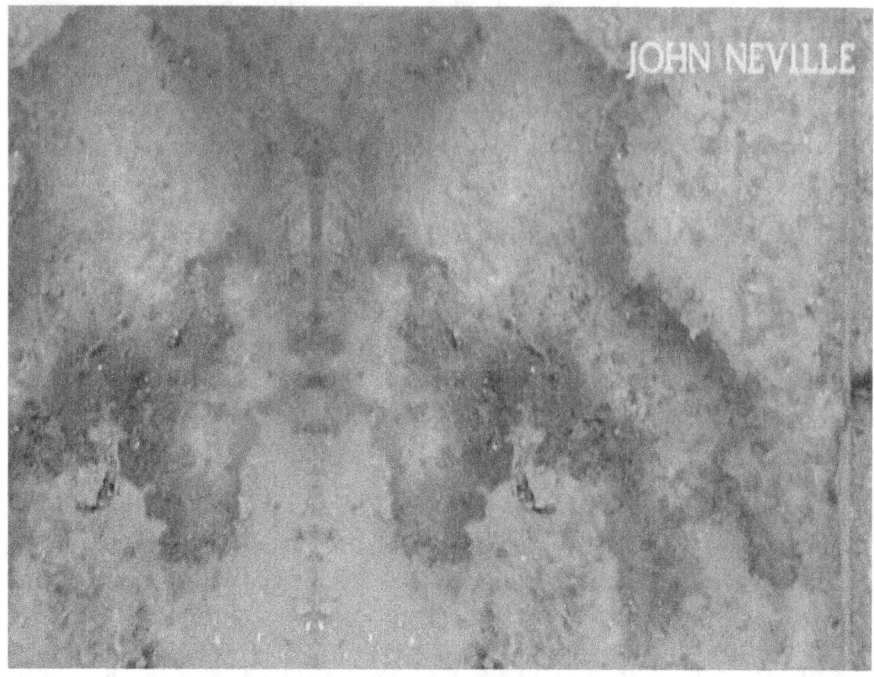
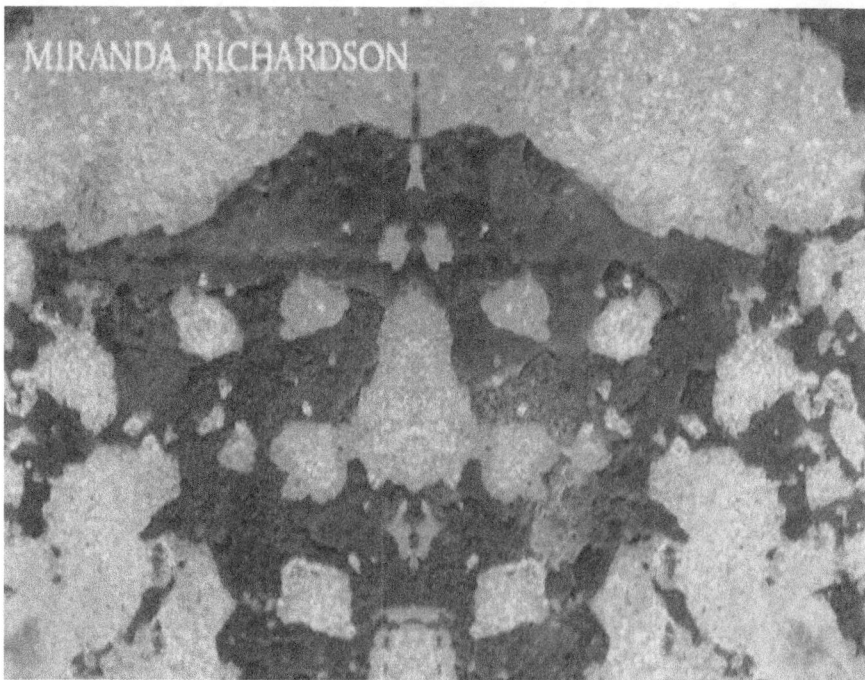

Figures 2.1 and 2.2 A series of stills taken from the opening titles of *Spider*. (Images courtesy of Adam Sheehan, © Cuppa Coffee Studios.)

The filmed 'surface-scapes' underlying each blurred or burnished shape that appears are equally important. It is possible to observe, in sequence, the texture of stone, wallpaper, fretwork, sandpaper and plaster: raw materials suggestive of construction, modernity and fabrication. In this sense, building and the most fundamental place of dwelling – the home – are undoubtedly implied here. Furthermore, these images introduce a specific kind of home that is equated with dereliction and neglect, as each shot conveys a process of stripping bare, erosion and unveiling that which is raw, moulding and decaying. This process of peeling away layers and textures recalls the shabby, papered interiors in the film, their post-war gloom hanging heavily over the events of the film as if an extension of Spider's repulsion. The transition from one shot to the next is established through a dissolve, a formal technique recalling the editing style of Marker's *La Jetée* which also relates each image back to the previous one, creating an impression of a fragmented yet cohering presence.

In addition to introducing a heightened awareness of physicality and form, Cronenberg prefigures the themes of the film's narrative. Through these images there is a dominant portrayal of modernity and dereliction suggestive of the film's dilapidated locations such as Mrs Wilkinson's halfway house, images of bricked-up windows and especially Spider's sombre and claustrophobic childhood home. However, breathing draws attention to a very different kind of spatiality as the film progresses. This spatiality evokes an Irigarayan place of dwelling associated with the maternal figure and can be traced during the final image within this sequence.

There are a few moments of darkness before we are able to view the final image contained in the film's opening sequence. Like the others before it, the image is uniformly monochromatic, consisting of the same limited palette of dull grey hues, containing a mass of imperceptible stains and markings. The most notable forms emerging from this thick, sculpted surface are two protruding dune-like shapes at the centre of the image. Spaced a little apart from each other, two raised, empty, circular forms or moulded 'holes' pierce through the screen's sculpted materiality. Before the appearance of this image we were placed at the periphery of such visions, the image always appearing fragmented and abstract, a kind of de-centring that Cronenberg emphasises throughout his sequence. However, the transition from one image to the next appears to slow down and build towards the shot of the sculptural 'holes'. Firstly, the circular forms constitute an 'opening' from inside, a gesture that is emblematic of a breathing body. Up until now the sequence has not contained any reference to this kind of fissure, but it emphasises the density of the image, a volume that is opened up, as if it were given access to air. Secondly, the doubling of the holes subtly introduces the mother and child of the film, or, rather, a filial gesture of orality. Certainly, these 'holes' are evocative of the two subjects' mouths, of the orifices necessary in order for breath to pass into and out of the body. However, it is not only the mouth or orality that is suggested here. The two 'holes' also form the imprint of olfaction in the film through the twinned orifice of the nose, the prefiguring of *Spider*'s olfactory as well as oral configuration of a breathing body. In these final moments of the title sequence, Cronenberg subtly foregrounds the corporeal as a simultaneously present and absent materiality, as suggested by the holes. This expressionist sequence, then, seems to allude to the human breathing body as a condition that can never fully close itself off from outside – an implicit conflict which haunts much of the film's events throughout.

The presence of surfaces in Cronenberg's work is also what compels Shaviro's phenomenological treatment of Cronenberg in his book *The Cinematic Body*, a model of thought which refers to cinema's affective power as one that is at work 'in the depths and surfaces of the body'.[26] For Shaviro, Cronenberg's cinema elicits rare sensations within the body of the spectator and it is *Spider*'s 'thematic embodiment and physical suffering of delirium'[27] that marks this film as resolutely Cronenbergian. However, the opening sequence of the film is suggestive not only of the 'flesh' but of the *air* in our flesh. Thus *Spider*'s opening titles gesture towards the interiority *beneath the surface* which makes this move from flesh to air most apparent.

I have shown how the opening titles gesture towards breathing in order to embed a sense of what lies beneath the surface of Cronenberg's 'bodily' imagery and, importantly, draws attention to the notion of the breathing nose and thus the importance of olfaction to the film's narrative. The next section of this chapter considers how the representation of the body in the diegetic space of the film emphasises the relations between breathing and the sensuousness of embodied existence. While I trace the relations between bodily trauma, breathing and mortality in order to develop thought on the interplay of breath and the senses in *Spider*, my exploration of the role of olfaction and breathing in the film will lead me to consider how to reconcile this particularly troubling evocation of breathing with Irigaray's positive conception of breath.

Olfactory Trauma

Once Spider has entered his room at the halfway house and familiarised himself with its new territory, Cronenberg immediately establishes a more explicit link between olfaction and breath: the very image of Spider smelling something in the air. In this early scene, Spider's body recoils in horror at the sight of a gas fireplace in his room. Although Spider's dialogue is invariably incoherent and inaudible, in this particular scene we clearly hear him enunciate the words 'gas, I smell gas . . .'. Following on from this exclamation, a hurried attempt is made to open a window, to let in some other kind of air, but the view only appears to block this escape: a gas tower whose giant steel structure seems to press against the frame of the window. Of course, it is not possible to smell an image, in the literal sense, but it is the sense of smell which represents a psychological threat to Spider, as well as the sensory experience itself which unsettles bodily and mental borders. These borders relate to maternal bonds once severed through Spider's use of gas to kill his mother, a lack of control over personal space, Spider's perception of his own body and its differentiation in the world.

The relations between borders and olfaction are usefully commented on by Marks in her writings on the intercultural borders which smell tends to disrupt. Recalling a particular memory of a train journey she once took between Ontario and New York, Marks describes the confiscation of an Indian-Canadian family's fragrant foods from home, snatched by customs officials when they crossed the border between Canada and the USA: 'I am convinced that a less *foreign*-smelling meal would have been safe. Smells do not respect walls or national borders: they drift and infuse and inhabit.'[28] The same is true of gas in *Spider*; it infiltrates physical space, fleshly borders which turn the inside out and the outside in. Indeed, to borrow from K-Punk, 'such is the logic of trauma', the memory of the past event overwhelmingly colouring one's perception of the present.[29] Above all, the representation of trauma in *Spider* tends to open up the boundaries between breath and the senses. Irigaray's thoughts on the intermingling of breath and the senses are useful in order to understand this particular 'logic' of trauma, to echo K-Punk's perspective on the film, and its implications for the theorisation of breath.

Irigaray's work, in her poetic discourse *Everyday Prayers*, gestures towards the olfactory senses as well as breath. In one text Irigaray contemplates 'the summer breathing . . . raising to itself a heady perfume/respiration de l'été . . . élevant vers lui un parfum enivrant'.[30] In alluding to air as well as rainfall, Irigaray reflects on the air becoming 'smooth, like a caress, its tender perfume smells moist'/'L'air est doux comme une caresse, son parfum tendre fleure l'humide'.[31] Irigaray invites a space for contact between breath and the senses, particularly smell, which may be contiguous but not continuous, underlining the potential tactility of breath. This is to say that air enters the nose and mouth and when we smell we are also breathing at the same time; indeed, we must breathe more deeply in order to smell.

Olfaction is part of the very fabric of the film, evoked through Spider's tobacco, earthy stained fingers, pinkish bath water which calls to mind the smell of copper rust, boiling pans of steamy, singed porridge, the lush cosmetic sweetness of Mrs Clegg's red lipstick and, above all, graphite – the smell of numerous pencils which scrawl incessantly across pages of Spider's journal. However, the parallel drawn by Irigaray between touching and smelling is also foregrounded in *Spider*. Indeed, the protagonist often appears to smell gas before instinctively, obsessively, touching his clothes, his body, with a hand that, in effect, grasps or reaches out for a smell. Cronenberg suggests the physical nature of smell, a notion that is made more explicitly thematic in Tom Tykwer's *Perfume: The Story of a Murderer* (Tykwer, 2006). In Tykwer's film, smell is so powerful that it embodies the strength of a physical slap; smell is the midwife, the thrust of the back of a hand, eliciting the first breath of life from the newly born protagonist Jean-Baptiste Grenouille. Smell, as a violent force, induces life itself in Tykwer's film, but for *Spider* it is the smell of gas that induces trauma since it *extinguished* his mother's life.

The sense of smell and its evocation of his mother's breathing is, for Spider, troubling and traumatic, but the question remains how to reconcile such violent connotations with Irigaray's more affirmative and, in my view, tender reflection on breathing. While on the surface Irigaray's thought might appear irreconcilable with Cronenberg's particularly violent evocation of breath, upon closer analysis it is possible to observe equal levels of intimacy in Cronenberg's representation. Although air contains a poisonous threat for Spider, it also carries with it the lasting memory of the mother which will always involve, in some way, feelings of love, its 'heady perfume' bittersweet, the breathing body's dull ache of a lost embrace. It is most telling, then, that the following day Spider visits what he believes to be the grave of his mother, a plot of soil on the allotments where he imagined her body to be buried by Yvonne and his father. Spider utters the words 'my mother', almost inaudibly, as he clings to the earth.

These words 'my mother' have their own affecting cadence, sighed out by Spider as if to articulate her loss not only through language, but through his breathing body. By contrast, the enunciation of the word 'air' occupies a largely negative position within the film's dialogue, thus air is gestured towards as distinctly unclean, abject – a bad air that is particularly associated with Yvonne.

Bad Air

Bill: '*You want air in those pipes.*'
Yvonne: '*We've got air . . . bad air. Can't you smell it?*'

Yvonne's dominant association with a 'bad air' is made overtly clear during a scene in which the adult Spider watches his father arriving at her flat and attempting to mend her plumbing. Here, bad air not only signifies the dank and repellent atmosphere of Yvonne's flat (a spatial awareness of breath, recalling my earlier discussion of *Felicia's Journey* and its morphology of the kitchen as the mother's breathing mouth), but provides the essential pretext in order for the sexual encounter to take place between Bill and his lover. Bill and Yvonne's dialogue resonates with a darkly sexual use of language spiked with a relentless use of innuendo that is, for Spider, amplified by a foul stench, the poisonous air that their relationship creates. Spider repeats Yvonne's reference to bad air, but this echo of her speech does not demonstrate an attempt to identify with her. Rather, in this moment the association is made clear and enunciated – Spider's memory of Yvonne is bound up with his memory of a disgusting air. Furthermore, Yvonne pollutes the air *outside*, but this infection is an externalisation of Spider's inner fears.

While Yvonne represents a pollutant air, *Naked Lunch*'s Joan possesses the ability to kill with her breath.[32] Joan breathes on the ants in her apartment, and it is not only the immediate extermination of the ants that our attention is drawn to, but the invisible act itself performed by Joan's breathing body as an active, yet (im)material exterminating force. Joan, an earlier example of the female breathing body as a poisonous, destructive force, precedes *Spider*'s representation of Yvonne, highlighting the significance of breathing as one that, as Irigaray implies, also has negative implications, of death as well as life that is engendered by women alone.

Importantly, Yvonne is associated with the smell of gas which represents Mrs Clegg's death in the film. This link between gas and mortality is significant to the mythological representation of hell, according to Connor in his article 'An Air that Kills':

> Bad or lethal air has usually been thought of as emanating from nature, rather than as the result of human device. The word 'influenza' preserves the belief in the malign influence of the stars, transmitted in the form of mephitic fluid or vapour. The fascinators or bewitchers of the medieval and early modern imagination were believed to have the power to blast and wither crops and cattle with their breath, often working in conjunction with the power of the evil eye. The basilisk, which could both immobilise its victims with its eye and destroy them with its mephitic breath, is the mythical embodiment of this belief. Hell, or the underworld, is regarded in many cultural traditions as a stinking or smoky place.[33]

Indeed, the older Spider endures throughout the film a kind of living hell through olfaction, compounded by the tormenting view of the gasworks from his bedroom window. Spider's increasing fear of gas reaches a climax in a later scene when he is compelled in terror to remove all of his clothing and replace it with newspaper held together by string. This reaction to gas suggests that Spider is plagued not only by an invisible smell/breath but, most importantly, by an *infection* that has attacked his body, his clothes. In defence of Spider's tendency to wear all of his clothes at the same time, a fellow resident at the halfway house suggests: 'Clothes maketh the man and the less of the clothes ... the less of the man.' Therefore, once clothes are shed, their touch and smell unbearable, Spider is, effectively, non-existent, 'absent'. Indeed, this view is also held by K-Punk in his reading of the film. He writes: 'he seems to want to make himself disappear. Everything about him – his mumbling speech, shambling movements – screams withdrawal, retreat, terror of the outside ... the outside is already inside. And the reverse.'[34] Thus Spider's troubled mind is outwardly expressed, and characterised, through its fusion of thoughts and objects into a drifting, oscillating view of the world.

This 'disappearing' might also be seen as a desire to vanish into thin air. In this sense, Spider yearns to be less visible, like breath, submitting to a corporeality *in absentia*, a body that is no longer only flesh but also air or, precisely, an 'air in flesh', as Irigaray suggests. However, the fact that Cronenberg foregrounds this 'air in flesh' through a male body suggests that his representation is not entirely in line with Irigarayan thought. Rather, Cronenberg implicitly opens Irigarayan thought to the male body, showing a way in which it might be possible to situate the masculine within a breathing encounter.

Spider's nakedness also draws attention to his visibly breathing body, previously veiled by clothing, and we view his exposed chest moving with the fall and rise of each breath. A passage from McGrath's novel also further implies the significance of air as a corporeal state of nothingness, a kind of *being in air* that, even when worn, the clothes merely emphasise: 'My clothes have always seemed to flap about me like sailcloth, like sheets and shrouds . . . and they always look vacant, untenanted . . . as though I were nothing.'[35] McGrath's writing tends to articulate Spider's existence through an invisible current of air that can only be made apparent through the movement of cloth on his skin, like the bandages worn by H. G. Wells's protagonist in *The Invisible Man* (a character also progressively plagued by mental instability). Cronenberg's film thus seems to visually interpret McGrath's allusions to invisibility, his metaphor for social anxiety, emphasising olfaction and the symbolic relevance of clothing, or rather its dual function to conceal as well as to reveal the breathing body of his protagonist.

Breathing marks an awakening of the body for Irigaray, and *Spider* allows us to reformulate her thinking. Breath becomes an awakening of Mrs Clegg/ Yvonne as a spectral body intoxicating Spider's own flesh: *himself* in her breath. While the prominent sense of longing in Irigaray's use of olfactory language, a desire to sense and feel the world she inhabits, is also comparable with *Spider*, this desire is always ambivalent since breath also represents the risk of contamination and infection, as Connor's thought implies.[36] In this way, Cronenberg's foregrounding of breath in *Spider* can be understood in the context of his thematic concern with the body as a site of transgression. Breathing is itself transgressive for Spider in the sense that his own bodily limits and boundaries are disrupted through the intake and exhalation of air. This 'micro-transgression' of bodily boundaries that is suggested by the locus of breathing in *Spider* also has implications for the way in which the gendered body is represented and for its portrayal of feminine and masculine identities.

According to Irigaray, women possess a more natural relationship with air, while men use their energy in order to construct and fabricate objects, putting their breath into things they produce.[37] This gendering of breathing that Irigaray theorises will be analysed in the next section according to the particular viewing processes and modes of identification that the 'film's body' calls into play, especially through the formal use of sound, editing, framing and depth of focus.

Film's Breathing Body

Cronenberg's use of film form offers ways in which to conceive of the film's body as one that 'opens up', as well as 'closes off', the locus of breath in the diegesis; our identification with Spider involves the film's form which heightens the contrasting sensations of anxiety and pleasure that the protagonist experiences. For Jo Smets, McGrath's novel comes to represent 'a final singing at the top of the lungs, until death – an acute lack of breath', but Cronenberg's film also opens itself up to breathing: the 'film's body', to quote Sobchack's use of the term, might be seen to articulate a lack of breath as well as, importantly, gaining access to air.[38]

As we have seen, breathing suggests an acute ambivalence: to breathe is to destabilise the boundaries of the body. I want to show how two scenes from the film manifest this ambivalence through their formal style. The first scene illustrates, through its use of framing, a heightening of suffocation that is felt by Spider when he encounters the presence of the gas tower. For Spider, the gas tower elicits memories of his mother and it is during these moments of recollection that the film's body opens up to the presence of air in the film's diegesis, heightening its manifestation in the film experience. The second scene raises questions about the opening up of air in the film and its resonances with maternal plenitude.

The first scene I am interested in takes place early on in the film when we view Spider gazing towards something, trembling, unable to move and in a state of shock that seems to enter his body from his feet upwards. While Spider cannot bear to look at the gasworks, he fails to escape the *feeling* of their presence. Thus Cronenberg's adaptation of McGrath's novel seems to draw out a relation between gas and heat, and subsequently claustrophobia and suffocation.

As well as signifying an olfactory presence in the film, gas is also primarily associated with heat, since it was the oven that enabled Spider to kill his mother. Yet breath is also a kind of heat, warm air given out by the body through the mouth. Halfway through the film, Spider's memories become intensely frustrating as he begins to experience repressed sexual feelings towards Yvonne. This tension builds towards a physical desire to escape as Spider rushes out of the halfway house and into the deserted street. It is here that he is brought face to face with the gasworks, amplifying his feelings of frustration, paranoia and fear.

While McGrath's novel is preoccupied with various forms of gas, Cronenberg reshapes this concern as sensitive to the nuances of air, and thus breath. Although McGrath admits that breathing had not initially occurred to him as an integral part of his story, he reflects:

> Gas most certainly became a highly developed trope in the novel ... The idea of gas arouses immense guilt in [Spider], but so traumatic was the death that he's repressed his memory of it, and the guilt has no real content. Simply, the gasworks arouses horror (the 'horror of multiplicity,' he says at one point, as his disturbed mind becomes entangled in the metalwork's repeating design of the structure) and he cannot look at it.[39]

The gasworks prompts a terrible anxiety which, in filmic terms, relates to a sensation of suffocation. This sense of shortness of breath or tightness of the chest is suggested in the diegesis when a fellow resident of the halfway house, Terence, rushes to Spider's aid and begins to shift his rigid body so that he is forced to turn away from whatever he is looking at. While ushering Spider away from the gas tower, he recalls an anecdote:

> Gasworks got you, have they? I'm not surprised. I knew a man once, he turned on the gas oven and then he changed his mind. Of course, it was too late. His head was stuck.

The most important aspect of Terence's story is his focus on the head, not as a symbolic reference to the psyche but as a way of emphasising the burden of embodiment. Furthermore, the oven is a signifier of heat which comes to stand for a smothering presence that parallels Spider's relationship with his mother. The head of the man is caught within the mouth of the oven, as if he were being breathed upon by the gas. Creed remarks in her reading of *Crash* that the concept of fusion is central to many of Cronenberg's films,[40] but while this scene connotes a physical convergence between man and object, it is most certainly also through 'breath' that this union is signified. The oven forms an abstract image of orality specific to breathing in the sense that it exudes warm air.

Cronenberg amplifies this smothering tension formally on screen through his framing of the scene. Throughout, he positions the camera at a very low angle, a cinematographic device conventionally employed in order to synthesise a hierarchical tension between the viewer and the subject within the frame. However, Cronenberg effects the reverse in this scene; the low angle does indeed make Spider appear larger, but only in the sense that the now tightly constructed framing of his upper body restricts the space in the image, corresponding to the sense of being trapped, as if his head is enclosed by the oven of Terence's story. Although subtly implied, Spider's head is 'stuck', both in the physical pressure of the frame as it appears to tighten around his body and in the trauma he experiences as a result of turning on the gas and killing his mother. Therefore, Cronenberg's choice of framing situates the viewer within the psychical space of the protagonist and the 'film's body' reinforces our identification with him.

While much of my analysis of *Spider* so far has concentrated on the symbolic resonance of bad air and breath in the film as it evokes a sense of dread, discomfort and paranoia, breath and air in *Spider* also correspond with the film's central theme of maternal goodness. The 'film's body' reflects such goodness associated with breathing, opening up the space of the film in a way that accords with the feelings of plenitude that Spider's memories of his mother elicit. Furthermore, the representation of maternal goodness in *Spider* closely relates to Irigaray's conception of feminine and masculine autonomy reached through a cultivation of breath. Indeed, Irigaray's view is that females 'communicate through air, through blood, through milk, and even voice before and beyond any perceptible thing'.[41]

During an early scene in which Spider recalls his mother remembering a moment from her own childhood, Cronenberg achieves a compelling, filmic duality between mother and child, relayed through a carefully composed and edited series of shots. It is not only through vision that this scene carries such potency; the female voice anchors this sequence's expression of 'air', of aural rhythms, temporality and its foregrounding of a subtle, completely respected and natural silence between mother and child.

Mrs Clegg sits at a table opposite her young son Spider. There is a small circular mirror on the table and she peers into it as she applies lipstick; her gaze shifts from Spider to the mirror, and in this moment she begins to narrate a story:

> I remember how I'd go across the fields in the morning; I'd see the webs in the trees – like clouds of muslin, they were. Spider's webs. Then, I got close; I'd see they weren't muslin at all, they were wheels. Great big shining wheels. And if you knew where to look, you could find the spider's egg bags, perfect little things, but after she laid her eggs, her work was done, she had no silk left. She was all dried up and empty.

Since my argument is that the whole film rests upon a pivotal moment of loss associated with breathing, this scene should accordingly, as a vivid memory of the mother, establish a fecund space within the film that most thoroughly makes manifest the breath of the mother. The most important way in which the mother's breath is foregrounded in this scene is through her voice and its formal creation of a particular space within the film: the circulation of her breath within the frame.

Psychoanalysis has made much of the mother's voice in the cinema. For example, Silverman has spoken of the maternal voice as a castrating threat, while the audio-visual theory of Chion locates a pre-symbolic, threatening malevolence: 'the voice not only envelops, but entraps the newly born infant'.[42] In both cases, however, the female voice is not acknowledged in terms which relate specifically to breath and air. The most natural rhythm that pre-exists language and sound remains undisclosed and thus the maternal voice is always already disembodied in the theories of Silverman and Chion, through her resounding lack of 'air'.[43] It is implied during the above scene that Spider has heard his mother's story many times over, as if a pleasurable lullaby, but this is not to say that he is enclosed in an envelope of 'pure sonorousness', as Silverman may claim.[44] Rather, Spider is encompassed within a *volume of air* created by Mrs Clegg's voice, a circulation of breath that is amplified throughout the formal space of the film. This 'air' carries a potent expression of feminine autonomy and breath in three ways, the first two of which refer to Mrs Clegg's gendered body on screen, within the diegetic space of the film, while the last refers to the 'body' of the film. Firstly, it is her own subjective storytelling; secondly, the content of the narrative evokes the very essence of womanhood itself: fertility, maternity, birth and the menopause; and finally, the positioning of each shot in the sequence privileges her point of view. Mrs Clegg is less an object than a speaking, breathing subject within the frame.

Much of Mrs Clegg's subjective positioning in the sequence is heightened by the formal composition of each image throughout her monologue. It is during this moment that four points are plotted in the three-dimensional space of the shot, heightening the image's illusory depth which, I argue, corresponds to an Irigarayan 'volume of air'. Cronenberg has often commented on the importance of wide-angle lenses and their ability to produce a depth of focus which tends to 'flatten' out the foreground and background.[45] Elaborating on his collaboration with the cinematographer Peter Suschitzky on *Spider*, Cronenberg explains that the use of wide-angle lenses serves to emphasise Spider's merging into the background when filmed against buildings and interiors, but when they are used to film Mrs Clegg's perfectly oval face, such thinning out of the film's illusory depth is countered by the editing of the sequence and circulation of Mrs Clegg's voice.[46] Most notably, there is a distinct change after the line which includes the phrase 'big shining wheels'. While Spider's repetition of Yvonne's reference to 'bad air' signified a negative association, his echo of Mrs Clegg's line here implies not only an identification with her, but also her association with a 'good air' that is suggested through the 'wheels' or, rather, their breast-like symbolisation of maternal plenitude.

The film cuts to a wider shot which incorporates the protagonist, but Mrs Clegg remains the focus of the image. We remain closer to her than to him in terms of our positioning within the field of vision. The line of the table, which also bisects the image, forms a diagonal arrow which points towards Mrs Clegg, effectively positioning both Spider and the mirror on the side of the mother. The lower left corner of the screen is occupied by Mrs Clegg's profile, the mirror is directly opposite her and Spider occupies the middle ground. Mrs Clegg's image is larger than the two other components of this triangular formation, emphasising her active/dominant role in the scene.

The focal point in the image is occupied by Spider, whose gaze is aimed at his mother. Mrs Clegg does not yield to Spider's gaze, retaining her autonomy as she attends to herself in the mirror. In this way, Mrs Clegg also controls time, using her voice to articulate a natural rhythm and pace that is echoed in the film's formal composition, a particular time and place, a volume of air that Spider associates with her goodness. The mirror also further opens up the space of the film by reflecting the maternal image, establishing the fourth point on the screen which reveals the other side of her face. This fourth point in the image can be understood as a doubling of the maternal presence, an affirmation of her surface image which casts a 'web', as it were, around the rest of the space of the image. Thus the mirror seals the space of the film in terms of its physical depth, since it denies any reference to the space beyond that which defines the maternal relationship. It does not reveal any area beyond the physical space of the mother so that the maternal presence is perpetually circulated through both the image's surface and its illusory depth.

The mirror also ensures that the maternal image is quite literally and symbolically *returned to her*. Indeed, in this sense, the image of the mirror also evokes the strategy of a web which weaves and encircles its territory rather like Mrs Clegg's enveloping of her child. Furthermore, this communication and circulation through air also opens up the space in the film, recalling Irigaray's thought on breathing and her affirmation of the maternal-feminine. Mrs Clegg's positioning of herself at the centre of the image while simultaneously reinforcing her subjective role through the use of her voice and the subject matter of her tale evokes an Irigarayan communication through air in a way that can be felt not only as a vocal presence, but made manifest in the film experience.[47] The use of mirrors or reflective surfaces in films often lends the viewer a privileged visuality, but Cronenberg is more interested in developing a physical response conveyed through the movement of the 'film's body' – a rhythm which corresponds with the slow beat of words, pauses for breath, uncertain overlaps and each shift in tone. The viewer's relationship to these images, then, begins and ends with the mother but, rather than appropriating her body, this particular sequence spins a web of its own which tends to revoke any sense of female objectification. The film is complicit with the mother's breathing body, sensitively attuning to her varying rhythms of breath and voice.

While Mrs Clegg is not objectified, the mirror is an object possessed by her that facilitates an opening up of the space within the frame, a formal amplification of the volume of air that she has created through her words. However, breath also bears a particular resonance with an object within the mise en scène that is closely related to Spider: the cigarette. By contrast, the cigarettes constantly drawn to Spider's mouth do not foreground breath in the same formal way that the mirror does in relation to Mrs Clegg. This containment of breath suggested by the cigarette is tainted by smoke, leaving a visible 'stain' that corresponds with a more material evocation of breath. Earlier, I described how *Spider* evokes a relation between the two subjects of the film (Spider and Mrs Clegg) that is precisely engendered through breath, but while the above scene has shown how this might be interpreted in relation to the mother and child of the film, Spider's individual, breathing body is also involved in a deterritorialisation through the objects he encounters.

The Lungs of the Film

I have already discussed Cronenberg's symbolic reference to staining in the opening titles of *Spider*, but there is also a prominent, literal staining of the body within the film's diegesis: the nicotine-stained fingers of its central subject. Certainly, the stains emphasise Spider's corporeal being: their fleshy, amber luminosity is striking against the oppressive, bleak tonality of the screen, drawing our gaze towards fingertips, nails and creases in the skin – details all brought into focus by the stain. It is also through Cronenberg's focus on Spider's stained hands that we are reminded of his withdrawal from the touch of others, comforted more by objects than the potentiality of human contact. Furthermore, the stains may also be seen to represent breathing. The stains on Spider's fingers resonate with breathing in so far as they are produced through smoking, an activity directly dependent upon the lungs. Spider's corporeal stains, a permanent discoloration of his flesh, cannot therefore be fully understood without thinking of the lungs as well as the cigarette as an object that unites the mouth, the hand and the skin in one culminating action inscribed by the stain. Of course, in a more literal sense, breath also passes through the cigarette directly from the mouth, an autonomous gesture entirely dependent upon the protagonist's active, physical engagement with the passive object. Yet it is the transference of the stain and its visible incorporation into the body that is uniquely bound up with the presentation of breathing in the film.

Considering the staining of Spider's fingers in relation to Cronenberg's structuring of his protagonist's subjectivity, the film theorist Patricia McCormack asks:

> What can we make of Spider's fingers, tattooed with the stain of the objects he inhales, creating a permanent, corporeal and visible intimacy between hand and cigarette? Where the 'normally' organised body would scrub the stains to restore the body to a hermeneutic 'whole', Spider's acceptance of the cigarette shows a different regard for the demarcations of what constitutes Spider's self, and an ignorance (volitional or otherwise) of what is signified by different indicators.[48]

According to McCormack, Spider's stained fingers constitute a continuous intimacy between object and subject. Unlike the other objects Spider interacts with, such as the jigsaw he pieces together, the shard of glass he retrieves from a shattered window, the twine he uses for webs or even his tattered notebook, the cigarettes leave a visible trace, or 'tattoo', as McCormack suggests, on his skin. In Cronenberg's 2007 film *Eastern Promises*, full-body tattoos feature prominently as bodily inscriptions of subjectivity that deliberately display an association with a particular social group (the Russian mafia). While the full-body tattoos in *Eastern Promises* signify, as Shaviro puts it, 'power, status and belonging',[49] the residual staining of Spider's fingers, like his hieroglyphic handwriting, offers an antithesis to the cultivated tattoos of Cronenberg's Russian gangsters. In fact, they have no purpose but to re-inscribe the processes of a physical compulsion (smoking) which must be 'worn' indefinitely. With the tattoo, sociality (and particularly fraternity, in the case of *Eastern Promises*) is inseparable from physicality, but for Spider the stain bears a very different significance with regard to his relationship with the outside world – it represents no wider social or political meaning, it is entirely subjective.

Like a fold between both object and subject, the stain materially reproduces an intimacy with the world that is also similar to an Irigarayan theorisation of breath. Yet, in her reading of Merleau-Ponty, Irigaray writes: 'Air is neither on the side of the subject nor of the object. It has neither objecthood nor essence. It has no objecthood because it has no single form of being.'[50] Breathing is thus also a form of deterritorialisation: nicotine stains create a material imprint of an activity which involves the lungs, the mouth and, importantly, warm air – recalling the association of gas with heat. Indeed, as heat also bears resonances with sexual desire in the film, especially Yvonne's warm air and her nakedness from the heat of her flat, these corporeal traces of the object (the cigarette) are also suggestive of breath in a way that can be theorised in relation to pleasure and sexuality in the film. Certainly, breathing is sexual for Irigaray in that it is part of our 'sexuate' identity as living subjects; this is not to say that when we breathe we are behaving in a sexual way, but rather that it is an important aspect of human subjectivity (including at the level of sexual being).[51]

For Spider, smoking is inherently sexual. Smoking has long been associated with an eroticism of the body since it draws attention to the mouth and creates an atmosphere of intimacy between bodies.[52] Indeed, the most famous example of cinema's codification of smoking as a signifier of sexuality may be observed in Irving Rapper's *Now, Voyager* (1942) when Paul Henreid lights two cigarettes and then offers one to his lover, played by Bette Davis. Smoking is a social activity and the sharing of cigarettes prompts close interaction and, importantly, physical contact; but breathing also becomes sexual through this association in *Spider*. Repressed sexual desire is signified through the act of smoking in the film and this is most overtly referenced in one particular scene when Spider fantasises about Yvonne.

Stretched out in a lush green field, Spider listens to two other men, inmates from the asylum, as they discuss their imagined sexual exploits. During this scene, one of the men attempts to explain his addiction to smoking, underlining the significant role of smoking in the film as a compulsion linked with sexual urges: 'every time I smoke a fag, my mother has it off with a sailor'. Simultaneously, we view Spider, closing his eyes for a moment and lovingly caressing a photograph of two nude figures. When Spider opens his eyes again, the smiling face of Yvonne gazes back at him from the photographs. Although Spider is not directly associated with the act of smoking in this scene, his sexual fantasy is led by the discussion between the two other men which is also, in turn, centred on the maternal figure. Therefore the stains are an index of a repressed sexuality. Furthermore, smoking makes breathing pleasurable in that it elicits an addictive, intoxicating sensation, released through inhaling and exhaling, and in this sense the stains on Spider's fingers are also an inscription of sexual pleasure articulated specifically through breathing.

In the final moments of the film we view Spider smoking a cigarette from inside a car that is to take him back to the asylum. Cronenberg cuts from a wide-angle shot of both Spider and the psychiatrist named John (Philip Craig), whom we know from earlier flashbacks, to a close-up of Spider's face peering out from the car window as he slowly exhales. These last breaths of the film are here used to emphasise Spider's resigned composure, a small gesture of dignity and acceptance of the return of, and contiguity between, old habits and the present in which Spider has sealed his own future. This contiguity is also implied through a dissolve to the young Spider seated in the same position as his older self, the indignant face of the child contrasted with the expressively calm resolve of the man. We watch the smoke linger in the air; its translucent immateriality smoulders at the edge of the frame, a cloud that also resembles a (partial) stain within the image. Like a shadow of the past trauma experienced by Spider, the smoke signifies an indelible history, an ultimately inescapable truth. Smoke marks a tenuous boundary between Spider's breathing body and the air, still tainted, but becoming part of a new shifting landscape: the potentiality of other breaths now scattered across a finally unfolding vista of tomorrow.

While the cigarette is a significant object for Spider, objects are also important to *Videodrome*'s foregrounding of breath, but in a way that is not, as with *Spider*, dependent upon physical contact with humans. In other words, in *Videodrome* the objects also come to represent 'bodies' that breathe.

Breathing Objects in a Video World

In *Spider*, the value of the cigarette is asserted, an object that, through its staining of the fingers, bears a particular resonance with breathing in the film. Again, with *Videodrome*, the status of the 'everyday' object is called into question. While Spider's relational behaviour towards objects is invariably tactile, the subject-object dynamic offered by *Videodrome* is less characterised by the same specificity of touch. Indeed, the most striking aspect of *Videodrome* is the film's portrayal of contact and communication with objects through breathing, breath that flows not only from the protagonist, Max Renn (James Woods), but more importantly from the objects themselves.

In an extraordinary set-piece from the film, a videotape begins to move, its increasingly amorphous materiality independently animated through what can only be described as respiration. Moreover, a television set also begins to pulsate and breathe as if it were becoming, in some way, a respiring organ. This rich, powerful suggestion of breathing thus presents many new questions about the way Cronenberg gestures towards corporeal subjectivity in *Videodrome*, both within the context of the film's quasi-religious thematic of the 'new flesh', where assimilation takes place between the body and technology, and in its vivid portrayal of sexual subversion. Certainly, gender plays an important part in the representation of these objects, along with the film's conception of the soul and transcendence reached through the material world.

In this respect, a considerable number of parallels can also be drawn between Cronenberg's foregrounding of breathing, in terms of gender and spirituality, and Irigaray's thinking. Most importantly, Irigaray claims breath cannot be assimilated to an object, but videotapes start to 'breathe' in *Videodrome*, rippling as if they were living flesh, and thus I consider the significance of breathing as it engenders a form of bodily subjectivity.

Videodrome is Cronenberg's sixth feature film, following on from the success of *Scanners* (1981) and preceding his seminal remake of Kurt Neumann's horror film *The Fly* (1958, 1986). Set within the austere office block premises of a local broadcasting corporation based in Toronto, *Videodrome* inhabits two worlds: the excessive, technological environment of the media, and the realm situated within its multiple screens, television sets and interfaces. In *Videodrome*, it is not the former that defines the limits and boundaries of the latter, for the status of the projected image is raised to a level of power capable of penetrating and transforming the living world and, above all, the human body. Technology thus dictates evolution, but for Cronenberg's protagonist, the television executive Max Renn, this most radical change comes at a heavy price. When Renn begins to seek out new ways to attract audiences and secure high ratings, he discovers an illegal channel transmitting highly graphic images of sexual violence and torture. Such images possess a heightened allure for Renn, their exoticism offering a compulsive form of visual stimulation. Renn eventually learns that Videodrome is rather more than an adult channel; it merely uses the alluring intensity of such images in order to subliminally transmit a signal embedded within its visual field which causes brain tumours.

Exposed to the full effects of the Videodrome channel, Renn starts to experience hallucinations which show him the plasticity of the human form. He also views his lover, Nicki Brand (Deborah Harry), being tortured during one of Videodrome's broadcasts, recalling the masochistic nature of their relationship which started soon after he had first encountered Videodrome. Communicating only through videotaped messages, Dr Brian O'Blivion (Jack Creley) urges Renn to 'surrender to the new flesh'. In the closing act of the film, Renn begins to understand O'Blivion's message – he starts to embody a human video machine. Unable to bear the physical transformation he has undergone, Renn shoots himself. In this last gesture, Renn's death is played out as an act of both sacrifice and emancipation, yet its deliberate ambiguity suggests that there is also nothing beyond carnality, the most absolute truth and enlightenment written only in the mortality of the flesh.

The breathing objects in *Videodrome* have been largely marginalised by critics, often limiting their discussion to a short reference.[53] Moreover, some critics have even described the objects in terms of an animation without taking into account that it is precisely through their representation of breathing that this animation is undoubtedly perceived. More generally, critics have commented on *Videodrome*'s thematic reference to the power and spectacle of the media, often viewed as a distinct engagement with post-modernism and the thinking of Marshall McLuhan.[54] Although post-modernist criticism of *Videodrome* has also drawn widely on the philosophy of Jean Baudrillard, Michel Foucault and Guy Debord, it is McLuhan's media theory that Cronenberg intended most to inform the iconography of the film. Indeed, *Videodrome*'s extreme, hallucinatory visions have often been described as an over-literalising of McLuhan's key concepts.[55] One of McLuhan's principal aims is to understand the medium, that is, the technological device, not as the carrier of messages, but as the very message itself.[56] Concerned less with the content of information systems, McLuhan theorises the mediated relation imposed on our bodies by forms of technology and its restructuring of embodied subjectivity, particularly in relation to touch.

Most interestingly, McLuhan's philosophy is brought into dialogue with Irigaray by the feminist thinker Sadie Plant in her analysis of 'cyber-feminist' stimulation. Plant argues that technology's multiple connections, switches and links allow for another kind of immersive touch that corresponds with 'the proliferating touch-point of women's speech and body-sex'.[57] In light of the centrality of touch or, rather, vision as an embodied experience in *Videodrome*, Plant's thinking offers a way of situating Irigaray within Cronenberg's postmodernist discourse. Working to uncover an alternative 'flesh' inscribed within *Videodrome*'s images of the fantastic, I question the role of gendered power structures embodied by technology in the film in order to negotiate a space for breath within the spectacular, an (in)visible circuitry engendered between both human and machine.

Respiring Interfaces

Immediately after Renn watches a 'snuff' video of Dr O'Blivion's murder, a number of extraordinary things start to happen, culminating in one of *Videodrome*'s most commented upon images: the fusion of Renn and his television set. This fusion between man and machine takes place when the television screen contracts into the shape of a large pair of lips. Originally viewed as a close-up video image of Nicki, the lips press against the surface of the screen, fleshing out a luscious embrace that consumes the protagonist's entire head. The television thus takes the form of a human receptacle, metamorphosing into a mouth that swells and pulsates as if it were living flesh. However, before this last moment of convergence, there are subtler references to a responsive and communicative respiring 'flesh', the most intimate of these embodied by breath. In fact, it is through the sound and materialisation of breath as a rhythmic modulation that the 'living' presence of the video cassette is first announced; this breathing is then transferred to the television set when the video is played.

Philip Brophy has also commented on the synthesised sound of breathing in *Videodrome*: 'The film foregrounds breath in both recognisable and abstracted states: from the synthetic noise of mock-human breath to actual breath analogue-filtered, to the synclavier simulating orchestral drones which historically symbolise vocal sighs and choral murmurs.'[58] While sound creates an ambivalent, human versus synthesised human tension relating to the diegesis, the film's 'breathing body', its formal properties, also emphasises the ambiguity of breathing as a subjective, and thus human, act.

Initially there are waves, gentle rippling motions as the audio vents of the television begin to respire. In place of an audio output of recorded sound, the television set begins to sigh, as if stirring from sleep. While one can argue that the eventual convergence between Renn and the television is central to the narrative plot of *Videodrome*, the development of proximity before this final, direct contact is equally important. Filmed separately, images of Renn's body are cross-cut with close-ups of the machine's breathing speakers. In making this link between Renn and the television set apparent, a comparison is also drawn between the two breathing 'bodies' contained within the same diegetic space. Renn's immobile, corporeal subjectivity is contrasted with the animated objectivity of the television, and it is through this precise representation that we become increasingly aware of breath, not in relation to the subject, but to the object. This is to say that breathing is exaggerated through the object, every physical and aural gesture amplified. As a result of this amplification, Renn's breathing is much less perceptible. Thus a considerable reversal, specifically performed through breath, takes place between subject and object, well in advance of the literal transformation of man into machine/machine into man.

If we know how the object respires, then we must also ask what kind of 'air' it breathes, since air is fundamental to any process of respiration. As much as the television set adopts a corporeal status through breathing, a crucial part of it is still a machine and therefore we must also ask what kind of air flows through this dimension of its being other than the oxygen we as humans need in order to survive. Unlike the celluloid breaths of Sobchack's analysis which I have discussed in the introduction to this book, the television set's breathing is not contained within its processing of images – it breathes through its body in a very literal way. We can consider the electrical charge of the machine as its 'pulse', its wires and circuitry suggestive of a possible network of veins and musculature, all moulded beneath a casing of poly-resin skin, but we must also think beyond the limits of the interior in order to include air within this schema of flesh. If air gives life, in the most literal sense, then with respect to the television set's sentient body it is Renn whose presence most directly gives this machine purpose and meaning within the film's narrative. It may be argued, therefore, that Renn fulfils the role of air in relation to the object. In this case, the television set is dependent on Renn; it breathes not for but because of him.

Unlike Sobchack's understanding of respiration as a material and repetitive process, the philosophy of Irigaray affirms air as a fluid and ephemeral space in which it is possible to enter a 'third ground', an inter-subjective, open encounter.[59] Sobchack touches upon such inter-subjectivity when describing her *cinesthetic* experience of figural patterns and abstraction in her analysis of *The Last Temptation of Christ*, but her theorisation tends to be dependent on these formal gestures. However, in view of Irigaray's thought on the inter-subjective relations that accord with breathing, the diegetic filmed breaths of *Videodrome*, then, also serve to establish an inter-subjective concurrency between man and (evolving) machine. While this inter-subjectivity is short-lived since the machine ultimately overcomes Renn, both through the scene's final images of fusion and through his violent transformation, it embeds a dynamic within the film that reveals an important part of the process of metamorphosis at work in *Videodrome*.

For Cronenberg, metamorphosis is suggested through extremely graphic images of physical transformation and their collective spectacle. Indeed, breathing objects are central to the representation of *Videodrome* and its overall critique of the scopic regimes pertinent to the media. In my reading of Egoyan's *The Sweet Hereafter*, I suggested how breathing relates to Egoyan's refusal to show the spectacle of the bus accident and the way in which this prompts viewers to 'hold' their breath in response to the tension that it creates. With *Videodrome*, vision is not refused, but rather displaced through breath. By becoming a 'breathing body', the television set is no longer the framed mediator of spectacle, but the spectacle itself within the frame.

The thinking of Irigaray locates the spectacle within a patriarchal economy of male objectification. Irigaray's examination of Western continental philosophy, particularly in her book *Speculum*, critiques Plato's equation of vision with truth and knowledge. In order to subvert this association, Irigaray invokes not an anti-ocular strategy, but rather a rewriting of philosophy with respect to its undisclosed debt to embodiment. Truth is thus a play of light on the eyes (vision) that prefigures the 'sensible corporeal' in which light is experienced as a sensuous engagement with the world. It is this particular touching of light on the eyes or, rather, vision as a tactile experience that has most resonance with the breathing objects of *Videodrome*.[60]

In addition to the visuality of the breathing objects, the sound of breathing also has implications for the role of sexuality in the film. The sound of breathing is often sexual in *Videodrome* but, most importantly, it embodies an alternative 'desiring touch', or what Irigaray might suggestively refer to as an assertion of 'the lungs as an organ of desire'.[61] This is literalised on the soundtrack when we hear the object exhale a current of air across Renn's face, its breathing rather less a simulacrum than a form of reciprocity in which Renn's gaze is returned through the bodily gesture of breath. While my reading of sexuality in relation to breathing in *Spider* focused more closely on the image-track, analysing the eroticised act of smoking in the film, *Videodrome* directly connotes a form of desire that is achieved most resolutely through the sound of sighing breaths. Of course, as Irigaray argues, no organ can truly embody desire if it is to be understood in a singular way, as a purely biological aspect of human subjectivity, yet the lungs, like the organ of the skin, enable the breathing object to perform and complete an (in)visible caress of the other (the subject, Renn). I refer here to my development of a model of haptics which follows a logic of the lungs. In my chapter on Egoyan I suggested that haptic theory needs to be developed in order to involve breathing, and my discussion of the lungs offers another way in which to open up the concept of haptics to the place of breath in film.

The lungs are also involved in a kind of embodied vision according to Deleuze.[62] In his reading of Francis Bacon's painting, Deleuze contends: 'his painting gives us eyes all over: in the ear, in the stomach, in the lungs (the painting breathes . . .)'.[63] This is not to say that vision takes over the other senses, but rather that Bacon's images enhance the other senses – sight stimulates them. For Deleuze, Bacon's painting appeals to the body as a whole, inviting an embodied response where the lungs also become an organ of perception. However, unlike the object (the breathing painting) of Deleuze's analysis, *Videodrome*'s breathing objects are experienced by the protagonist Renn as distinctly gendered forms of being, since the sounds which accompany the images of the objects evoke the breathing, desiring voice of Nicki. Thus Cronenberg asserts the objects as specifically 'feminine'. It is therefore most striking that breathing is explicitly involved in this representation, since an affirmation of the feminine through breath is also highly Irigarayan. Yet gender is also mobilised in *Videodrome*, and critics such as Martin Ham have remarked on Renn's transformation into a machine as a 'feminisation' of the subject, most notably through the wound that appears in his chest where videotapes are later inserted, its shape according with a female morphology of the body.[64] In this sense, Renn gains a breathing body in a way that never existed before, reaching a state of being through breath that is only accessed through his own feminisation. One might call this a kind of transcendence, a fresh potentiality of *Videodrome*'s 'new flesh'.

Feminine Transcendence

It is made clear by Dr O'Blivion during his videotaped messages that the 'new flesh' refers to a rebirth of mankind, reprogrammed as 'the video word made flesh'. This transformation is itself implied throughout the film as a form of spiritual transcendence reached through the material world, namely that of the televisual image. To become at one with the 'video word' is therefore not to cease being in existence, but rather to become immortal (also reminiscent of Egoyan's use of the video image in *Felicia's Journey* where Hilditch refers to his victims as 'angels' preserved forever on film). However, the transcendental can also be discussed through further contemplation of *Videodrome*'s breathing objects and Irigaray's particular conceptualisation of the soul. For Irigaray, breath ensures the junction between soul and body:

> The breath is necessary for entering into the presence of a human as human, more than language and in a different way. Indispensable for

life, breath is also the means, the medium to accede to spiritual life as an irreducible dimension of human subjectivity.[65]

Certainly, breathing corresponds with a kind of bodily subjectivity in *Videodrome* that is irreducible. Breathing engenders life in *Videodrome*, not in a purely biological way but in relation to a subjective being. In the scene preceding Renn's encompassing embrace by the televisual lips, breathing is suggestive not only of a human presence but of a female body, and this also has a particular resonance with Irigarayan thought. Since the breathing television set conveys the possibility of the transcendental, it is most interesting that the feminine soul enunciates this position through breath and that the male subject in *Videodrome* is able to reach transcendence through his feminisation. According to Irigarayan thought, the scene in which Renn is 'transformed' would thus suggest that breath is the junction between soul and that of the televisual body, which becomes the breathing body of the 'new flesh'.

Ultimately, breathing fleshes out a path toward transcendence, prescient of Renn's inevitable fate, but in order to reach this stage of being he must endure a process of feminisation. Most notably, when Renn discovers that Barry Convex is responsible for the *Videodrome* channel, a vagina-like opening appears in his stomach, allowing Convex to programme him by inserting a breathing video cassette into it. Through this act, Renn is programmed to assassinate Bianca O'Blivion, Dr O'Blivion's daughter. Although I am in agreement with Martin Ham's view that Renn is feminised by the Videodrome signal, this scene also amounts to Renn's containment of breath as a form of irreducible bodily difference.[66] Irigaray asserts breathing as a specifically feminine form of engendering difference since it is the woman's maternal right to share her breath with a child in a way that respects two irreducible subjects. Renn's violent act of impregnation can thus be seen to reflect Irigaray's model of thought, but with respect to a male subjectivity. On one level, the video cassette as a breathing body conveys a fear of pregnancy from a male perspective where breath embodies a foreign object, unnatural and abject, while on another, more contextual level in relation to the role of the technology in the film, breath is implied as part of a programme, associated with a form of assimilation and totality. We might, then, conclude that this evocation of breathing – Renn's containment of the breathing video cassette – relates to an autonomy that is at once affirmed and negated.

Earlier in this book, I referred to Lloyd's sociological analysis of breathing as a form of body modification that relies less on the visual perception of change, but in *Videodrome* breath is not ornamental, it calls into question what it means to be an autonomous subject.[67] When the breathing body of the videotape is inserted into Renn's gaping chest, the programme that the breathing tape 'plays' restricts Renn's autonomy. However, this insertion also leads to Renn's reclaiming of his autonomy when he painfully removes the tape from his body. Renn's desire to separate the tape, this breathing body, from his own suggests that he respires again for the first time as he has been reborn, not through the 'new flesh' of Convex's project, but in terms which relate closely to an Irigarayan flesh, a transcendence reached through his own feminisation.

Reflecting on Cronenberg

As we have seen, the film experiences offered through *Spider* and *Videodrome* are ordered by a complex physicality that involves breathing. This physicality and its shaping through the filmed, breathing bodies and objects of *Spider* and *Videodrome* are reflected not only in the narrative of the films and the depiction of the human body on screen, but also in the viewing relations and the formal style of each film. Most importantly, my exploration of Cronenberg's films has considered how breathing has implications for the discussion of the gendered subject and the significance of the senses to our understanding of the place of breath in cinema.

While this chapter has considered how the representation of diegetic bodies on screen suggests ways of interpreting the shifting of bodily boundaries, especially in relation to Irigaray's thought on the sexed, breathing body and the interaction between the senses and breathing, my analyses have also shown how the 'film's body' and the viewer's identification processes are organised according to such radical portrayals of physicality. In my analysis of *Spider*, the 'film's body' can be seen to represent a sexed, breathing body which amplifies the diegetic representation of bodily discomfort as well as pleasure. The film's breathing 'body' is thus frequently complicit with the diegetic breaths contained within the images themselves. In addition to the filmed bodies of *Spider*, my exploration of objects such as the cigarette shows how the material world and its tangible presence constitute an Irigarayan interplay of physical sensation and breathing. My discussion of the cigarette and its external signification of the lungs foreshadows my analysis of the deterritorialisation of bodily boundaries which are engendered by breathing videotapes in *Videodrome*.

What is emphasised by this chapter is the importance of the formal use of editing and the close-up to my theorisation of the film's breathing 'body'. In what follows, such formal aspects will be re-examined, refocusing on Irigaray's inter-subjective conceptualisation of breathing that is based on a dynamic of sharing and the implications her thought bears for the theorisation of the viewer's breathing body. Attention is drawn to the viewer's breathing which becomes implicated in the film experience. This specific focus on the viewer's breathing body involves rethinking the particular issues of suffering in the flesh and mortality that I have gestured towards in this chapter's engagement with Cronenberg's thematic concerns. Taking these concerns with embodied suffering forward, the next chapter will approach the issue of filmic realism and the role breath plays in the representation of 'real' bodies: the crack in the voice, the jarring textual qualities of breath and its overall suggestion of an unbearable closeness that the cinema of Lars von Trier richly evokes.

Notes

1. See Jean-Luc Nancy, 'Icon of Fury: Claire Denis's *Trouble Every Day*', Eng. trans. by Douglas Morrey (2001), *Film-Philosophy*, 12:1 (2008), available at <http://www.film-philosophy.com/2008v12n1/nancy.pdf> (accessed 20 July 2008).
2. See Luce Irigaray, *An Ethics of Sexual Difference* (London: Continuum, 2004), p. 108.
3. *Dead Ringers*, dir. David Cronenberg, Canada/USA, 1988.
4. See Williams, 'The Inside-Out of Masculinity: David Cronenberg's Visceral Pleasures', in Michele Aaron (ed.), *The Body's Perilous Pleasures: Dangerous Desires and Contemporary Culture* (Edinburgh: Edinburgh University Press, 1999), pp. 30–48 (p. 32).
5. Ibid. p. 32.
6. See, in particular, Irigaray, *The Way of Love* (London: Continuum, 2004), p. 67.
7. See Irigaray, *Everyday Prayers* (Nottingham: Nottingham University Press), p. 56 and p. 146.
8. See Shaviro, *The Cinematic Body: Theory out of Bounds* (Minneapolis: University of Minnesota Press, 1993), p. 8.
9. See Sobchack, 'What My Fingers Knew: The Cinesthetic Subject, or Vision in the Flesh', *Senses of Cinema*, 5 (2000), available at <http://sensesofcinema.com/2000/5/fingers> (accessed 7 December 2011).
10. I refer here to Marks's model of identification as 'a bodily relationship with the screen' in 'Loving a Disappearing Image', in *Touch: Sensuous Theory and Multisensory Media* (Minneapolis: University of Minnesota Press, 2002), pp. 91–110; Nicole Brenez's sensual reflection on the films of Philippe Grandrieux and the classical film theory of Jean Epstein, 'The Body's Night: An Interview with Philippe Grandrieux', *Rouge*, 1 (2003), available at <http://www.rouge.com.au/1/grandrieux.html> (accessed 7 July 2009); and Martine Beugnet's *Cinema and Sensation: French Film and the Art of Transgression* (Edinburgh: Edinburgh University Press, 2007). See also Joseph Mai, 'Corps-Caméra: The Evocation of Touch in the Dardennes' *La Promesse* (1996)', *Contact!*, special issue of *L'Esprit Créateur*, ed. Martin Crowley, 47:3 (2007), pp. 133–44; Sarah Cooper, 'Mortal Ethics: Reading Levinas with the Dardenne Brothers', *Film-Philosophy*, 11:2 (2007); and Daniel Frampton's discussion of film as a thinking body in 'Film Phenomenology', in *Filmosophy* (London: Wallflower Press, 2006), pp. 39–48.
11. See Sobchack, *The Address of the Eye: Phenomenology and Film Experience* (Princeton: Princeton University Press, 1992), p. 207.
12. See Martine Beugnet, 'The Practice of Strangeness: *L'Intrus* – Claire Denis (2004) and Jean-Luc Nancy (2000)', *Film-Philosophy*, 12:1, pp. 31–48 (p. 43), available at <http://www.film-philosophy.com/2008v12n1/beugnet.pdf> (accessed 5 August 2011). It would also seem that Beugnet is particularly sensitive to relations between breath and the senses. See, for example, Beugnet's reference to deep breathing along with a distant rumbling and the many variations of the wind which affirms an 'aesthetics of sensation' in her essay 'Evil and the Senses: Philippe Grandrieux's *Sombre* and *La vie nouvelle*', *Studies in French Cinema*, 5:3 (2005), pp. 175–84 (p. 180). See also Beugnet's thoughts on Chantal Akerman's filmic adaptation of Marcel Proust's *La Prisonnière* (*La Captive*, 2000) and a passage from the novel which describes the protagonist Albertine listening to breathing and its rhythm of the sea in 'Filming Obsession: Chantal Akerman's *La Captive*', in Martine Beugnet and Marion Schmid (eds), *Proust at the Movies*, Studies in European Cultural Transition Series (Aldershot: Ashgate Publishing, 2005), pp. 168–205 (p. 186).
13. See Irigaray, *Everyday Prayers*, p. 146.

14. See Irigaray, 'The Invisible of the Flesh: A Reading of Merleau-Ponty, *The Visible and the Invisible*, "The Intertwining – The Chiasm"', in *An Ethics of Sexual Difference* (London: Continuum, 2004), pp. 127–53.
15. Ibid.
16. See, for example, William Beard, *The Artist as Monster* (Toronto: University of Toronto Press, 2006); Scott Bukatman, *Terminal Identity: The Virtual Subject in Postmodern Science Fiction* (Durham, NC: Duke University Press, 1993), pp. 85–92; Christine Cornea, 'David Cronenberg's Performing Cyborgs', *Velvet Light Trap*, 52 (2003), pp. 4–14; Lia M. Hotchkiss, '"Still in the Game": Cyber-transformations of the "New Flesh" in D. Cronenberg's *eXistenZ*', *Velvet Light Trap*, 52 (2003), pp. 15–32; Michael Thomson, '*eXistenZ*: bio-ports/boundaries/bodies', *Legal Studies*, 21:2 (2001), pp. 325–43; Parveen Adams, 'Death Drive', in David Grant (ed.), *The Modern Fantastic: The Cinema of David Cronenberg* (Trowbridge: Flicks Books, 2000), pp. 102–22; Helen W. Robbins, 'More Human Than I Am Alone', in Steven Cohan and Ina Rae Hark (eds), *Screening the Male* (London: Routledge, 1996), pp. 134–50; and Marcie Frank, 'The Camera and the Speculum: David Cronenberg's *Dead Ringers*', *PMLA*, 106:3 (1991), pp. 459–70.
17. See Creed, 'Woman as Monstrous Womb: *The Brood*', in *The Monstrous Feminine: Film, Feminism and Psychoanalysis* (London: Routledge, 1993), pp. 43–58. See also Creed's reading of male masochism in Cronenberg's cinema in 'Dark Desires', in Cohan and Hark (eds), *Screening the Male*, pp. 118–33; for Creed's reading of the wound as fetish in *Crash* see 'The *Crash* Debate: Anal Wounds, Metallic Kisses', *Screen*, 39:2 (1998), pp. 175–9.
18. See McGrath, *Spider* (London: Viking, 1991).
19. See, for example, William Beard, 'Spider', in *The Artist as Monster*, pp. 471–504; Mark Browning, *David Cronenberg: Author or Filmmaker?* (Bristol: Intellect, 2007); Reni Celeste, 'In the Web with David Cronenberg: *Spider* and the New Auteurism', *CineAction*, 65 (Winter 2005), pp. 2–5; Kevin Jackson, 'Odd Man Out', *Sight and Sound*, January 2003, available at <http://www.bfi.org.uk/sightandsound/feature/72> (accessed 5 June 2010). Browning also presented a paper on *Spider* entitled 'The Child in Time: Cronenberg's Use of Chronology in *Spider*' at the 2004 *Screen* annual conference, Glasgow.
20. See K-Punk, 'She's Not My Mother', at <http://k-punk.abstractdynamics.org/archives/003227.html> (accessed 5 June 2010).
21. For a useful physiological account of the olfactory sense, see Donald Wilson and Richard Stevenson, *Learning to Smell: Olfactory Perception from Neurobiology to Behaviour* (Baltimore: The Johns Hopkins University Press, 2006).
22. For a useful commentary on the issue of time in *Spider*, see Celeste, 'In the Web with David Cronenberg'.
23. Named after its inventor, Hermann Rorschach (1884–1922), a Swiss psychiatrist.
24. See Anthony Kaufman's interview with David Cronenberg, 'David Cronenberg on *Spider*: Reality Is What You Make of It', *Indiewire*, 2003, available at <http://www.ralphfiennes-jenniferlash.com/article.php?id=89> (accessed 8 December 2011).
25. Cronenberg's early narratives centered on the themes of bodily infection and decay in films such as *Shivers* (1975), *The Brood* (1979) and *Videodrome* (1986); this exploration evolved into other examinations of transformation and metamorphosis in films such as *The Fly* (1986), *Dead Ringers* (1988), *M Butterfly* (1993) and *eXistenZ* (1999).
26. See Shaviro's introduction to *The Cinematic Body*, p. 8.
27. See Shaviro's internet blog *The Pinocchio Theory* for an entry on *Spider*, available at <http://www.shaviro.com/Blog/?p=76> (accessed 5 May 2010).
28. See Marks's conclusion in *The Skin of the Film: Intercultural Cinema, Embodiment and the Senses* (Durham, NC: Duke University Press, 1999), p. 246. For Marks's

other key writings on olfaction see, for example, her analysis of the brothers Quay film *Institute Benjamenta*, 'The Quays' *Institute Benjamenta*: An Olfactory View', in *Touch*, pp. 127–40; see also Marks, 'Thinking Multisensory Culture', *Paragraph: Journal of Modern Critical Theory*, special issue on 'Cinema and the Senses', ed. Emma Wilson, 31:2 (July 2008), pp. 123–37.

29. See K-Punk, 'She's Not My Mother'.
30. See Irigaray, *Everyday Prayers*, p. 56.
31. Ibid. p. 106.
32. This characteristic of Joan's character is also a particular point of interest for Beard, although his thoughts reflect on the broader significance of breathing in the context of the film's themes of monstrosity and perversion. See Beard, *The Artist as Monster*, p. 310.
33. See Connor, 'An Air that Kills', an online except from a paper first given at the 'Death by Technology' conference, Birkbeck College, 30 May 2003, available at <http://bbk.ac.uk/english/skc/gas> (accessed 5 May 2011).
34. See K-Punk, 'She's Not My Mother'.
35. See McGrath, *Spider*, p. 50.
36. See Connor, 'An Air that Kills'.
37. See Irigaray, 'The Way of Breath', in *Between East and West: From Singularity to Community* (New York: Columbia University Press, 2001), pp. 73–92 (p. 84).
38. See Smets, 'Memory can be a terrifying thing', available at <http://www.writemen.com/pages/writing-print-article-Spider-E.html> (accessed 5 October 2011).
39. These comments are taken from McGrath's correspondence with me via email, dated November 2007. I am indebted to Mohsen Shah, the personal assistant to McGrath's literary agent at Rogers, Coleridge and White, for helping me to get in touch with him.
40. See Creed, 'The *Crash* Debate: Anal Wounds, Metallic Kisses', p. 177.
41. See introduction to *Luce Irigaray: Key Writings* (New York: Continuum, 2004), p. xiii.
42. See Kaja Silverman, 'The Fantasy of the Maternal Voice: Paranoia and Compensation', in *The Acoustic Mirror: The Female Voice in Psychoanalysis and Cinema* (Bloomington: Indiana University Press, 1988), pp. 72–100 (p. 72); Michel Chion, *The Voice in the Cinema* (Columbia: Columbia University Press, 1998), ed. and trans. Claudia Gorbman from the French *La Voix au cinéma* (Paris: Cahiers du cinéma, 1982).
43. One theorist who has respected the role of air in vocality is Theresa M. Krier, whose work on cultural nostalgia suggests that the shelter provided by maternal sound, her singing, 'encompasses the child within a volume of air shaped by her voice', constituting 'long-lived and haunting topoi'. See Krier, 'From Aggression to Gratitude: Air and Song in the *Parlement of Foules*', in *Birth Passages: Maternity and Nostalgia, Antiquity to Shakespeare* (New York: Cornell University Press, 2001), pp. 109–38 (p. 109).
44. See Silverman, 'The Fantasy of the Maternal Voice', p. 72.
45. See, for example, Cronenberg's interview with David Schwartz at the Museum of the Moving Image, New York, 10 January 2003, available at <http://www.movingimagesource.us/files/dialogues/2/63883_programs_transcript_html_204.htm> (accessed 8 December 2011).
46. See, in particular, Cronenberg's comments in interview with Anthony Kaufman in 'David Cronenberg on *Spider*'.
47. I refer to Irigaray's remark 'she communicates through air' expressed in the introduction to *Key Writings*, p. xiii.
48. See McCormack's essay 'Phantasmatic Fissures: *Spider*', *Senses of Cinema*, 27 (2003), available at <http://www.sensesofcinema.com/2003/feature-articles/spider> (accessed 8 December 2011).

49. See Shaviro's blog entry on *Eastern Promises*, available at <http://www.shaviro.com/Blog/?p=601> (accessed 11 October 2008).
50. See Irigaray quoted in Connor, 'Next-to-Nothing', *Tate Etc*, 12 (Spring 2008), available at <http://www.tate.org.uk/tateetc/issue12/air.htm> (accessed 12 September 2009).
51. See, for example, Irigaray's writings in 'The Way of Breath', pp. 73–92.
52. For a more detailed discussion of smoking in films see Dr Lesley Owen and Kenneth Mackinnon, *Smoking in Films: A Review* (London: Health Education Authority, 1997).
53. See Shaviro's reference to 'breathing flesh' in 'Bodies of Fear', in *The Cinematic Body*, pp. 126–55 (p. 138); see also Scott Bukatman's reference to the breathing television set in '*Videodrome*' in *Terminal Identity*, pp. 85–92 (p. 89).
54. See, for example, William Beard, '*Videodrome*', in *The Artist as Monster*, p. 124; Scott Bukatman, '*Videodrome*', in *Terminal Identity*, pp. 85–92; Frederic Jameson, 'Totality as Conspiracy', in *The Geopolitical Aesthetic: Cinema and Space in the World System* (London: BFI, 1992), pp. 9–82; Shaviro, 'Bodies of Fear', in *The Cinematic Body*, pp. 126–55.
55. For work engaging with the philosophy of Baudrillard see Martin Ham's article 'Excess and Resistance in Feminised Bodies: David Cronenberg's *Videodrome* and Jean Baudrillard's *Seduction*', *Senses of Cinema*, 30 (2004), available at <http://www.sensesofcinema.com/2004/30/videodrome_seduction> (accessed 8 December 2011).
56. See, in particular, Marshall McLuhan, *McLuhan: Hot and Cool*, ed. G. E. Stearn (New York: Dial, 1967).
57. See Plant, 'On the Matrix: Cyberfeminist Stimulations', in Gill Kirkup et al. (eds), *The Gendered Cyborg: A Reader* (London: Routledge, 2000), p. 270.
58. See Brophy, *100 Modern Soundtracks*, BFI Screen Guides (London: BFI, 2004), pp. 246–7.
59. See Irigaray, *Being Two: How Many Eyes Have We?* (Rüsselsheim: Christel Göttert Verlag, 2000), p. 22.
60. The notion of light as a form of touch in Irigaray's work is thoroughly explored by Vasseleu in her book *Textures of Light: Vision and Touch in Irigaray, Levinas and Merleau-Ponty* (New York: Routledge, 1998).
61. I refer here to a conversation with Irigaray during my participation at her 2007 seminar at Liverpool University.
62. See Deleuze, 'Hysteria', in *Francis Bacon: The Logic of Sensation* (London: Continuum, 2005), pp. 32–9; Eng. trans. by Daniel W. Smith from the French *Logique du sens* (Paris: Les Éditions de Minuit, 1969).
63. Ibid. p. 37.
64. See Ham's article 'Excess and Resistance in Feminised Bodies'.
65. See Irigaray, *Being Two: How Many Eyes Have We?*, p. 19.
66. See Ham, 'Excess and Resistance in Feminised Bodies'.
67. See Lloyd, 'Life in the Slow Lane: Rethinking Spectacular Body Modification', *Journal of Media and Cultural Studies*, 18:4 (2004), p. 555.

3. TOWARDS INTER-SUBJECTIVITIES OF BREATH AND THE BREATHING FILM VIEWER: LARS VON TRIER'S 'GOLD HEART' TRILOGY

Interdependency is no longer reduced to questions of possessing, of exchanging or sharing objects, cash, or an already existing meaning. It is, rather, regulated by the constitution of subjectivity. The subject does not invest its own value in any form of property whatsoever. No longer is it objecthood, having or the cost of having that governs the becoming of the subject or subjects and the relation among them. They are engaged in a relationship from which they emerge altered, the objective being the accomplishment of their subjectivity while remaining faithful to their nature.[1]

Luce Irigaray

From its first breath, the lived-body constitutes both an intrasubjective and intersubjective system.[2]

Vivian Sobchack

This chapter explores the relationship between on-screen bodies, the sounds they make and the body of the viewer – what the film theorist Tarja Laine might call a 'triadic communality'.[3] Central to the way in which I draw attention to a viewing experience shaped by the acoustic, and visual, orientation towards the communality of breathing will be Lars von Trier's filmic coupling of bodies and their articulation of an Irigarayan inter-subjectivity; this reflection on the inter-subjectivity of breathing places special emphasis on what Tamazin E. Lorraine has described as a moment in which it is possible for 'the subject to become engendered on the basis of the other rather than being reduced to the image, ideal or illusion of the other'.[4]

While the key concern of the previous chapter in this book was to approximate the differences and concordances between breathing objects and subjects and their corporeal status, this chapter asks what might come of such relations when thought through as an inter-subjective encounter – the coming together of two breathing subjects. This inter-subjective dimension of breathing forms the very basis of Irigaray's conceptual thinking regarding the social and ethical implications of embodied being, a facet of her theoretical model which was outlined earlier in my introduction to this book.[5] The breaths shared between two people, or a community of breathing bodies, symbolise, for Irigaray, a vital aspect of existence which constitutes the foundation for all bodily, linguistic and environmental linkages pertinent to human life. This is to say that all humans enter into a dialogue with each other through breathing, a relation that is established the moment we take our 'first breath', as Sobchack puts it.[6] However, the very notion of *two* breaths is complicated by the many refractions of subjectivity which the cinema grants us. The previous chapter foregrounded ways in which to conceive of breathing bodies in Cronenberg's films according to the figuring of bodies in the film's diegesis, the formal suggestion of the film's 'body' and questions of gender that arise as a result of analysing depictions of physicality made manifest in *Spider* and *Videodrome*. This chapter on von Trier's films aims to examine the role of bodies in the context of their possible couplings and parallels. My overarching concern with the notion of breathing as an inter-relational dynamic will also lead me to examine more fully the possibility of the film viewer as a differentiated, breathing subject. Thus, while previous chapters acknowledged the importance of the film viewer, this chapter fully addresses questions concerning the viewer's position as a breathing subject. It is my interest in the film viewer and the diegetic presence of on-screen inter-subjectivity, as well as understanding how both are implicated in each other, which will be the focus of this chapter on von Trier's 'Gold Heart' trilogy.

The question of the 'breathing film viewer' will be privileged here as I begin to pursue the implications of Irigaray's thinking for the embodied viewer. In the first chapter of this book I recalled the viewer's embodied experience of witnessing the bus accident/Stephens's monologue in Egoyan's *The Sweet Hereafter*, and in the subsequent chapter on Cronenberg I examined his development of claustrophobic and suffocating sensations which worked to mirror his protagonist's physical and psychical trauma in *Spider*. These filmic instances seem to elicit some kind of shift in the viewer's embodied perception, often quite literally actualising the 'breathtaking' spectacle of film itself. In this sense, changes in the viewer's breathing occur as a direct consequence of the film. As I have already made clear, films can make us feel out of breath, or even prompt us to hold our breath, but here I want to explore this particular aspect of film viewing in depth.

Following the thought of Marks, we might conclude that the breathing body of the viewer participates in a kind of *visuality* of breath – a way of looking which perceives through a breathing body.⁷ However, the philosophy of Irigaray will allow me to determine the ways in which the dual act of 'looking and breathing' might configure a dimension of inter-subjectivity applicable to embodied film viewing. Most useful to theorising the flow of breath inhabiting our bodies as film viewers is von Trier's 'Gold Heart' trilogy of films. Each instalment of von Trier's trilogy enables me to develop my model of *breathing visuality*, focusing on each film's unique way of positioning the breathing film viewer. While von Trier's trilogy prompts me to re-examine co-existences between our breathing bodies and those on screen, it also draws attention to the potentially inter-subjective nature of viewing, as well as hearing, bodies that breathe.

The main trajectory of my analysis of von Trier's 'Gold Heart' trilogy will begin with an examination of the inter-subjective audition of breath in *Breaking the Waves*. This exploration of sound and its corresponding visuality in *Breaking the Waves* will draw on the film's formal and diegetic structuring of a breathing encounter between filmic bodies and the body of the viewer. Centring on the notion of the breathing film viewer and its prompting of a breathing visuality, a large part of this chapter is dedicated to the Irigarayan, inter-subjective elements of *Breaking the Waves*, in relation to both the constraints enforced by the Dogme 95 rules and the emotional, affective core of the film. My treatment of *Breaking the Waves* will examine the schema of inter-subjectivity involved in the visual and aural experience of breathing in the film, hypothesised through my concept of breathing visuality – a term which will in this chapter help me to clarify my differences from Marks's primarily 'tactile' model of haptic visuality. Questions of the hapticity of sound are then reframed through the musical aspects of von Trier's *Dancer in the Dark*. Taking as its focal point the performance and representation of three musical interludes, this section opens up a space for the theorisation of the breathing voice in song through engagement with Irigaray's significant contemplation of music in her philosophy of breath. *Dancer in the Dark* brings into play relations between breath, motion and emotion, leading me to consider how breathing visuality might represent a viewing relation organised by movement and kinaesthesia. Finally, a section on *The Idiots* centres on the embodied silences of the film and the performance of intimacy which will lead to conclusions about the communality of breathing and the ethics of sharing one's breath with another.

A Prelude: von Trier's Element

Von Trier's early experimental film *Element of Crime* begins with images of muslin sheets billowing in the wind, dense with shadows. Minarets and slabs of stone walls denote Cairo. The images are gauzy, drifting like semi-conscious thoughts; the camera pans away from the muslin and retreats smoothly through the sharp square of a window. We see the muslin framed by the window and then we hear voices, but they are not in the room with us. They play out from another room in the film. These images spill over into each other like a mirage that emerges from the ether before the first scene of the film begins.

Element of Crime opens with an obese Asian therapist in Cairo talking to a British expatriate. We learn that the British man, clothed in a crumpled linen suit, is suffering from crippling headaches and the shamanistic therapist is about to offer a cure. The British man will be hypnotised in order to soothe his pain, a treatment which will return him to a place that haunts his waking life: Europe. The man, private detective Harry Fisher (Michael Elphick), will go back to Europe but, as his languid voice foretells, 'it is not the same'.

Element of Crime is ostensibly a detective story following Fisher's investigation into the 'Lotto murders' whose victims are young girls selling lottery tickets. Fisher pursues the child-killer, Harry Grey, after coming across the first victim – 'a little girl, lying down on the harbour'. This figuring of a 'lost' child persists throughout von Trier's film and is very much at the heart of its most harrowing sequences, including Fisher's witnessing of the child's autopsy and his (implied) fantasies of her murder. The breathing child of Egoyan's *The Sweet Hereafter* and *A Portrait of Arshile*, then, is now refigured as a different kind of memory through the diegetic representation of a suffocated, murdered child in von Trier's *Element of Crime*, recalling the point of interest with which this book began. One cannot begin to think about breathing in von Trier's films without first mentioning the little girl of Trier's dystopian epic. She is a portentous symbol, an idea as much as an image, which drifts throughout von Trier's narrative of dystopia as a most awful and unforgettable sign of uncertainty and loss. Indeed, as Wilson also contends, 'the phantom presence of the missing child subtends, unsettles and dictates his Dogme films', but this is also a child whose breath has been directly, violently taken away from her, and it is this child which might be key to further understanding von Trier's later work.[8]

In her recent book *The Cinema of Lars von Trier: Authenticity and Artifice*, Caroline Bainbridge describes the filmmaker's thematic adoption of hypnosis and its psychical manipulation of memory and experience in *Element of Crime* as a trope which resurfaces in his subsequent films *Epidemic* (1987) and *Europa* (1990). Collectively, *Element of Crime*, *Epidemic* and *Europa* come to stand for von Trier's 'Europa' trilogy whose overarching theme examines the symbolism of post-war Europe, but it is the staging of hypnosis in *Element of Crime* which leads to the recollection of a suffocated child, a breathless body. According to Bainbridge's highlighting of the centrality of corrupted thoughts and the uncertainty of memories in *Element of Crime*, the suffocated child of the film's narrative trajectory might be seen to reflect the psychical damage resulting from Fisher's defective memory: an endlessly tormenting image which can be neither fully understood nor explained. However, Fisher's recall of a suffocated child in *Element of Crime* also provides a helpful point of departure for thinking about von Trier's aesthetic and its appeal to the viewer, not only as a sensorial experience that relates to breathing, but as a way of embedding a kind of consciousness that plays on the dimensions of mortality pertinent to breathing.

While the police enquiry into the dead girl's suffocation drives much of the film's neo-noir plot, we are also reminded of the importance of breath through the film's atmospheric use of silence and wind, not only conveyed through sound but also visually alluded to in the mise en scène. Echoing filmmakers such as Tarkovsky and Parajanov, *Element of Crime* is rich with images of silent rooms, stillness softly interrupted by gusts of wind blowing through thin sheets of billowing muslin, chattering windows, dust settling beneath chimney flues and disintegrating tunnels.[9] Air is unclean, pestilent, in *Element of Crime* (indeed, this marks the subject matter of *Epidemic*'s narrative which centres on the aftermath of a miasmic plague), but it is nonetheless a means of travel and communication. In several scenes we view a subterranean network of transparent tubes carrying messages to employees within government offices, like airwaves stretching out far beyond the walls of the city, while voices carry in hollow buildings like enormous gramophones. Filmed in sallow, golden tints, human bodies appear also to be starved of air, clammy, as we view close-ups of skin sweating filthily, barely soothed by electric fans and occasional winds. Osborne (Esmond Knight), a scholarly ally of Fisher's, is seen at the start of the film inhaling vapours in a bowl from beneath a misted sheet of plastic, but the same stiff sheeting eerily covers dead bodies in the film, lending a macabre intensity to such quiet inhalations. Furthermore, Fisher's voice, narrating drowsily while under hypnosis, is lethargic, wheezy and breathless; his visions hint at an airy realm he has no access to in Cairo. Thus while water, reflected as flickering undulations on walls, flooding cavernous basements and speckled over the perspiring, sickly bodies of von Trier's protagonists, is obviously the key elemental motif in *Element of Crime*, it is water's coupling with air which gives the film's mise en scène its hypnotic aura. More broadly, von Trier's latest depiction of the natural world in *Antichrist* (2009) and *Melancholia* (2011) seems more deliberately suggestive of an uncertain and perverse universe, and both these films are testament to the evolution of von Trier's particularly metaphysical aesthetic.

Following *Element of Crime*, the evocation of the breathing child is also most notably foregrounded in von Trier's Danish television production *Medea* (1988). Von Trier's adaptation (with a screenplay written by Carl Theodor Dreyer) of the Euripides myth adopts a poetic, tonal aesthetic owing much to its grainy, translucent images which resulted from von Trier's transference of the original three-quarter-inch video footage to 35mm film and then back to one-inch videotape.[10] *Medea* culminates in the harrowing infanticide of Medea's children, and their death not only recalls the suffocated victim in *Element of Crime* but serves as a precursor to *Dancer in the Dark*'s final traumatic scenes in which Selma is publically hanged. Furthermore, we view close-ups of Medea's (Kirsten Olsen) anguished face and, especially, her gasping mouth as she ties a noose around each of her son's throats. Not only do these hushed images, coupled with various shots of sun-bleached grass flickering in the wind and gusts of air on the soundtrack, convey emotional intensity, but the very fabric of the film becomes implicated in the depiction of sacrifice and trauma. Indeed, as we shall see during my discussion of the 'Gold Heart' trilogy, the film's form will play an important role in my theorisation of a filmic visuality which involves the locus of breathing, and this will lead me to contemplate the breathing film viewer.

Although stylistically and conceptually entirely separate from the 'Gold Heart' trilogy (I will elaborate more on these differences later), *Element of Crime* and *Medea* most notably prefigure von Trier's development of an aesthetics which draws on images and iconography evoking air and breath. It is this contextual inheritance of air in *Element of Crime* and *Medea* which can be loosely traced through to the richly suggestive mise en scène of each of the 'Gold Heart' trilogy's instalments. However, while breathing is evoked through the mise en scène of the 'Gold Heart' films, the trilogy is, more importantly, the focus of this chapter because of the way in which sound becomes more crucially involved in such filmic depictions. Thus, while the importance of the filmic image is certainly not denied here, it is the sound of bodies and its corresponding visuality in the 'Gold Heart' trilogy which more deeply embeds viewing relations ordered by breathing. These viewing relations prompted by the sound and image of breathing in von Trier's 'Gold Heart' films especially encourage inter-subjective responses which call on the viewer's identification with a filmed, breathing body. The contours of such viewing relations, stimulated through the filmic sound and image of breathing, are fleshed out in order to develop my concept of breathing visuality.

While this chapter's prioritising of the film viewer builds on the foundations of haptic enquiry analysed in Egoyan's films and the bodily discourses of breath found in the films of Cronenberg, light is also shed on the specificity of trauma, loss and catharsis central to the viewing experience of von Trier's films. Here, breathing emphasises the fragile mortality of each of the film's protagonists, the 'golden hearted', as well as their endurance of suffering in the flesh.

Golden Hearted

Von Trier's 'Gold Heart' trilogy consists of three films: *Dancer in the Dark*, *The Idiots (Idioterne)* and *Breaking the Waves*. The most widely viewed and critically acclaimed of von Trier's corpus of films, the trilogy follows his earlier 'Europa' triptych and precedes his thematic exploration of American society in *Dogville* (2003) and *Manderlay* (2005).[11] Both *Dancer in the Dark* and *Breaking the Waves* were nominated for Oscars, for best music and actress respectively, while *The Idiots* received the prestigious FIPRESCI critics award.

The opening film of the trilogy, *Breaking the Waves*, is the first to submit to the rules of filmmaking constituting the Dogme 'Vow of Chastity' established by von Trier and his compatriot Thomas Vinterberg (well known for his feature debut *Festen* (1998) and his big-budget sci-fi epic *It's All About Love* (2003)). Unlike the epic scale and artifice of films such as *Europa* and *Element of Crime*, the Dogme 95 manifesto was designed to challenge dominant modes of film production and its ten rules forbid artifice: props and sets are not permitted and genre films are also prohibited. In order to further emphasise the importance of authenticity, both sound and location are also required to be real and therefore never fabricated or reproduced. While, strictly speaking, *Breaking the Waves* is not a Dogme film since it does not submit to all ten rules (locations were often fabricated using studio sets, for example), it is important to bear in mind the role of the movement when reflecting on its position within von Trier's corpus of work. In fact, *The Idiots* was von Trier's first official Dogme film. The final part of the trilogy – *Dancer in the Dark* – represents a break from the Dogme movement but, as we shall see, there are also traces of the Dogme sensibility which form some of the foundations of this work.

The trilogy's relationship with Dogme filmmaking is important since it is through the conditions enforced by its rules that both the breathing body of the viewer and that of the film's content become involved in the film experience. For example, the limitations of sound-recording devices and the restriction of sound editing enable an uninterrupted, unrefined quality of live sync sound that captures the lived, breathing body of the performer, while the highly improvised, fragile formal quality of each film owes much to Dogme's insistence on hand-held cameras, which encourage actors to pay less attention to camera set-ups and to concentrate on each other's performance.[12]

While the constraints enforced by the Dogme rules certainly shape the viewing experience offered by *The Idiots* and *Breaking the Waves*, the specificity of the trilogy's subject matter and the motivation behind its conceptualisation must be acknowledged. In general, much has been written from a psychoanalytic – and often feminist – perspective on von Trier's portrayal of the female protagonists at the centre of his trilogy,[13] but few analyses have been led by questions that address the role of the viewer and identification processes. Thus it is important to note the way in which attention is drawn to viewing relations in the work of Bainbridge and, in particular, Laine's reflection on von Trier in her 2007 book *Shame and Desire: Emotion, Intersubjectivity, Cinema*.[14] Both Bainbridge and Laine are interested in examining von Trier's investment in the affective bonds of cinema and, in this respect, my work might be seen to build on Bainbridge's approach to narrative trauma and Laine's highlighting of the significance of inter-subjectivity to the viewing of von Trier's films. While Bainbridge persuasively demonstrates how emergent themes of love in the 'Gold Heart' trilogy shift each film's articulation of trauma towards a heightened level of feeling experienced by the viewer,[15] the work of Laine shows how von Trier's representation of the 'cinematic' emerges from a kind of 'in-between' space of inter-subjectivity.[16] However, my difference from both Bainbridge and Laine lies in the fact that I want to rethink the emotional complexity of narrative trauma, as well as the sensuous world of each film, according to an alternative model of inter-subjectivity that breath uniquely affords.

While the symbol of a gold heart calls to mind a universal motif of goodness, the title of the 'Gold Heart' trilogy refers directly to a well-known tale in Danish folklore, a story von Trier admits to being enthralled by as a child.[17] The story of *Golden Hearted* (*Guld Hjerte*) tells the tale of a little girl who willingly gives away her possessions until she has nothing left, but her faith in goodness is rewarded and at the tale's close she is showered with gold coins that fall miraculously from the heavens. Taking this story as a point of departure, each narrative trajectory of the 'Gold Heart' trilogy interrogates the principles of goodness that are emphasised by the tale and the fate of its heroine. Thus the neat symbol of the gold heart hints at the limits of virtue and its flawed mechanisms. Most importantly, the question of maintaining faith in goodness is key to von Trier's trilogy and his fascination with this concept has implications for the viewer, whose experience is as much a form of endurance as it is cathartic. In these terms, breathing is also part of von Trier's schema of morality, as well as his gesture towards belief beyond the material world, a theme most explicitly conveyed through the references to religion in *Breaking the Waves*. Breathing is inherently bound up with von Trier's physical and emotional awakening of the viewer, who also, in turn, becomes ethically implicated in the transformative world of the film.

Empathetic Images: *Breaking the Waves*

Breaking the Waves was awarded the Grand Jury Prize at Cannes and earned Emily Watson an Oscar nomination for her performance as Bess. Set on a remote coastal village in Scotland within a strict Calvinist community, *Breaking the Waves* opens with Bess confessing her love for Jan (Stellan Skarsgård), an outsider and non-believer whom she has come to know through his visits from the nearby oil rig, where he is stationed as an engineer. Minutes into the film, Jan and Bess are married, but this happiness is abruptly compromised when Jan returns to work and is soon after involved in an accident which leaves him severely injured. Paralysed and doubting his virility as an adequate lover, Jan encourages Bess to leave him, but she refuses. Appealing to her child-like innocence, Jan lies to Bess, leading her to believe that if she takes a lover his condition will improve. Fatally for Bess, Jan's condition does improve immediately after her first encounter with another man. Taking this as a sign from God, Bess continues to offer her body to other men, but when Jan's condition worsens again she convinces herself that only the sacrifice of her own life will truly save her husband from death.

The breathing body is diegetically present in a number of ways in *Breaking the Waves*. For example, the microphone that Dodo (Katrin Cartlidge), Bess's sister in-law, uses when giving a speech at Jan and Bess's wedding emphasises an acute sense of on-screen sound which enables the viewer to hear her choked, anxious breaths fracturing her efforts to remain emotionally restrained. Also, when Jan and Bess make love their energetic, overtly audible heavy breathing serves as a potent sign of the emancipatory nature of their sexual encounters, enunciating Bess's rapturous liberation from the joyless conditions of her patriarchal community. Then, much later in the film, when Jan lies in his hospital bed we are able to listen to his weak body's shallow, faintly surfacing breaths undermining his stoic endurance of physical pain. No doubt these filmic moments where the breathing body is foregrounded contribute towards the film's fleshing out of its narrative discourse, but they offer limited scope for reflection beyond the analysis of their function within the diegesis. Breathing does, however, figure as a more central aspect of the way in which we perceive the film's lead protagonist, Bess, who occupies a significant position both within the film's form and in the viewing experience as a whole.

During one of the final moments in *Breaking the Waves* we view Bess making her journey towards a large ship; this is to be the last time we see her before she makes her ultimate sacrifice for Jan, and the subtle sound and image of her breathing serve as a measure not only of her fragile emotional state but of the transient and fleeting nature of her mortal being. Bess knows she will be brought to her death by the inhabitants of the ship and is therefore deliberately voyaging towards her executioners, a passage towards death that also recalls *Dancer in the Dark*'s conclusion in the gallows. The passage also emphasises the film's thematic hagiography which often dwells on the procession or public display of the female martyr, subverted here by von Trier, given the absence of a crowd or gathering in this scene.[18]

There are two sequences that make up these penultimate views of Bess: one just before she boards the boat, and another immediately after she has become its sole passenger. While the sound of breathing features explicitly in the second sequence, an aspect which I return to later in this chapter, the breathing body is not heard but formally suggested in the scene preceding it. Thus while the first sequence attunes the viewer to a form of heightened, interior consciousness embedded in the film's 'body', that is, the formal style of the film, the second sequence draws attention to breath as an 'internal sound' that prompts a different experience of Bess's breathing body. Above all, my view is that von Trier creates a portrait of an Irigarayan, breathing subject whose being cannot be objectified.

A few seconds before Bess boards the boat, we see her in a medium shot framed with the mossy, Hebridean coast behind her on either side of the screen; she is clearly dishevelled and overwhelmed, but her patient resolve, the focal point of this scene, clearly reflects a determination to regain composure. There is very little movement in the frame except for a few strands of hair that sweep across Bess's face while the rest of her body is motionless. We hear nothing except the soaring cry of seagulls circling the harbour bay. Then there is a small but significant movement: Bess inhales deeply and we view her mouth open a little, her head rises upwards, her shoulders move and her whole body lifts for the briefest of moments. Therefore breath is suggested more through vision than sound as a bodily act that compels movement; Bess's physical and emotional exertion are here matched by the co-ordinating image of her drawing breath. Contrastingly, in the scene that follows attention is drawn more to the prominent aurality of Bess's breathing, but here the visual representation of this expressive sigh is underpinned by a formal gesture: the image quivers and loses focus precisely when Bess inhales. Suddenly, the static framing of the image is affected by Bess's breathing: it slips slightly out of focus and then recovers composure. Although one might argue that this register of movement embodied in the film's form is simply characteristic of the lightweight hand-held camera that von Trier employs, it seems that this perceptible instability conveyed through the film's form is, rather, more of a deliberate gesture by the filmmaker. Thus von Trier uses a combination of formal attributes in order to provoke in the viewer similar feelings of disorientation to those felt by Bess. Significantly, the timing of these formal effects appears to suggest a concurrency with Bess's breathing body. If the momentary blurring of the image corresponds with the rush of oxygen entering Bess's body, then the image's switch back into sharp focus might be understood as a kind of exhalation. In other words, the particular formal aspects of *Breaking the Waves* seem to suggest a movement of release, or rather literal recomposure, that is synchronous with the body in the film's diegesis.

In her book *The Tactile Eye*, Jennifer Barker remarks on the 'breathing of lenses',[19] but her view of 'cinematographic' breathing differs from what occurs in *Breaking the Waves*. While Barker's reflection on the embodied dimensions of cinematographic equipment implies a kind of visual contraction suggestive of breathing, *Breaking the Waves* makes manifest a reciprocal point of contact between the film and the body on screen. Further, although we are unable to feel Bess breathing in a literal sense since screens cannot breathe (with the exception, that is, of those that I have described in Cronenberg's *Videodrome*), the image's loss of focal stability seems not only to reflect Bess's breathing body but to sharpen our own awareness of breaths we take as film viewers. Bess's breathing awakens our bodies to a shift in conscious, bodily perception. Indeed, to a certain degree, the discreet change in focus creates an interval which evokes a sensation of relief, albeit visual, in the viewer and therefore this freshly configured perspective echoes the 'feeling' that Bess's restorative breaths also grant her. In sum, Bess's emotive sigh is a fitting example of the way in which breath becomes the focus of the film and works to foster an interval of mutual, embodied experience between the viewer and the subject on screen. Such an 'interval' of experience might accord precisely with a breathing visuality. To this end, the intensity and fervour of the scene, its palpable trauma, can be visibly detected in the image, trembling like an empathetic imprint of Bess's 'feeling'. This filmic imprint of breath, arriving at a point of emotional relief in the film (diegetically suggested through Bess's sigh), shores up the very possibility of perception articulated through a breathing body, a perspective that is derived from breathing in the diegesis and the formal aspects of the film.

While breathing is alluded to visually in the scene I have just discussed, the next scene places emphasis on film hearing rather than film viewing. Although my term 'breathing visuality' tends to suggest an exclusive focus on the visual dimensions of film viewing and its resonances with breathing, my discussion of the following scene shows how it is more widely applicable to the viewing experience as a whole. Breathing visuality is a viewing experience that reacts and responds to the film's images and it invites a sensual appreciation of the filmic foregrounding of breathing.

On screen, we see Bess's pale, almost translucent face, while in the background we view the coast and flat, silvery sheets of water. This image is crosscut with the distant view of the ship, underlined by thinning peaks of waves. The soundtrack is reflective of earlier solitary scenes with Bess, her voice split into two as she asks questions of God and then answers them in her own voice, but it is rather more the formal use of sound than the content of this 'monodialogue' that privileges a kind of aural perception of breathing. However, before we attend to the relations between film hearing and breathing, it is necessary to sum up the way in which the scene is filmed, thus providing a context in which to understand the noise of breath heard by the viewer.

On the soundtrack, the first line is hesitantly spoken by Bess: 'Father, why aren't you with me?' Following this line we cut to an image of the ship and then back again to Bess. While this cross-cutting emphasises the narrowing path towards death for Bess, it also draws attention to the spaces of silence which pervade her speech. The cross-cutting lends a pace to the visuals, a well-measured cadence which parallels the vocal patterns and pauses contained on the soundtrack; silences are therefore amplified and prolonged by the visuality of the scene, and it is this cultivation of silence through sound and image that closely relates to the presence of breath in the scene. Importantly, the use of silence in the scene seems to act as a substitute for the body that the close cropping of Bess's face prevents us from viewing. Thus what is heard on the soundtrack articulates an altered perception of corporeality, one that privileges the sound of breathing. Most importantly, for about eight seconds during the scene there is no speech – a relatively short amount of time which takes on greater significance due to the limited amount of action taking place. Throughout this pause in Bess's speech, our attention is entirely focused on every fluctuation of her breathing: its soft-sharp-soft rhythm and its build-up towards a lengthy gasp. Furthermore, the ambient sound of squawking seagulls, the lapping of water against the side of the boat and its weight tilting lightly (recalling the watery ambience of *Element of Crime*) provides a range and depth of noise which does not affect the audibility of Bess's breathing body.

Accompanying these breaths on the image-track, the right side of the screen is immersed in sunlight, giving an impression of the sea as a shifting backdrop of whiteness. Almost glowing, the light illuminates one side of Bess's face and

Figure 3.1 Moments before Bess exhales.

Figure 3.2 Bess inhales and the film 'breathes' with her. (Images courtesy of Trust Films.)

scatters highlights throughout the image – a constant reminder of her purity and transcendence that is accentuated through her tentative breaths. In this respect, the most crucial difference between von Trier's filmic depiction of the martyr and Carl Theodor Dreyer's *La Passion de Jeanne d'Arc* (*The Passion of*

Joan of Arc, 1928), one of the film's strongest formal influences, is the sound of breathing which von Trier establishes in *Breaking the Waves*.

While parallels can certainly be drawn between von Trier's use of the close-up and Dreyer's tightly framed images of his martyr's face, the lack of sound in Dreyer's early silent cinema denies the viewer the same kind of visual and aural access to breath that von Trier offers in *Breaking the Waves*. Indeed, on the excessive number of close-ups in Dreyer's film, the critic Gary Morris describes their precise effects on the viewer as 'suffocating', but this sensation is diffused in *Breaking the Waves* through von Trier's inclusion of the diegetic sound of breathing, in turn releasing some of the tension that the close-up creates.[20] Although it might be argued that Dreyer effectively compensates for the lack of sound in his film through his formidable formal style and, in particular, the recurrent image of his martyr's open mouth and her almost palpable, gasping breath, von Trier's inclusion of breath on his soundtrack introduces a dual layer of meaning in relation to both the symbolic narrative of the film's diegesis and its role as an affective device. Breath signifies another kind of vocalisation of Bess's suffering within the diegesis which also has implications for the viewer who hears the sound of breathing. Ultimately, by offering the viewer this register of breath on the film's soundtrack, von Trier pushes the limits of the diegesis from inside the film's mise en scène, creating an Irigarayan breathing body from his formal and contextual construction of the scene.

For Chion, the diegetic sound of breathing is categorised as an inner dimension of film sound – it emphasises a moment on the film's soundtrack that is resolutely interior. Chion identifies the sound of breathing, along with heartbeats and groans, as physiological, *objective-internal* sounds, while the soundtrack's representation of mental voices and memories reflect what he terms *subjective-internal* sounds.[21] However, as Irigaray suggests, breath is also a subjective expression of being that can initiate communication more meaningful than the mere noises that are analogous to our sensible existence. Irigaray's philosophy of breath thus leads me to posit a theory about the sound of breathing in the cinema which can produce effects relating to a more subjective-internal aurality. Indeed, listening to Bess's breathing in *Breaking the Waves* requires a particular perception of breath as a subjective-internal sound. Although Bess's breathing is not the same as a mental voice or memory that Chion offers as examples of subjective-internal sounds, its containment of vocal and bodily nuances presents us with an immediate sense of Bess's state of mind as well as her physical being that constitutes a subjective perspective. We could term Bess's breathing, then, an active, non-verbal, internal-subjective sound, but this would liken it to other bodily sounds such as coughing or even screaming. More appropriately, Bess's breathing creates an intermediary internal sound between conscious expression and involuntary, unintentional corporeality: authentic life in the flow of being.

Internal sound situates the viewer within close proximity to the subject on screen; it is used to connote the possibility of 'nearness' that can be either physical or symbolically suggestive of a character's interiority. The particular sense of nearness and proximity offered through the internal sound of Bess's breathing raises questions about the apprehension of space as sound, especially the audition of an aural field which prompts a kind of haptic hearing. This form of haptics tends to require the viewer's hearing body to experience, fragment by fragment, the sound of Bess's breathing, encouraging a sensitivity to, and embodied perception of, hearing breath as contact between self and world articulated through textures of aurality.

Hearing the 'Grain'

> Wherever and however we locate ourselves in the theatrical space (straight on, obscenely, or obliquely), whether blind or not to the images on screen and pervaded by sound, we are intensely attentive to the heightened sense of our own material being – to the film's resonance in our flesh, blood, bone, viscera, breath, heart rate.[22]
>
> Vivian Sobchack

Film viewing makes us acutely aware of our own material being, as Sobchack argues. Thus the breathing body of the viewer experiences bodily resonances between what is filmed and shown on screen and felt in their chest, their lungs. For Sobchack, it is the horror genre which especially prompts an attentiveness to breathing, but it is the representation of the traumatised body in *Breaking the Waves* which emphasises a haptic relation. The previous section showed how concurrences between the film's form and the filmed body come to represent a breathing visuality and its suggestion of inter-subjectivity – empathetic images which also shape identificatory processes. This section suggests how hearing the 'grain' of a breathing body posits a dimension of breathing visuality informed specifically through sound and its haptic implications. My examination of Bess's subjectivity will lead me to consider how her presence in the film elicits a space of inter-subjectivity that can be observed on screen and in the film experience itself.

For Marks, haptics is a negotiation of a visual field in terms that remind us of tactility and our material engagement with the world. Currents of physicality in the film image (the visual field) elicit an appropriately tactile response. While Marks does not entirely rule out the implications for the hearing body of the viewer when engaged in haptic vision, it seems that questions are left open about the relevance of 'navigating' textures of noise.[23] Thus currents of physicality in the soundtrack must also be thought alongside the image-track as an important aspect of haptic perception. Most striking are Marks's thoughts on film hearing which suggest a tantalising engagement with breathing in order to clarify her perspective on haptic sound. Although Marks's gesture to breath is brief, her analysis is richly suggestive. She writes: 'The aural boundaries between body and world may feel indistinct: the rustle of trees may mingle with the sound of my breathing, or conversely the booming music may inhabit my chest and move my body from the inside.'[24] Marks's underlining of breath is vital given its minimal presence within film theory, and her emphasis on the way it shares its sounds with other noises recalls von Trier's deliberate enfolding of Bess's breath within the elements where voice and body also become inseparable through sound.

Irigaray also places special emphasis on the nuances of breathing as a kind of bodily intimacy characterised by discretion, a small movement that attends to a less reactive and more tentative sound which does not overcome the 'body' of the other. Rather, breath creates two important spaces: intervals between our own words and between ourselves and others. She writes:

> Respect for the negative, the play of the dialectic between us, would enable us to remain ourselves and to create an oeuvre with the other ... This alchemy needs measures, words ... It implies a culture of breath, a becoming between earth, fire and water which overcomes inertia, submersion, ice, fire, and void, one where air subsists, an indispensable matter for life ...[25]

This furtive space between words, or 'alchemy', as Irigaray suggests, is also an elemental contemplation which opens up a natural interaction with the world. Furthermore, the elemental interplay between breath and air suggests a dimension of materiality. Thus, while Marks and Irigaray share an interest in the way in which breathing marks an indistinct boundary between inside and outside, resonating in the body, Irigaray's philosophy offers a way towards thinking about our aural perception of breath as a new form of hearing the materiality of the body.[26]

The materiality of the voice, in particular, has been the subject of investigation for Phil Powrie in his article on François Ozon's *5x2* (2004). Powrie makes a fascinating connection between Barthes's concept of the grain of the voice and the audible textuality of the film's soundtrack, which he examines as an instance of haptic hearing.[27] As my introduction to this book suggested, I share Powrie's interest in the Barthesian concept of the materiality of the voice, but while Powrie's emphasis is on what he refers to as the 'gravelly' voice of the male singer featured on the soundtrack of Ozon's film and its signification of male melancholia, my focus on Irigaray's theorisation of breathing sheds light on a different materiality of the voice, uncovering a new kind of haptic possibility in *Breaking the Waves*.

Von Trier uses sync sound throughout the film in order to produce a live or highly naturalistic effect, and it is through this particular formal aspect of *Breaking the Waves* that breathing is most explicitly registered. Images of von Trier's visceral films are often noted for their graininess, their textural, kinetic density that charges each moment with an immediate energy, but the audio track also produces something that is comparable with this impression of the visual field. Primarily, von Trier's employment of sync sound in *Breaking the Waves* captures an aspect of Watson's performance that allows us to trace the relationship between speech and breath or what would normally be considered as the inaudible or silent pauses between dialogue. Von Trier's use of sync sound creates within these silences pockets of expression that are usually banished or minimised through the manipulation of sound levels, such as in the scene I have discussed above. Thus the 'alchemy',[28] to quote Irigaray's use of the term, of aural spaces is here gestured towards by von Trier. Indeed, in *Breaking the Waves*, the level of breathing can often be as audible as the level of speech, a sound that contributes towards our impression of Bess as an embodied subject whose voice enunciates *through* and *with* her body.

Bess's 'bodily' enunciation of breath can be observed during the moment just after she asks 'Father, why aren't you with me?' when we are able to detect both the visual and the audio suggestion of her breathing body. This corporeal 'touching upon', as Irigaray suggests, draws attention to the immutable presence of breath that rests between language and words. On the image-track, we see Bess in close-up detail: her lips part, her nostrils contract, frown lines around her mouth crease, her eyes blink and she swallows the cold air. However, these delicate traces of emotion are more profoundly embodied through the soundtrack and therefore, in this sense, hearing is prioritised above vision. Although it is Bess's face that is physically close to us in its proximity to the camera, the dominance of breathing on the soundtrack penetrates beyond the surfaces of the flesh and its suggestion of sensations, encouraging the viewer to experience the inner intensity of the body.[29]

While von Trier's use of the close-up provides a visual register of breathing, it is rather an 'acoustic close-up' of Bess's breathing which offers a profound sense of the palpability of her body. In order to understand the acoustic nature of breath more closely, it is useful to consider Barthes's remarks on the sensuous sounds of the body, the aurality of the mouth and, importantly, breathing. In my earlier treatment of Egoyan's *Felicia's Journey*, Barthes's theorisation of breath as the 'soul' illuminated my reflection on the breathing bodies captured on video in the film, but his writings in the 1975 publication *The Pleasure of the Text* also shed light on closely miked sounds of speech which enable us to hear 'the breath, the gutturals, the fleshiness of the lips, a whole presence of the human muzzle'.[30] For Barthes, the formal device of close-miking enables speech to be lined with a fleshy resonance, but the rich foregrounding of the sound of breathing in *Breaking the Waves* suggests a texture created specifically through respiration.

Barthes's identification of breath on film soundtracks reminds us of the voluptuousness of bodies, but his thoughts also tend to make assumptions about the universality of such noises. Thus it is important to describe the specificity of Bess's breathing. On the soundtrack, the exasperation of Bess's body is felt through the sound of her quickening, laboured breaths; we hear the gently ascending and descending passage of air through the body, the shaft of breath escaping the mouth and its unsteady, uneven faltering and rising. We perceive the sensation of air against the back of the throat and the tightening of the chest as gasps rapidly increase.[31] Attuned to this momentary rhythm, the sound of breathing creates another dimension of the lived body on screen for the viewer; it lends a volume and shape, a hapticity, through its suggestion of a human physicality that can almost be felt and touched.

As a more concretely surfacing bodily sound heard on the soundtrack, Bess's breathing creates a textuality that is not smooth but 'grainy'. This embodied encounter between Bess's breathing and my own body is precisely inter-subjective in so far as it provokes me to think about and feel my own breath through what is audible on screen. In preserving my subjectivity through breathing, I do not possess the image, rather, it breathes *with* me, and I call this an inter-subjective encounter. Furthermore, the breathing subjectivity of Bess might therefore be described as a way of inviting the breathing film viewer to act in a way that is empathetic, physical evidence of film's powerful, emotive qualities. Indeed, the work of psychologist Hugo Münsterberg illuminates current debates on the body in the cinema, given his acknowledgement that in sharing the emotions of the subjects on screen we simulate these so that 'all the resulting sensations from muscles, joints, tendons, skin and viscera, from blood circulation and breathing, give the colour of living experience to the emotional reflection in our mind'.[32] While Münsterberg's last reference to breath seems to suggest that it is the least, or most discreet, physical response felt by the body of the viewer, Chion is also keen to emphasise a connection between hearing and the viewer's own breathing: 'breathing noises in a film can directly affect our own respiration'.[33] Chion's observation, along with Münsterberg's cognitive plane of thinking, leads us to consider what is at stake when our breathing bodies react to what is experienced in the cinema. Their thinking posits theories which encourage us to ask what might happen if we hold our breath in empathy with Bess, sharing her shallow little breaths and thus reaching a bodily synchronicity with the film's subject. Our perception of *Breaking the Waves* is rendered more complete at this level of bodily discourse between film and viewer and it is Bess's breathing body that underscores this particular instant of embodied experience in von Trier's film.

Yet, despite the possibility of the viewer's breathing, too, quickening while viewing *Breaking the Waves*, my body also breathes in a way that is almost silent, muted, compared to the multidimensional recording of breath that I hear in the cinema. My body can never compete with the Dolby Digital Surround that envelops me with Watson's breaths. In his book *100 Modern Soundtracks*, Brophy describes the cinema auditorium as a 'cinesonic womb' where the 'curvaceous film theatre returns us directly to a psycho-physical zone of uterine impressions: deep rumbles, pink noise, shifting timbres, spatial reflections, swelling rhythms'.[34] According to Brophy's description, one could also suggest, then, that the cinema is comparable with the space of inter-subjectivity that Irigaray evokes through her contemplation of the intra-uterine sharing of breath.

However, unlike the exchange of oxygen between mother and child in Irigaray's model of thought, the air that the viewer breathes is different from Watson's. The filmed breaths the viewer experiences engender a mimetic, sensory passage between two bodies, attuning to Watson's, but it is the air passing between viewer and the viewed subject which allows each body to remain 'faithful to their nature'[35] since it is breathed within separate spaces. In this sense, the viewer is physically empathetic with Bess, but this empathy can never lead to the appropriation of the space in which she breathes. This most important matter of spatial difference prompts questions surrounding notions of place and the role of the environment in the production of a breathing 'sound'.

While the sound of Bess's breathing comes from her body, it cannot be separated from the space that it resonates within and, in particular, the live or, as Jeffrey Pence puts it, 'wild' sound of the external elements that the film's coastal setting provides.[36] Von Trier's exterior locations reverberate with the sound of the sea, the rain, the wind and the air (air, too, has a sound, as Chion has also suggested),[37] situating Bess within a highly receptive and reactive realm of being, a kind of breathing inside the current or, rather, waves of sensation. To be inside such waves is to be gripped by the momentum of change, of alternating shifts in the atmosphere, but the breathing body is not submerged by these aural resonances, rather it is brought to the surface through our awareness of peripheral sound. When breathing becomes foregrounded it creates an aural shudder that is evocative of a sensual bodily being. For example, like the images we view, this breathing textuality heard on the soundtrack is not smooth, but 'grainy'. The presence of ambient or peripheral sound, often understood as natural or atmospheric noise, aids this 'graininess' since it possesses a proximal relationship with breath. Woven together, the breathing body resonates throughout the elemental, aural spaces of *Breaking the Waves* which become haptic through von Trier's employment of digital, sync sound.

Love and Sorority

The diegetic representation of inter-subjective relations between Bess and other central protagonists also foregrounds breathing as a bodily exchange or interaction. These breaths demarcate a furtive space of intimacy which keeps the viewer alive not only to the breathing body, but to the relationship between two subjects.

The most explicit way in which breathing is suggested as an act shared between two occurs during a scene in which Jan telephones Bess from the oil rig during their first time apart. Aware of her own and Jan's body, Bess asks: 'I can hear you breathing. Can you hear me [breathing]?'[38] The film cuts to a medium close-up of Jan's face leaning over the large telephone handle, his eyes wide open, and then it cuts back again to Bess listening, her eyes tightly closed, her nose touching the receiver. This scene seems to suggest the ways in which desire has a transformative effect on the everyday, a notion that is also explored in *Dancer in the Dark* through Selma's (Björk) imagining of its musical sequences. Furthermore, the digitally enhanced panoramas that von Trier uses as chapter headings throughout *Breaking the Waves* serve to collectively signify a detached and 'agonising banality', as von Trier's collaborator Per Kirkeby has claimed, contrasting the personal and individual depth of experience of the everyday that breath in this scene symbolically evokes.[39] Thus breath also assists in the creation of an alternative romance inscribed in an authentic world that characterises the film's involvement with the Dogme aesthetic. For Bess, the sound of breathing allows her to drift amongst her dreams: she closes her eyes to recall the body it brings to life for her, inspiring the memory of love. However, while Jan's breathing is the only sound Bess requires in order to be transported to her private realm of fantasy, subsequent scenes depicting the lovers' telephone conversations show Jan to be less sensitive to the sensuality of silence occupied only by their gently breathing bodies. For Jan, a way back into language, and into less subtle means of communication, is required in order to prompt his desire for Bess when they are parted from each other. However, listening is rather more pleasurable for Bess in that it requires not words, but sensitivity to Jan's body as well as her own.

Bess's awareness of breath as an inter-subjective gesture of love between men and women also recalls Irigaray's thoughts on the possibility of transcendence in the flesh. According to Irigaray: 'Carnal love becomes a spiritual path for energy, the flesh becomes spirit and soul thanks to the body itself, loved and respected in its difference, including at the level of breathing.'[40] When Bess asks Jan to listen to her breathing she reflects a belief in the potential of their separation as one that might be transfigured into an indelible instant of unity and, as Irigaray's thinking implies, spiritual liberation. Bess seeks nourishment not from a contaminating closeness or appropriation: breath is the preservation of the self, nourishing an interior vision inspired by Eros. However, these breaths are only made possible through the technological mediation of the telephone, where the strange experience of a loved one's disembodied voice prompts the sudden urge to anchor its immateriality in something one can 'touch' again: a reassurance that renders our solitude bearable. Marks suggests, drawing on Irigaray's critique of Merleau-Ponty, that 'the loss of the sense of touch creates a feeling of being an orphan in the world',[41] but if listening to breath can prompt a different kind of aural tactility, then it also holds the promise of renewing our social contract with the world. This theme of sociality symbolised through the sound of breath will be more fully explored during my discussion of *The Idiots*, where the body is denied personal expression while subjected to 'communal' living.

Such moments of quietly affecting exchanges between Jan and Bess conveyed through the soundtrack of *Breaking the Waves* are thrown into relief by the contrastingly oppressive, man-made noises created by machinery that occasionally overpower their breathing bodies on the soundtrack. Most memorably, when Jan is late for his wedding ceremony to Bess, his arrival by helicopter completely wipes out the sound of Bess's frustrated voice and breaths as she rejects Dodo's attempts to comfort her. We see Bess shout 'get off me' in close-up before her mouth contorts into an exaggerated scream, but the sound is masked by the fiercely whirring helicopter propeller. Moreover, the offscreen and on-screen sound of the screeching, chopping blades of the propeller, combined with the image of Bess fitfully attacking Jan when he finally arrives and the highly mobile camerawork with which this scene is filmed, all contain suggestions of violence that prefigure the physical torment that Bess and Jan's marriage will bear. Posited within this violence, the haunting image of Jan and Bess's coupled, muted breaths offers a view that subjects their bodies to the forces of the exterior world embodied by the totalising presence of the helicopter: a prescient reminder of their human mortality caught up in the film's mythic proportions of chaos and disaster.

The image of Bess and Jan's muted breaths is the antithesis of Irigaray's thought on love as it is 'inscribed in breath'.[42] Von Trier's obscuring of the sounds of the couple's breathing bodies suggests that he refuses the consecration of desire that Irigaray's thought on breathing implies, a gesture that amounts to the suffocation of the two subjects whose inter-subjective relation is scrutinised. The negative impact of such images is also 'felt' by the embodied viewer. Certainly, it is impossible to avoid feelings of discomfort that mark our experience of this scene as our ears are subjected to the helicopter's churning blades, a sound whose volume shatters everything and disorients our hearing throughout the rest of the sequence. Furthermore, given the scene's diegetic focus on domestic conflict, it follows that Bess and Jan's drowned-out voices and breaths produce affects that are unsettling for the viewer as they work to expel us from the action, contradicting the inclusive nature of the close-ups that here dominate von Trier's portrayal of the couple. Since we are unable to hear the voices and movements of Bess and Jan, we are momentarily exiled, repelled by the noise of the helicopter, its inhuman threat, and the ambivalent, soundless image of von Trier's lovers. Paired with an inhuman, mechanical sound, Bess and Jan's bodies seem more vulnerable yet, perversely, less human since we are denied the very sound that tells us that they are alive. In this context, the troubling image of Bess and Jan's muted coupling is deathly, a *memento mori* placed before the viewer foretelling of their own anguish or viewing 'unpleasure', to quote Bainbridge, as well as the trauma that awaits its breathless, filmic subjects.[43]

While the central love affair between Jan and Bess offers ways in which to hear, as well as view, the coupling of Irigarayan breathing bodies, the relationship between Bess and Dodo presents sorority as an Irigarayan sharing of breath and of love between two bodies of the same gender. These 'breaths' of love between women feature as a continuing motif in the 'Gold Heart' trilogy and the relationships between Selma and Cathy and Susanne and Karen, but they are most suggestively felt in *Breaking the Waves*. In her analysis of von Trier's cinema, Wilson also comments on the representation of comfort between women present in both *Breaking the Waves* and *The Idiots* explaining how each depiction of sorority fits an image of both suffering femininity and angelic maternity.[44] The role of breathing in von Trier's construction of female goodness can be read as a motif of embodied suffering. Irigaray's philosophy enables such a portrayal of femininity to be analysed from the perspective of subjective being, negotiating a space for reflection on female friendship beyond terms of objectivity.

For Irigaray, sorority must be sought not through a desire for plurality or multiplicity, but through a positive engagement with the other's difference. This respect for difference also exists at the level of breathing, engendered through sociality and communality where each subject listens and attends to the other's embodied being. Indeed, in her text 'The Redemption of Women', she writes that women 'must keep a part of breath available for a relation of interiority with the self and for a language of communication and exchange with one's own gender'.[45] Von Trier's privileging of breath and its implicit involvement in the representation of love between Dodo and Bess is highly suggestive of Irigaray's concern not only with a need for a relation with others of the same sex through breath, but also for the individual articulation of corporeal subjectivity as it might be suggested through the breathing body. Bess and Dodo experience each other's physical as well as emotional difference in a way that is articulated through their breathing bodies and it is this reflection of sorority in *Breaking the Waves* that is specifically Irigarayan. Breathing together, Bess and Dodo call on each other for strength, recalling earlier scenes such as when they pray together when Jan is first admitted into hospital and their brief, but compassionate, exchange when Bess awaits Jan's phone call in the telephone booth. These scenes between Bess and Dodo are rarely commented on by critics, but the foregrounding of breath during their last meeting, in particular, is a genuinely moving testament to the exceptional portrayal of unrelenting, unconditional female friendship at the heart of *Breaking the Waves*.

In one of their last scenes together, Dodo tells Bess that Jan is dying, Bess reassures her that she has done the right thing, and before they part she tells her: 'thank you, Dodo, I know that you love me'. Bess's proclamation resounds beyond the words shared between her and Dodo: it becomes bodily, urgent – an action unbound and set in motion through the sound of short gasps of breath escaping into the air. We also begin to hear Dodo's breathing, a sign that she has been moved, but this response does not require confirmation in words. Bess's emphasis on acknowledging Dodo's love, rather than declaring her own, presents an ethical response to love that is most reminiscent of Irigaray's poetic text in *Everyday Prayers*. On knowing and sharing love, she writes: 'Why do you weep? I do not know/Because I love you?/Would I venture to say "because you love me"?/It would be even more touching.' ('Pourquoi pleures-tu? Je ne sais pas/Parce que je t'aime?/Oserais-je dire "parce que tu m'aimes"?/Ce serait encore plus doux.')[46] The intention of the phrase 'you love me' is, as Irigaray affirms, 'more touching' since it emphasises the position of the other as the subject rather than object of dialogue: the very basis of Irigaray's philosophical approach to inter-subjectivity. Thus it follows that Bess's admission to Dodo – 'I know that you love me' – corresponds with Irigaray's ethical mode of address, and the sound of Dodo's faltering breath confirms just how much she has been moved by such a gesture.

Breathing might, then, seem to embody the loss that Bess experiences, but it also works to focus our attention on Dodo's loss and her devotion to Bess, her restrained speech and body language giving way to feelings of love which overflow and break the surface of her body as gentle tremors of air. The breaths registered during these moments thus emphasise not only an inter-subjective relation, but also an ethereal yet physical bond between the women. Such a calling into play of both carnal and transcendental relations might be seen to evoke Irigaray's concept of the *sensible transcendental*: the 'material texture of beauty'[47] which mediates between bodily matter and the abstract, spiritual realm.[48]

While the diegetic representation of breathing contributes towards the narrative investment in the thematic depiction of female suffering, the tender intimacy suggested through the sound of Bess and Dodo's breathing also implicates the embodied viewer, transcending the parameters of the diegesis. Most notably, breathing and its 'vocal grain' is emphasised through the formal positioning of the camera. Indeed, the camerawork appears to 'nestle' within the space that Dodo and Bess's crouched bodies occupy.[49] From this framing, we are asked to share their embrace and dwell amongst their hushed breaths. Such an invitation, made by von Trier, limits our impartiality as mere observers. In a sense, Bess and Dodo breathe 'on' the camera as well as in the space that it occupies and this produces effects that relate to a real, lived experience, creating an awareness not only of the body but of the breathing body. This is further implied through von Trier's relatively static composition which also appears to adopt the stillness of the bodies in the frame. Thus we become involved and entangled within the emotion of the scene through our perception of breath as it is explicitly heard on the soundtrack and carried through the formal framing of the scene.

In *Breaking the Waves*, breathing is not only a *memento mori* of Bess's final sacrificial act; it is evoked in ways which suggest the importance of bonds which ground life in meaningfulness, as the inter-subjective, shared breaths between Bess, Jan and Dodo convey. Film viewers who come into contact with the diegetic breaths of *Breaking the Waves*, through sight and sound, as we have seen, enter into a bodily dialogue with the film which pushes the limits of trauma and emotion. Like the role of the little girl, found suffocated in *Element of Crime*, breathing in *Breaking the Waves* becomes symbolic of the possibility to sense another's loss and to be acutely aware of the fragile breath of another human being.

'IF LIVING IS SEEING, I'M HOLDING MY BREATH': *DANCER IN THE DARK*

> If living is seeing, I'm holding my breath
> In wonder – I wonder
> What happens next?
> A new world, a new day
> to see.[50]
>
> (Lyrics from 'A New World')

While the sound of two breathing bodies in *Breaking the Waves* compels us to re-examine the diegetic relationship between love and goodness central to the film's contribution to the 'Gold Heart' trilogy, the role of breathing in *Dancer in the Dark* is specifically associated with one subject, or one voice, as it were, embodied by the female protagonist Selma Ježková. This evocation of breath takes place during *Dancer in the Dark*'s musical sequences where Björk's distinctively passionate and euphoric vocality is marked by the sound of her breathing-in-song, a characteristic use of her voice that is also observed by Daniel M. Grimley as a 'breathy' presence.[51] With these interludes, von Trier takes the intensity of the breathing body suggested in *Breaking the Waves* and creates a Dogme-esque musical that reshapes voice and body, breath and lyric. While the musical aspects of *Dancer in the Dark*, especially Björk's use of her voice as a kind of breathing-in-song, propose new ways in which to analyse the audition of hearing a breathing body, the choreography and filming of Selma's singing body present an increasingly inter-subjective viewing experience. *Dancer in the Dark* shows how breathing visuality works to elicit a response to breathing bodies predicated on their movement and the textural properties of the voice when it is heard in song.

The narrative that contextualises the music of *Dancer in the Dark* takes place in the American state of Washington in the mid-sixties. Selma, a Czech factory worker, is determined to use her meagre income to save for an operation that will save her son Gene (Vladica Kostic) from blindness he genetically inherits from her. Friendships are formed while sharing shifts at the factory with a shy admirer, Jeff (Peter Stormare), and an older French female colleague, Kathy (Catherine Deneuve). Bill (David Morse), a police officer and Selma's landlord, attempts to steal her savings in order to pay off his debts. When Selma confronts Bill, suspecting his theft, a struggle ensues in which he is accidentally shot with his own gun. Overcome by guilt and the knowledge that he will be imprisoned, Bill forces Selma to kill him. Soon after, Selma is arrested and accused of murder, her good intentions to absolve Bill of misery resulting in her own demise. In jail, Selma pleads with Kathy and Jeff to ensure Gene has the operation, since it has been decided that she will be executed. Her harrowing death closes the film, leaving the viewer in darkness before the credits roll.

The way in which Selma is executed, as Grimley also remarks, further emphasises the fact that her being is especially vocal and breathy, the hood she is forced to wear before being hanged 'impeding her breathing and singing, but not her vision which she had already lost through blindness'.[52] However, beyond the literal stifling of Selma's breath at the end of the film and its amplification through blindness, the presence of breathing in many of the film's musical sequences raises important questions about Selma's desire to sing and the philosophical interpretation of blindness as Selma 'dances in the dark'. Von Trier has claimed that the musical numbers subvert conventions of the musical genre which often carry no threat. Instead of such frivolity, his sequences underscore Selma's important truth: 'celebrating and cultivating what it means to be human'.[53] As the most fundamental sign of Selma's humanity, breathing becomes part of an interior world of sensation independent of a need for 'vision'. For example, when Kathy goes to watch a musical at the cinema with Selma she acts out the dance steps on the palm of Selma's hand in a scene which conveys the importance of touch now that sight is unreliable, but breathing also importantly figures in this relation between living with or without sight. Indeed, at the film's close, the words that ring out repeatedly during 'A New World', the soaring orchestral piece which accompanies the credits, make the link between sight and breath most apparent: 'if living is seeing, I'm holding my breath'.[54] Since the musical sequences foreground breath through Selma's vocal enunciation, the lyrics we hear at the end of the film consequently imply that such interludes should be viewed as moments when Selma is not 'seeing' and therefore not 'holding her breath'. Indeed, the images Selma views, an 'internal landscape',[55] as Peter Travers remarks, are all in her head. Despite the vibrancy of the musical interludes, they are ultimately tinged with some sort of loss and melancholy that is symbolically equated with Selma's increasing blindness throughout the film.[56]

During an early sequence in which Selma is seen to operate machinery drowsily, before slipping into one of her fantasies, breathing marks Selma's entry into her dream-state of consciousness as the rhythm of the machines slowly metamorphoses into clusters of hypnotic beats. The very first image that introduces the sequence is of Selma at shoulder height with her rubber-gloved hand pressed against the lever she operates. Selma's eyes close and her head collapses forward, nudging her gloved hand. While we begin to hear a prolonged buzzing sound and a whirring thud, a noise that seems to evoke the sensation of weariness and the jolt of waking that Selma has just experienced, a resounding 'clunk' functions rather like a delayed sound effect that underlines the silent image of her head knocking against the machinery. Then a close-up shows Selma sighing, followed by a visible smile: in profile, we see her cheeks plump and shadows form around her mouth while the light rise of her chest tells us that she is drawing breath. Von Trier then cuts abruptly to the midriffs of Selma's co-workers, the breathing torsos whose operation of the machines becomes rhythmic and sequential, merging with the analogue components that they continue to assemble. Rapid editing cuts from one action to the next, offering a multidimensional perspective that climaxes in the first words of musical number 'Cvalda' sung by Selma.[57] Through this change in the speed and frequency of the alternating images, the diegetic world of the film gathers a velocity that serves to stir the beating heart of the breathing film viewer.

On the introduction of the musical sequences in *Dancer in the Dark*, von Trier has remarked on the explanation that Selma was 'dreaming' as one that is too easy and a 'little trick' he felt uncomfortable with using.[58] In retrospect, von Trier has suggested that he would have preferred to be more daring and get the characters singing spontaneously 'for no reason', as they do in classical Hollywood musicals. However, 'Cvalda's' smooth and nuanced introduction is highly effective and the place of breath in this journeying towards Selma's interior dream world suggests that it is the bodily act associated most of all with her first surrender to the 'music'.

As we begin to adjust to a beat established by the editing that echoes Selma's sensitivity to the rhythms of the diegetic sound, the images convey the feeling of a rush of blood to the head that Selma seems to experience when she first enters the trance-like state of her dreams. Breathing is central to this shift in embodied experience. While my discussion of *Breaking the Waves* shed light on the breathing film viewer's sensitivity to the sound of breathing in the film's diegesis, *Dancer in the Dark*, then, prompts questions relating to the concordances between the filming and suggestion of breath, movement and music. Marks makes clear the way in which her term 'haptic visuality' draws from other forms of sense experience, primarily touch and kinaesthetics, but the breathing visuality of *Dancer in the Dark* introduces a kinaesthesia of sound to Marks's haptic theory.[59] Indeed, the concept of kinaesthesia, the physiological condition of movement, offers a way in which to re-examine the figuring of motion in the film and the dance sequences in the film, tracing their sonic, bodily imbrications in the soundtrack.[60]

While the image of Selma slowly breathing opens 'Cvalda', the vocal presence of breath persists throughout the howls of excitement that escape Selma's suddenly animated and gracefully choreographed movements. Von Trier's decision to alternate between various shots gained from a network of cameras positioned on set might be seen to undervalue Vincent Paterson's (*Evita, The Birdcage*) choreography.[61] However, this sequence, in particular, strikes a good balance between the bodies in the frame and their kinetic presence as fragmented images in the edit. In addition to the frequencies and juxtapositions of the various dancing figures on screen, breathing forms part of the non-verbal pattern of 'Cvalda'. Yet 'Cvalda's' articulation of breathing must be distinguished from what we hear during *Breaking the Waves* as well as in the rest of *Dancer in the Dark*'s non-musical sequences. 'Cvalda' offers the first sound of breathing in the film that is explicitly conveyed in song, a harmony that can only be reached through the pitch and timbres of Selma's singing voice: a vocal range that music encourages.

Yet, unlike the use of sound in *Breaking the Waves*, the breaths that are heard on *Dancer in the Dark*'s soundtrack are not 'live', but part of a 'cleaner' sound. Furthermore, Selma's breaths, here, are joyful elations rather than the peaks of embodied suffering that Bess's breathing comes to stand for. Nevertheless, this is where *Dancer in the Dark* offers the viewer a different experience of the breathing body in the 'Gold Heart' trilogy. Von Trier foregrounds breath as a melodic presence expressive of an emotional depth that reaches beyond the words of the song or, as Irigaray suggests, 'a music made from breath and soul . . . a voice which creates passages – between the universe, the world and the beating of one's own heart, the pulse of one's own blood, the alternation of inhaling and exhaling which gives one's own life its pulse'.[62] Indeed, Irigaray's use of the term 'pulse' resonates with 'Cvalda's' drumming beat and the importance of breath as the mediator of such rhythms.

While *Breaking the Waves* tends to situate Bess's breathing within a rich, acoustic soundscape where it can be heard alongside the sound of water, seagulls and other ambient reverberations, 'Cvalda' positions Selma's breathing body amongst a series of colliding and co-existent mechanical beats and groans. Although the title refers to the affectionate Czech name Selma gives Kathy that translates as 'big and happy', the song becomes emblematic of Selma's escape into another consciousness which uses the sounds of industry, trains, engines, cogs rolling and unwinding, as a bridge between the two realities that merge with her liberated, breathing body. Unlike the deafening sound of the helicopter in *Breaking the Waves*, breathing is not masked, but brought into the foreground of our aural perception, following a duality of interaction between the machinery and Selma's body and voice. A space of mediation, or bridging harmony, is allowed to develop between Selma's breathing and the patter of noise from the machines. While obvious comparisons might be drawn between the human body and the machines we hear, closer examination of this sequence suggests that von Trier attempts to find a common, corporeal ground between Selma's voice and the analogue machines, her breathing intertwining with the heavy blocks of metal that 'tap out a beat' for her to sing to.

The lyrics of 'Cvalda' also privilege the sound of the machinery through its repetition of onomatopoeia which, in turn, crystallises physical sensation: 'Clatter, crash, clack! Racket, bang, thump! Rattle, clang, crack, thud, whack, bam!' 'Cvalda' is, then, a kind of aural mapping of space, in much the same way as Selma comes to know the world once her sight starts to diminish, a sonogram of the factory floor. These images tend to approach the viewer not 'along the skin',[63] as Marks has written of the haptic nature of film viewing, but as a fluid, kinaesthetic acoustic. This perception of breath suggests a model of breathing visuality advanced through the audition of breath and movement and their correlative mapping on screen.

This breathing visuality connoted through a kinaesthetic presence of breath on screen and on the soundtrack is also motivated by the inter-subjective nature of Selma's voice interacting with the machinery. More specifically, the two melodic themes that dominate this sequence, Selma's child-like whispers and yelling and the blunt, dull thronging of the machinery, present a kind of acoustic inter-subjectivity that occurs between two radically different 'bodies'.

Of course, the more recognisable, human duet occurs between Selma and Kathy, but it is the intertwining forces of voice, breath and metal that persist throughout. In her book *The Way of Love*, Irigaray emphasises the inter-subjective nature of breathing as a chorus in song. She writes: 'to be sure, to sing together is a sharing of breath'.[64] Von Trier's development of a dialogue between human voice and the factory it resonates within accords with the practice of singing together, but this occurs between a human breathing body and a machine. We might consider, then, that the machinery possesses a different corporeality whose synchronised movements evoke an alternative breathing body. Thus the machine's 'breathing body' connects, through its beat, its 'pulse', with Selma's little gasps and primal cries. While an alternative perspective might perceive such a joining together of human and machine as a distinct embodiment, and critique, of capitalism in the Western world, the prospect of both bodies being able to breathe as individuated beings tends to suggest a form of liberation through music which resists subordination to the system of production that the factory could otherwise stand for. A similar comparison between the labouring body and the breathing body is made by Kimsooja, as the introduction to this book suggested. In her work *To Breathe*, Kimsooja evokes the thread-like nature of breathing in order to draw parallels between the fashioning of life itself and the weaving machinery which symbolises the work undertaken by much of the labour force in Korea today; while Kimsooja's work appears to emphasise the objectivity of the breathing body, like the material fragments of the yarn, the interaction between machine and voice in *Dancer in the Dark* foregrounds a more inter-subjective relation.

In sum, the logic of 'Cvalda's' breathing visuality, then, spins out from the diegetic, vocal presence of breath within the performance of a song, but the sequence is also particularly narrativised by motion as it is filmed on screen and conveyed through the formal devices of editing and cross-cutting. Thus the trajectory of motion, the movement of bodies and machines, underpins the cultivation of Selma's breathing which signals her lapse into the dream-like world of the musical. This 'dreaming' is celebratory and affirmative, it is emotive, but breathing, motion and emotion are more tightly organised around the music of *Dancer in the Dark* during the performance of the song 'I've Seen It All'. This second musical interlude of the film demonstrates how the concept of breathing visuality can be useful in articulating viewing responses to the concurrent depiction of motion, emotion and breathing as evoked through the body of the singing subject. In 'I've Seen It All', the breathing body of Selma co-ordinates the viewer's movement through the space of the film and this orientation is driven principally by emotion.

'I'VE SEEN IT ALL': BREATH, MOTION AND EMOTION

The Latin root of the word emotion speaks clearly about a moving force, stemming as it does from *emovere*, an active verb composed of *movere*, 'to move', and *e*, 'out'. The meaning of emotion, then, is historically associated with 'a moving out, migration, transference from one place to another.'[65]

Giuliana Bruno

If breathing is diegetically introduced through 'Cvalda', then 'I've Seen It All' begins to forge closer links between Selma's breathing, her singing body, the formal properties of the image and the body of the viewer. These connections between the filmed body, film form and the viewer are characterised by proximal relations which motivate a concordance between motion and emotion. Motion and emotion, for Bruno, are conjoined parts of the same physical and psychical geography or *psychogeography*, where emotion materialises as a moving topography.[66] But the representation of space that is pertinent to breathing in 'I've Seen It All' refers to traversing a human body rather than an expansive location. The viewer is positioned as a 'satellite' in orbit around Selma's breathing, singing body, and thus movement towards and away from Selma comes to represent a kinaesthesia of motion and emotion, a 'voyaging' which also serves to alert the viewer to his or her own breathing body.

Through this awakening of the viewer's breath, the film's most beautiful theme becomes an elegy for Selma, drawing us towards partial glimpses of her body and 'voice' which invest the film, for the viewer, with a sense of her spirit, her essence as a memory of 'feeling'. On the voice and memory in the text 'Before and Beyond Any Word', Irigaray writes: 'The vocal message is written with the body itself . . . and is written on or in the body or the being of the other, which will remain the support of it, its memory.'[67] Hearing Selma, her voice and breath are 'written' in our bodies. In order to understand this bodily inscription further, close attention must be drawn to a key moment in 'I've Seen It All'.

'I've Seen It All' takes place after Selma has lost her job and must walk home along the railway, risking her life as she depends on her sense of hearing and touch (her feet nudging the tracks as she goes along) in order to avoid oncoming trains. Jeff, Selma's admirer, follows her and soon realises that she cannot see where she treads. Jeff confronts Selma about her eyesight, but all she can say is 'I'll be fine', the ominous phrase that is also famously uttered by the heroine of von Trier's 'Gold Heart' Danish folktale.

The sequence begins with a close-up of Selma, her large, thick glasses concealing most of her features. We hear a locomotive train approaching and its wheels begin to gather a rhythmic pace as they pass. This off-screen sound cue introduces the musical number. In the first shot of the musical sequence, von Trier cuts to a wide-angle view of Selma and Jeff on the tracks as the train drifts on behind them. Selma takes off her glasses and in one graceful movement she lets them drop. What follows is a series of alternating shots from numerous angles, creating the feel of the earlier kaleidoscopic, colour-saturated sequences that mark them out separately from the rest of the film's formal aesthetic.

As with the other musical sequences, we gain an omniscient view of the action that cannot be continuously traced to any single fixed point of reference associated with a character's position within the diegesis. Indeed, these images are Selma's imaginary creations, a cinema reel unspooling inside her head, and thus she is rarely seen from the perspective of Jeff, whose view would conflict with her fantasy since he does not share her imagination, unlike the viewer. This is to say that the camera adopts an omniscient position rather than showing us Jeff's subjective perspective, and this fluidity and mobility of camera movement emphasises the way in which the sequence conveys Selma's breaking free from the rules and restrictions of reality. The relationship between emotion and bodily motion is thus fleshed out in the film through a series of formal and vocal gestures, but it is the role of Selma's breathing body and voice which informs the scene's vibrant yet also melancholic aesthetic.

During one particular series of images which accompanies the chorus of the song, our attention is drawn to Selma's breathing as an instance visible both within the mise en scène and through the editing of the sequence, intensely heightening this moment for the viewer. First of all, the chorus contains explicit breathing sounds which form punctuation marks between the words, but following its first appearance Selma's voice becomes less restrained. On the image-track, we see Selma's profile, her mouth open in a blurred image of her entering and leaving the shot. Von Trier's snapshots of Selma's body, especially her face and mouth, appeal increasingly to a tangible proximity. This visceral navigation around Selma's body posits the viewer inches away from her hair, skin, teeth, lips. She embraces us, but this grasp of the viewer is completed through her sharing of breath with the breathing body that responds to her image; ourselves in her breath.

Selma's breathing body is multiplied over several images like a collage of the same heady instant. As the chorus ends, we see Selma's whole body, a shivering image of her beige cardigan and green dress, before we are pulled towards the hem of her flowing dress, peering at her bare legs and thighs. This shot of her thighs is not voyeuristic or intrusive; it tends to foreground the wave of air that her body, exhilaratingly, seems to emit, her skirt bristling against her skin in a gust of wind as if her breathing has swept up her body into a tornado-like vacuum. Then, we see two images of Selma's upper body, inversions of each other. The words of the song, at this point, are barely perceptible, an 'emanation' of the character reserved only for such moments within these dream sequences.[68]

When Selma's voice reaches a crescendo, we face her side-on, the frame just resting on the line of her nostrils. We see Selma's mouth stretched wide open on the far right of the screen, the lines of her mouth creasing in extreme close-up. This is followed by the sight of Selma's skirt in close-up, Jeff's ear and shoulder just recognisable behind its lurid green fabric. The last image which underlines the sound of Selma hitting the highest note in the song is filmed from above, an 'altitude' that, for Irigaray, corresponds with a cultivation of breathing.[69] Far from signifying vertiginous detachment, Selma's direct address to the camera during this aerial shot realigns her within a position of control and knowingness (recalling Bess's gaze towards the camera within the first few minutes of *Breaking the Waves*). We catch glimpses of Selma – half of her face, the stretched skin of a wide open mouth, a patch of green or the weave of a beige cardigan on the edge of the frame – but this view corresponds more with von Trier's communication of the emancipatory nature of singing than an objectification of Selma. Most importantly, the rhythm of the editing, the speed with which we view this succession of shots, is like a burst of energy. Combined with the dominant emphasis on Selma's breathing body and mouth, the editing of the sequence serves to elicit an acute awareness of breathing, and of bodily euphoria.

The abstract views of Selma's body, a collective of disorientating and surreal, even spectral, visions, relates her being more to sensation than to an optical image; we experience the vitality of such images as a sign of Selma's most positive and powerful affirmation of life. Indeed, mise en scène plays an important part in the foregrounding of Selma's body, but its formal effects, through editing and framing, aids our perception of the rhythm and flow of breathing. Unlike the Hollywood musical's dependence on mise en scène in order to accentuate or reveal emotional states felt by the protagonist, I would argue that von Trier evokes an emotional kind of breathing, accentuating Selma's psychical experience more through film form than the mise en scène.[70]

'My Favourite Things': Troubling Objects

While the musical number 'I've Seen It All' contains the most powerful and celebratory suggestion of breathing as it is conveyed through song, Selma's desperate attempt to reconnect with the feelings of joy that music brings her in 'My Favourite Things' is no doubt the most melancholic and painful to watch. In the pallid quarters of her cell, this song is sung not as part of a dream sequence but as a real event in the film, and as a consequence of this realism it features none of the rich tones or frantic editing of multiple perspectives that the other musical numbers contain. The music in 'My Favourite Things' is willed into existence through Selma's tapping and knocking on the walls of her prison cell and the use of the particular song, 'My Favourite Things', is suggestive of Selma's nostalgia, as well as our own, for a lost dream: the chance she had of starring in an amateur production of *The Sound of Music* (Robert Wise, 1965). The tone of the song becomes mournful, but it is Selma's breathing that emphasises this sadness, mirroring the penultimate scenes before Bess's sacrifice in *Breaking the Waves*.

The scene opens with Selma placing a hand against the wall of her cell, her head turned away from us, her hand raised to the greying concrete. We cannot hear her breathing. Instead, our attention is turned to Selma listening out for something. She suddenly kneels on a bench before climbing towards the wall.

We see a small vent near the ceiling and Selma directs her head towards it, her shadow looming near the black shape of the back of her head. There are echoes of music, of movement passing in corridors and other indistinct noises that reverberate in the air, from the depths of the prison. These multiple sounds of bodies and indistinct noises suggest a community, a sound of living, breathing life, beyond Selma's cell.

In close-up, Selma's entire head covers the vent. Then something strange occurs that we know cannot be happening for real. A faint chorus of voices sings, the music carrying through the vent as if a great auditorium had been set up inside the prison and was screening one of her favourite musicals. It is a sound soaked in nostalgia, as well as being full of lightness and air. In view of von Trier's examination of the figure of the martyr throughout his trilogy of films, the chorus evokes a choir of angels. However, while flecks of golden sunlight cast a divine aura over Bess's head in *Breaking the Waves*, announcing her celestial redemption, Selma's experience of the rejoicing voices only briefly gestures towards the possibility of transcendence beyond the material world. The chorus of voices breathes life back into Selma.

The distant voices are accompanied by three close-ups of the cell which focus on several items in the mise en scène: neatly folded towels on a shelf, the ceramic rim of the lavatory and piled white pillowcases. I will return to these images later in order to make sense of their position within the film's form, but at this stage it is important to acknowledge their abstract composition and the way these formal effects emphasise the disorienting and transformative power of the music Selma 'hears'. These close-ups frame Selma's first attempts to sing into the vent: 'raindrops on roses'. This phrase is followed by an encouraging, small smile. Then Selma's voice begins to break and she repeats the next lines of the song twice before she begins to cry. Pulling herself together, Selma bangs her flat palms against the wall and closes her eyes in concentration. Her breathing is shallow, almost silent. However, as she reaches the chorus ('these are a few of my favourite things...') she sighs deeply and we see her legs tucked underneath her, her shoe pushing at the wall. She picks up some energy and jumps off the bench, skipping over her bed and spinning around, tapping as she goes. Cultivating her breathing gives Selma the strength to release her repressed emotion and, momentarily, vanquish her feelings of dread as she awaits execution, but the viewer has limited access to such recovery given the formal strategies von Trier adopts in order to remind us of Selma's building anxiety.

We know already from my earlier analysis of scenes at the end of *Breaking the Waves* that breathing can become entangled in expressions of suffering, breaths caught up in tears and gasps of pain and, in the case of Bess, this turmoil is perhaps closer to catharsis than it is to grief. However, in *Dancer in the Dark*, Selma's final scenes are much more founded upon unbearable devastation, for the character and for the viewer. Although Selma finds temporary respite from the insurmountable trauma she suffers, the scene remains a deeply troubling experience for the viewer and the sound-image of her breathing is not enough to generate the same feelings of catharsis for the viewer that the character is able to produce through her relationship with music. While Selma is seen to press her face towards the vent in order to hear the music, the viewer is not granted the same kind of proximity to the noise which offers peaceful sanctuary to Selma. The image of Selma curled up against the vent suffices only as a pictorial register, but the breathing film viewer is still stifled by the harrowing nature of the scene and its oppressive framing. Indeed, working against Selma's alleviation of despair through music, the formal properties of the scene such as the tight framing of the prison cell and the close-up, frozen-in-time shots of its contents, seem to counter her attempts to regain her 'breathy', impassioned being.

While the images of the cell are visually unappealing, von Trier's insertion of shots focusing on the cell's contents in close-up seem to act, both literally and suggestively, as an overt point of visual disturbance for the viewer. This intrusion weighs heavily on the rest of the sequence and contributes towards the viewer's troubling experience of the scene. Questioning this difficult tension within the formal aesthetic of the film may offer ways of addressing the role of suffering in the film and its implications for the breathing film viewer.

The representation of the cell is stark, emphasising the harshly lit interior and its monochrome colour palette of off-white hues and sickly yellows, recalling, in particular, the Gothic, milky tones of the hospital in von Trier's earlier television series *The Kingdom* (*Riget*, 1994). Selma frequently appears against a backdrop of the cell wall and this creates an impression of interior space that is without curves, corners or lines, 'flattened out' to form an indistinct environment that clings and enshrouds Selma's slight frame. In this respect, the uneven tones of the wall and its beige opacity prematurely evoke the hood that will, as Grimley points out, stifle Selma's breathing before execution. Furthermore, the grey cardigan Selma wears not only doubles the effects of the walls, acting as a further layer that consumes her body, but marks her out as a weary shadow hovering in the foreground of the murky cell. While the representation of the cell conveys a sense of unease that links the moment closely with Selma's death, the series of shots depicting objects in the cell cryptically embeds tension in the film's form.

The uniformly pressed towels, the white pillowcases and the lavatory are abstractly rendered and refused the status of the innocuous everyday. Now unfamiliar and quietly unsettling, von Trier's photographed still lifes seem to pull the viewer immediately into a temporal drain or 'dead-time'. This sense of duration conveyed through the tightly framed and ordered objects tends to recall the unsettling iconography often seen in the films of Chantal Akerman, the concreteness of the objects in Selma's cell similarly translating as a kind of intent concentration on the familiar. Yet the objects in *Dancer in the Dark* do not invite us to 'touch the interior physiognomy of space',[71] as Bruno writes of Akerman's framing of objects; rather, the objects negate the possibility of departure.

On the nature of familiarity and the filming of objects, David Trotter writes: 'Familiarity is life lived in extreme close-up, by means of a racking of focus which never allows one plane to settle into coherent relation with another. Familiarity is all texture.'[72] While close-ups of objects, for Trotter, evoke familiarity through their texture, von Trier's static close-ups work to defamiliarise such everyday objects, thus troubling the logic of Trotter's argument. Familiarity is thus risky here and, in this sense, the objects appear immovable, inescapable, intensifying the constrictions of the cell.

When von Trier cuts to the objects within the mise en scène, the 'micro-montage' appears not only to deconstruct and disenable the sense of familiarity associated with such everyday artefacts, but also to disturb the on-screen space of the film. This shift in the film's formal composition is produced by von Trier's camera angles which emphasise the objects as flat optical images, a 'striated' perspective, as Deleuze and Guattari would concur.[73] This notion of flatness contrasts the perception of texture required in order to produce a sensation of haptic visuality and thus the optical effects von Trier adopts resist bodily perception.

Unlike the other sequences like 'Cvalda' and 'I've Seen It All', the striated prevails over the haptic here and the viewer's contact with the breathing body in the film is limited to its acoustic and narrative point of reference. Shifting focus away from Selma's body to such numbing close-ups of objects, distance is placed between the viewer and the character in the film and, in contrast to the extreme close-ups of Selma's body in 'I've Seen It All', we are, perhaps cruelly, denied any kind of human proximity, offered instead stagnant objects which repel us. While the culmination of extreme close-ups of Selma and her reaching of a high note suggests a euphoric, breathing visuality in 'I've Seen It All', the close-ups of objects in 'My Favourite Things' break off our engagement with Selma and serve to block any way in which we might want to come into contact with her through such means of viewing perception. Viewing relations here are more threatening than cathartic.

In order to further analyse the kind of repulsion associated with the filmed objects, one must retrace the experience of viewing such images and their ability to get under our skin. While composition and editing are formal aspects key to understanding the cryptic nature of the micro-montage, colour also plays an important part in the representation of these objects and their meaning within the film. Unified by the same spotless condition, a white or bleached sterility works to emphasise an erasure of human contact, washed out or scrubbed of the fragments of human subjectivity that once touched them and now no longer exist. Hence these artefacts are rather less 'favourite things' than objects of displeasure and, even, revulsion.[74] Indeed, it is no coincidence that such objects are unified by their 'whiteness', reminding the viewer nauseously of sanitation, the daily rituals of life that they represent, and how irreconcilable with death these 'habits' truly are.

White is also traditionally associated with spiritual purity, but unlike the gleam that illuminates Bess when she travels towards the pirate ship to her death in *Breaking the Waves*, white is here coupled with formal effects in order to produce feelings of anxiety for the viewer. As if hesitantly consuming a last supper, something morbidly turns in the pit of my stomach when I view the micro-montage, my lips part, dryly, aghast, my breathing slows down and my heart beats a little faster. We might not consciously register the threat of such objects, but it is nonetheless an important sense of unease which is felt by the body of the breathing viewer. It is most telling that one reviewer of the film, the online film critic Nathaniel Rogers, observes a direct connection between his body and Selma's: 'By the end of the film I felt like I could only breathe if Selma could – the shifts to Selma's musical world became my own flood of emotion and relief.'[75] In this sense, breathing can be considered part of our identification with Selma, but in my view it is our proximity to her body which underscores this viewing relation. When this proximity to Selma is broken, as my analysis of the micro-montage suggests, we are more likely to feel such loss of physical connection in terms that relate to a kind of suffocation.

Perhaps, then, through this prickling sense of what might be described as a suffocating revulsion, von Trier prepares the viewer for the overtly harrowing images that are to follow at the film's close as Selma is ripped away from us. Selma's death thus symbolises the price of identification, our view of the gallery watching her hanging body only serving as a further reminder of our complicity in von Trier's indictment of cinema as purely 'entertainment'.[76] Unlike Selma's diegetic responses to trauma, her own last rites provide some source of hope for the character, but we are prevented from mediating such grief. The film's form exposes the breathing film viewer to a psychical and material terrain of 'doubtful' images which rouse intense emotions and deepen the pathos of Selma's rendition of her favourite song. Indeed, exhaling, a gesture that suggests physical relief, seems most inappropriate at the end of the film; it would seem that our bodies only permit us to take small, stifled breaths as the film cuts abruptly to the credits. For a few moments, there is no noise at the end of *Dancer in the Dark* and the breathing film viewer is immersed in silence.

While a chilling diegetic silence marks the difficult end of *Dancer in the Dark*, and indeed the extinguishing of Selma's last breaths, silence *generates* our perception of the female protagonist's breathing body in *The Idiots*. The next section will consider how the role of silence in *The Idiots* sheds light on an ethical dimension of my model of the breathing film viewer, drawing attention to a new social and filmic contact which emerges through the locus of breathing and silence in the film.

The Idiots: Engendering Breath through Silence

As we have seen in my analyses of *Breaking the Waves* and *Dancer in the Dark*, my concept of breathing visuality corresponds with a kind of perception sensitive to the protagonists' breathing bodies and the formal amplification of such breaths through the style of each film, or what I have analysed as the 'film's body'. Breathing visuality suggests a form of embodied perception in which the breathing body of the viewer participates in the act of vision. While my conceptualisation of the breathing film viewer and breathing visuality has so far involved engagement with the representation of catharsis and suffering pertinent to the subject matter of von Trier's *Breaking the Waves* and *Dancer in the Dark*, the representation of communality in *The Idiots* prompts questions about the ambivalence of belonging and separation from others, and this leads me to consider the ways in which the breathing film viewer is engendered in terms of an ethical relationship with the image.

In my readings of *Breaking the Waves* and *Dancer in the Dark* I have reflected on the relations between the breathing body in the frame and the breathing film viewer which may represent an inter-subjective model of identification with the film. In this section, the representation of on-screen silences in *The Idiots* will lead me to consider how breathing is implicated in the ethics of viewing the emotional trauma of the film which, unlike in *Breaking the Waves* and *Dancer in the Dark*, barely fissures the surface of the film until the very end.

The Idiots explores the relationships between a group of young people taking part in a social experiment which requires them to revert to child-like beings or 'idiots', faking disability to the outside world. The ideology of the idiots' role-playing or 'spassing' encourages inhibitions to be freed, but as the film unfolds we learn that this new-found sociality comes at a heavy price. The film centres on Karen (Bodil Jørgensen), a newcomer to the group of 'idiots'. We learn that Karen has recently endured a miscarriage and has not yet recovered from this anguish. In an effort to be accepted by her new 'family', she begins to try to release her 'inner idiot', as the character Stoffer (Jens Albinus) demands of her, and it seems that the group provides some sort of way towards healing. However, the group's activities start to get out of hand and the social experiment draws to a close. Karen returns home and, proving her faith in the group, becomes an 'idiot' in front of her husband and the rest of her horrified family. While *The Idiots* can be seen to represent von Trier's interest in exploring the nature of anarchy and authenticity, it also sheds light on the ethics which lie at the very heart of his films. Our perception of such ethics is shaped by the role of trauma in *The Idiots* and its articulation through the locus of breath in the film.

While both *Dancer in the Dark* and *Breaking the Waves* end in the deaths of their protagonists, *The Idiots* culminates in a moment that does not depict the death of its central character but is nevertheless just as unbearable to watch. Earlier in this chapter, the scenes of infanticide in von Trier's *Medea* were discussed in order to suggest how close-ups of the protagonist's gasping mouth and heaving chest called attention to the breathing body and its harrowing register of trauma, underscored by silence and an intermittent howl of wind. Such hushed silences are recalled in *The Idiots* when we view many close-ups of Karen's face, grimacing, sighing, upon her return to her family home. Here, in the private hospitality of close relations, Karen achieves something none of her fellow 'idiots' could bear. This final scene takes place in silence, as we view Karen dribble cake from her mouth in close-up detail before she is slapped by her husband Anders (Hans Henrik Clemensen). Yet, while it may seem that the silence at the end of *The Idiots* bears negative implications, it is Karen's triumph in achieving the release of her 'inner idiot'. Indeed, it is fitting that this last, courageous effort by Karen to become an 'idiot' takes place in silence since she is so strongly associated with this muteness throughout the film.

Karen takes her place on a green sofa and is framed alongside her family. She sits at the far end of the sofa, her knees almost touching the edges of a small coffee table upon which cakes and tea are laid out with napkins. The camera zooms in on Karen's face and we see her hand reach out for a cream cake resting on a delicate saucer. The odd angle at which Karen's arm is bent towards the saucer hints at what is to come: she is becoming child-like and awkward and thus about to 'spass'. On the soundtrack, there is no family chatter, lively banter or nervous laughter as Karen returns home; she is met with stoic, disgruntled faces and an unbearably uncomfortable silence emphasised by the occasional clinking of china cups. Slowly, Karen begins to leak cake from her mouth, its lumpy mess dripping from the middle of her lower lip. Then dark, syrupy streaks of tea run from the sides of her mouth, trailing over her chin and coagulating with the crumbs of cake around her lips. Karen releases her 'inner idiot', behaving like an infant and horrifying her family, before being led away by Susanne (Anne Louise Hassing), another member of the group of 'idiots' whose role was to bear witness to Karen's 'spassing'.

The formal qualities of the above scene depicting Karen's 'spassing' isolate her from the rest of her family and enclose her within a space only she controls. For example, the mise en scène draws attention to the small piece of cake through the similarly creamy shade of wallpaper which serves as a backdrop to Karen's soft, lined face. Her synthetic, yellow cardigan seems to overwhelm and dull the sheen of her gold wedding ring as she holds the saucer and, to the left of the image, an orange glow enhances the red tones in Karen's hair, reinforcing her vivid presence. Certainly, it is significant that the lighting and use of colour during this scene tends to emphasise Karen's presence and greatly contrasts with the dreary brown and beige tones of the wider shots which feature her family. The silence which follows such images is disturbing because it prompts viewers to focus on Karen's mouth full of cake, a diegetic silence which is created and controlled by Karen since her family are now too disgusted to speak. While the leaking of food from her mouth is a deliberate attempt to lose control, the formal qualities of the image suggest that Karen remains in control of the space of the film and it is this ambivalence which structures the viewer's ethical response to the film.

Much has been written on Karen's gentle yet ambivalent silences, but it would seem that such considerations have paid less attention to the sound of her breathing which is also heard in the film, a different kind of embodied gesture that is 'appeased and attended', as Irigaray suggests.[77] Karen's silence, her subjective consciousness, offers a way in which we can understand more about silence as an important aspect of breathing and its implications for my concept of breathing visuality.[78]

While my readings of Bess in *Breaking the Waves* and Selma in *Dancer in the Dark* have focused on their articulation of breathing as an aspect of vocality, emphasising the importance of their voices and their self-expression, Karen often retreats into silence and avoids enunciation of her thoughts, especially her pain. Furthermore, her quietly reserved and controlled persona sharply contrasts with the noise of the group of 'idiots', whose collective presence is often marked by incessant chatter, child-like giggling and laughter. On Karen's need for silence, Hanna Laakso writes: 'She does not believe that the authenticity of being lies in externalised behaviour. For her, silence is a guarantee of her non-theatricality and authentic existence.'[79] Thus Karen's silences can be understood, paradoxically, as a commitment to the group's ideology, but since she is often observed in isolation from the group, her behaviour bears more of an ethical implication for the viewer than for the other members of the group in the film. Certainly the style of the film, especially its cinematography, tends to situate viewers face-to-face with Karen. Above all, it is the evocation of Karen's silence during one particular scene from *The Idiots* which can be seen to attune the viewer to his or her own breathing body. In Irigarayan terms, Karen's silences call to mind a possible respect for oneself and for the other within their respective limits, a proximity which preserves the breathing film viewer and the breathing body of the protagonist in the film.[80]

In addition to the final scene in the film, Karen also elicits a space of silence in the film experience during an early scene in which she attempts, in private, to call her husband and fails to respond to his concerned voice, lost for words. In close-up, we view Karen's face in profile, her eyes filling with tears. The camera zooms in on her face and within moments she gasps uncontrollably as she cries, her subtle breathing accompanied by the sound of birdsong that serves only to foreground her breath more acutely. The camera lingers on Karen's face, her eyes slowly blinking in the light, and her trembling features. We bear witness to her fragility and are exposed to the depths of her pain. While Susanne bears witness to Karen's 'spassing' at the end of the film, the viewers become the implicit witnesses during this earlier scene. Tracing every shift towards 'external' behaviour, to quote Laakso's analysis of the film, the camera frames Karen as she bows her head and grimaces before releasing a whimper, her eyes close and then she covers her face with her hands, hiding from us. As she raises her head, her eyes look up, avoiding our gaze. Karen's visible and audible despair starkly reflects the pressures of the adult world, contrasting with the tantrums and infantile volatility that the 'idiots' act out in public.

The close-ups of Karen as she quietly weeps recall the images of Medea as she commits infanticide. Medea's body stands limp yet also controlled, masking her pain as she frowns and her eyes roll up towards the sky. In *Medea*, von Trier cross-cuts between a close-up of its protagonist standing near branches of the tree she will use to hang her children and the expanse of desolate land which stretches out beyond the horizon, images overlaid with the sound of wind bristling through the sparse terrain. Medea's face is also often viewed from a high angle in close proximity to her dead child whose legs dangle in the foreground of the image, her face just above them. In *The Idiots*, Karen stands within an empty room near a window, but it is the interiority of her mind which is evoked through such silence and use of framing. Like Medea, Karen is caught within a still and silent realm, but unlike Medea's quiet acceptance of her fate, Karen's silence is more overtly suggestive of catharsis and release.

Medea and Karen are also counterparts in the sense that they both feel anxiety towards the loss of their children. While Karen did not, like Medea, murder her child, these characters share the same trauma of loss since Medea believes it is her fate to commit infanticide. Their silences contribute towards the representation of embodied suffering and the corporeal nature of trauma.

Karen's silence and her alienation is also inscribed in the 'body' of the film, that is, its formal composition. When Karen's hands close around her face, the image dissolves momentarily, underscoring her retreat into silence. The dissolve corresponds with the image of Karen's bowing head, serving to suggest a lapse of clarity and focus which, combined with the on-screen silence it accompanies, intensifies Karen's introspection and inner turmoil. While the dissolve can be seen to pinpoint the emotional trauma of the scene that lies beyond representation, it also marks a pause within the 'body' of the film which, in turn, tends to disrupt our engagement with Karen's breathing body. The dissolve prompts the viewer to contemplate his or her own breathing rather than Karen's alone, positing a proximity between Karen and the viewer. The viewer not only watches in silence but is sensitive to the breaths which also occupy such audible spaces, and this point of contact with the film is made while safeguarding the subjectivity of each breathing body involved in this filmic encounter.

Karen's Theme

While silences are created in order to reinforce Karen's interiority and our perception of her suffering and gradual recovery from trauma, we also first encounter this character in silence as she rides a wagon through a quiet park. According to the Dogme rules, non-diegetic music is forbidden: 'music must not be used unless it occurs where the camera is standing'.[81] *The Idiots* follows this rule with the exception of its opening sequence; the first few images of Karen are accompanied by a version of 'Le cygne' ('The Swan') by Camille Saint-Saëns, played on the melodica wind instrument (the movement was originally composed for the cello). 'Le cygne' was intended to evoke the smooth gliding movement of a swan through water and thus von Trier's use of the music underlines the physicality of Karen as she rides serenely through the park. Above all, von Trier's use of an arrangement of 'Le cygne' composed for a wind instrument identifies Karen's character with a breathy presence, similar to Selma's embodiment through music. Furthermore, the figure of the swan is generally regarded throughout popular culture as a symbol of transformation and enchantment, especially if we recall the narrative of Pyotr Ilyich Tchaikovsky's *Swan Lake*. In this context, Karen's journeying through the park and her theme's connotations transport her to new territory in which she will be transformed, and it will be her 'spassing' which will denote such physical and metaphorical changes.

The sweeping, gliding evocation of a swan's graceful movement through water can also be comparable with the way in which Karen encounters her new group of friends and her isolation amongst them. Karen is swept along with the tide of movement and action which results from her encounter with the 'idiots', but she continues to observe and be carried along as events unfold. 'Le cygne' is a pertinent theme for Karen since it conveys her passivity and calm, objective position within the group. Furthermore, the theme highlights the subtle fissures in the group's overt, liberal-spirited communality: Karen represents a point between self and other and foregrounds the importance of safeguarding such inter-subjectivity.

Von Trier's choice of music also offers insight into the social commentary underpinning the narrative of *The Idiots*. Indeed, 'Le cygne' is the thirteenth movement of Saint-Saëns's *The Carnival of the Animals*, and if Karen is the swan then the rest of the group must also have their animal counterparts. In this sense, von Trier is reminding us of the animality of the group and their absurdity; he is 'poking fun' not only at the political ideologies that the group negate, but at their own anarchy. Also in agreement with this view is Thomas Beltzer, whose profile of von Trier emphasises the fact that he was raised in a commune.[82]

In sum, von Trier encourages a communality between the viewer and his lead protagonist that takes place during the film experience of *The Idiots*. Indeed, it is the locus of breathing that is suggested through the viewing experience of *The Idiots* which differs from the representation of on-screen communality that is contained within the diegesis of the film. Furthermore, it is the visual, as well as aural, representation of Karen's silent body which enables us to share her emotional intensity and slow, cathartic release from pain. The kind of breathing visuality that is suggested by Karen's silence corresponds not with the actual image of her breathing body in the diegetic space of the film, but rather with the visual and aural field of proximity that silence affords between viewer and the filmed body on screen.

Concluding Thoughts

To return to Marks's thoughts on breathing and the inter-subjectivity of hearing, the breathing body safeguards a space for reflection, interiority and exchange without compromising one's own subjective being as a differentiated body in the world of conscious perception. While this chapter has paid attention to the diegetic construction of inter-subjectivity on screen, it has also emphasised the role of the breathing film viewer and developed thought on the haptic implications of such a viewing position. In my analysis of *Breaking the Waves*, I have shown that breathing might not only offer a new dimension to haptic hearing, but might also suggest a breathing visuality, a way of *sensing* the breath of an other as an image on screen. This perception is not tactile, nor is it haptic, in the sense that Marks describes, but it offers a model of visuality sensitive to breath in the inter-subjective terms Irigaray has fleshed out. Following this model of thought, *Dancer in the Dark* opens up evocations of breath to interpretations of music and harmony as well as discord. While my reading of *Dancer in the Dark* has explored the significance of music and the singing voice to my model of the breathing film viewer and breathing visuality, my engagement with a key moment from *The Idiots* suggests how silence prompts a different viewing response to the diegetic, breathing body and its inscription in the 'body' of the film.

What emerges through my engagement with von Trier's 'Gold Heart' trilogy is the role of breath as a signifier of the very immediacy and urgency that is characteristic of his particular aesthetic in which bodies possess a vitality and spirit, igniting the screen with their presence. The locus of breath in the content and form of von Trier's trilogy of films invites the viewer to attune to the diegetic bodies on screen, and this form of identification is bound up with the cathartic nature of each narrative. Breathing visuality pinpoints the acute moments in von Trier's films which tend to evoke suffering or intense emotion; my model of film viewing suggests another layer of the visceral experience of von Trier's trilogy and, above all, embeds the film viewer's breathing within the film experience.

Notes

1. See Luce Irigaray, 'A Breath that Touches in Words', in *I Love to You: Sketch for a Felicity Within History* (New York: Routledge, 1996), p. 127.
2. See Vivian Sobchack, *The Address of the Eye: A Phenomenology of Film Experience* (Princeton: Princeton University Press, 1992), p. 41.
3. See Laine, 'Triadic Communality', in *Shame and Desire: Emotion, Intersubjectivity, Cinema* (Oxford: Peter Lang, 2007), pp. 70–3 (p. 70).
4. See Lorraine, *Irigaray and Deleuze: Experiments in Visceral Philosophy* (Ithaca: Cornell University Press, 1999), p. 108.
5. See, in particular, Irigaray, 'The Way of Breath', in *Between East and West: From Singularity to Community* (New York: Columbia University Press, 2002), pp. 73–92.
6. See Sobchack, *The Address of the Eye*, p. 41.
7. I refer here to Marks's term 'haptic visuality' which first appears in her book *The Skin of the Film: Intercultural Cinema, Embodiment and the Senses* (Durham, NC: Duke University Press, 1999), p. xi.
8. See Wilson, 'Dogme Ghosts', in *Cinema's Missing Children* (London: Wallflower Press, 2004), pp. 123–38 (p.133).

9. For a more detailed exploration of dust and film's materiality, see Claire Thomson's fascinating article 'A Cinema of Dust: On the Ontology of the Image from Dreyer's Thorvaldsen to Ordrupgaard's Dreyer', available at <eprints.ucl.ac.uk/4963/1/4963.pdf> (accessed 2 December 2010). I am very grateful to Thomson for alerting me to the existence of this article.
10. For a more detailed discussion of the processing techniques used by von Trier to achieve particular visual effects, see Dorothy Ostrawoska and Graham Roberts, 'The Element of Childhood from Children's Television to Dogme 95', in *European Cinemas in the Television Age* (Edinburgh: Edinburgh University Press, 2007), pp. 87–106 (p. 89).
11. Von Trier's *Antichrist* and the comedy of manners *The Boss of It All* (2006) were made in the period between *Dogville* and *Manderlay*. On the significance of the 'Amerika' and 'Europa' trilogies and von Trier's use of symbols such as Europe or the USA in order to portray individuals that have 'become victims of destiny', see Torben Grodal's insightful article 'Frozen Flows in von Trier's Oeuvre', *Northern Lights: Authorship, Creativity and Intentionality in the Media*, 3 (2004), pp. 129–68.
12. See rules 2 and 3 of the Dogme 'Vow of Chastity': 'The sound must never be produced apart from the images or vice versa (music must not be used unless it occurs where the scene is being shot)', and 'The camera must be hand-held. Any movement or immobility attainable in the hand is permitted (the film must not take place where the camera is standing; shooting must take place where the film takes place).' An abridged version of the rules can be found at <http://cinetext.philo.at/reports/dogme_ct.html> (accessed 4 January 2012).
13. I am referring to Lisa Coulthard's feminist reconsideration of the 'Gold Heart' trilogy through Jacques Lacan's discussion of the essence of tragedy entitled 'The Tragedy of Love: Lars von Trier's Suffering Heroines', paper presented at the Locus of Tragedy conference at the University of Antwerp, November 2006; for an alternative, strictly Lacanian, perspective see Slavoj Zizek's article 'Femininity between Goodness and Act', which views the paradoxes of feminine sexuality at play in *Breaking the Waves* as a film that 'enables us to avoid the fatal misreading of Lacan's notion of feminine *jouissance*', available at <http://lacan.com/frameXIV3.htm> (accessed 4 May 2011). For a broader feminist critique of the representation of religion in particular, see Irena S. M. Makarushka's 'Transgressing Goodness in *Breaking the Waves*', *Journal of Religion and Film*, 2:1 (April 1998), available at <http://www.unomaha.edu/jrf/breaking.htm> (accessed 3 May 2011).
14. See Laine, *Shame and Desire*.
15. See Bainbridge, *The Cinema of Lars von Trier: Authenticity and Artifice* (London: Wallflower Press, 2007), p. 119. My review of Bainbridge's book appears in *Film-Philosophy*, 12:1 (2008), available at <www.film-philosophy.com/2008v12n1/quinlivan.pdf> (accessed 12 June 2011).
16. Laine's model that I specifically refer to here draws on the psychoanalytic thought of Kurt Lewin in order to show how a 'hodological' field of human energy is created through the absence of sets in *Dogville*. See Laine, 'Lars von Trier, *Dogville* and the Hodological Space of Cinema', *Studies in European Cinema*, 3:2 (November 2006), pp. 129–41.
17. See von Trier's 1996 interview with Christian Brad Thomsen in Jan Lumholdt (ed.), *Lars von Trier: Interviews* (Jackson: University Press of Mississippi, 2003), pp. 109–10:

> a picture book about a little girl who goes out in the woods with some breadcrumbs in her apron and on her way she gives away both her food and her clothes. And when the rabbit and the squirrel tell her that now she doesn't have a skirt on, her answer is the same every time: 'I'll be alright.'

18. For a fuller reflection on *Breaking the Waves* as a hagiography of its central protagonist see Theresa Saunders, 'Both/And Holiness and Mental Illness', in *Celluloid Saints: Images of Sanctity in Film* (Atlanta: Mercer University Press, 2002), pp. 201–3.
19. See Barker, *The Tactile Eye: Touch and the Cinematic Experience* (Los Angeles: University of California Press, 2009), p. 3.
20. See Morris's article on Criterion's DVD release of *The Passion of Joan of Arc* in *Bright Lights Film Journal*, 27 (January 2000), available at <http://www.brightlightsfilm.com/27/joanofarc.html> (accessed 3 October 2011). See also, in particular, the classical film theory of Béla Balázs, whose extensive theorisation of the close-up as a filmic expression of subjectivity that reveals the soul found an exemplary model in Dreyer's framing of his protagonist. See Balázs, 'The Close Up', in *Theory of Film: Character and Growth of a New Art* (New York: Dover Publications, 1970), p. 55.
21. See Chion, *Audio-Vision: Sound on Screen* (New York: Columbia University Press, 1993), p. 76.
22. See Sobchack, 'Thoughts on Seeing (most of) *The Descent* and *Isolation*', *Film Comment*, July-August 2006, pp. 40–1 (p. 41). *The Descent*, dir. Neil Marshall, UK, 2005.
23. Indeed, I am very grateful to Marks for her stimulating comments on earlier drafts of this chapter's exploration of the haptic implications of sound.
24. See Marks, *The Skin of the Film*, p. 183.
25. See Irigaray, *I Love to You*, p. 148.
26. See Marks, *The Skin of the Film*, p. xi. See also Barker's exploration of the concept of haptic visuality in *The Tactile Eye*, p. 24.
27. See Powrie, 'The Haptic Moment: Sparring with Paolo Conte in Ozon's *5x2*', *Paragraph: A Journal of Modern Critical Theory*, 31:2 (2008), pp. 206–22.
28. See Irigaray, *I Love To You*, p. 148.
29. On the numerous close-ups of Bess's face in the film, Jeffrey Pence observes a tension between the intrusive nature of these shots and the narrative's framing of her actions. See Pence, 'Cinema of the Sublime: Theorizing the Ineffable', *Poetics Today*, 25:1 (2004), pp. 29–66 (p. 49). I tend to view von Trier's employment of the close-up as an evocation of the concepts of Balázs and Dulac, implying an intimate engagement with the character's 'soul' rather than an invasion of personal space, and thus they are key to the film's overarching transcendental style.
30. See Roland Barthes, *The Pleasure of the Text* (New York: Hill & Wang, 1975), p.67; Eng. trans. by Richard Howard from the French *Le Plaisir du texte* (Paris: Éditions du Seuil, 1973).
31. Von Trier's focus on the breathing features of Bess's face especially calls to mind a passage from Jean Epstein's essay 'Magnification': 'It's not even true that there is air between us ... a breeze of emotion underlines the mouth with clouds.' See Jean Epstein, 'Magnification', in Richard Abel (ed.), *French Film Theory and Criticism Volume 1* (Princeton: Princeton University Press, 1988), pp. 235–40 (p. 239).
32. Quoted in Grodal, 'Cognitive Identification and Empathy', in *Moving Pictures: A New Theory of Film Genres, Feelings and Cognition* (Oxford: Oxford University Press, 2002), p. 81.
33. See Chion, *Audio-Vision*, p. 34.
34. See Brophy, *100 Modern Soundtracks*, BFI Screen Guides (London: BFI, 2004), p. 2. Brophy's view is also echoed by the film sound editor Walter Murch in his introduction to Chion's *Audio-Vision*, where the infant's first impression of sound is referred to as the 'swash' of its mother's breathing (p. vii). I also thank Brophy for his help with this research via several email messages in 2008.
35. See Irigaray, 'A Breath that Touches in Words', in *I Love to You*, p. 127.
36. See Pence, 'Cinema of the Sublime', p. 50.

37. See Chion, 'On-the-Air Sound', in *Audio-Vision*, p. 76.
38. See von Trier's script, *Breaking the Waves: Lars von Trier* (London: Faber and Faber, 1996), p. 51.
39. See Kirkeby, 'The Pictures between the Chapters in Breaking the Waves', in *Breaking the Waves: Lars von Trier*, p. 12.
40. See Irigaray, 'The Way of Breath', in *Between East and West*, p. 75.
41. See Marks, 'The Memory of Touch', in *The Skin of the Film*, pp. 127–93 (p. 149).
42. See Irigaray, 'May 5th', in *Everyday Prayers* (Nottingham: Nottingham University Press, 2004), p. 130.
43. See, in particular, Bainbridge's use of this term at the close of her article 'The Trauma Debate: Just Looking? The Work of Lars von Trier', *Screen*, 45:4 (Winter 2004), pp. 391–400 (p. 400):

    The role of affect is crucial here, highlighting the way in which the mechanism deployed in the experience of unpleasurable trauma can be put to use in the context of unpleasurable cinema to provide a pleasurable sense of mastery and self-awareness. It can be argued that this is the appeal of moments of unpleasure in cinema.

44. See Wilson, 'Dogme Ghosts', in *Cinema's Missing Children*, p. 134.
45. See Irigaray, 'The Redemption of Women', in *Luce Irigaray: Key Writings* (New York: Continuum, 2004), pp. 150–64 (p. 162).
46. See Irigaray, *Everyday Prayers*, pp. 98–9.
47. See Irigaray, *An Ethics of Sexual Difference* (London: Continuum, 2004), p. 75.
48. For a useful analysis of the sensible transcendental in Irigaray's philosophy, see Tina Chanter, *Ethics of Eros: Irigaray's Re-writing of the Philosophers* (London: Routledge, 1995), p. 180.
49. See Brophy, *100 Modern Soundtracks*, p. 4.
50. Written by Björk, Sjón and Lars von Trier.
51. See Grimley, 'Hidden Places: Hyperrealism, Björk's *Vespertine* and *Dancer in the Dark*', *Twentieth Century Music*, 2:1 (2005), pp. 37–51 (p. 45).
52. Ibid. pp. 41–2.
53. See the interview with von Trier included on the Film Four/Channel Four DVD release of *Dancer in the Dark*, 2007.
54. Von Trier's comments in interview confirm that the inclusion of this song at the end of the film was entirely Björk's idea: 'She already had made her mind up on the prospect of future hope. She'll have to stand by all that. I wouldn't have done anything like it.' See Jan Lumholdt's interview 'There Will Be No Fun Poking Today', in *Lars von Trier: Interviews*, p. 165.
55. See Travers's review of the film for *Rolling Stone* magazine (2000), available at <http://www.rollingstone.com/movies/reviews/dancer-in-the-dark-20001006> (accessed 14 December 2011).
56. Ibid.
57. It is well known that von Trier used 100 static cameras during these musical numbers in order to create the feeling of spontaneity. This method of working which leaves some of the film to chance is also followed in von Trier's post-modern comedy *The Boss of It All* (2006) where the computer program Automavision was used in order to co-ordinate random positions. For more on von Trier's experimental use of Automavision in *The Boss of It All* see Sheila Johnston's interview 'Lars von Trier's Funny Turn', available at <http://www.telegraph.co.uk/culture/film/starsandstories/3671331/Lars-Von-Triers-funny-turn.html> (accessed 14 December 2011).
58. See the interview with von Trier included on the Film Four/Channel Four DVD release of *Dancer in the Dark*, 2007.

59. See Marks, *Touch: Sensuous Theory and Multisensory Media* (Minneapolis: University of Minnesota Press, 2002), p. 2.
60. I have written elsewhere, in greater depth, about the relations between kinaesthesia and haptics. See Quinlivan, 'Material Hauntings: The Kinaesthesia of Sound in *Innocence* (Hadzihalilovic, 2004)', *Studies in French Cinema*, 9:3 (2009), pp. 215–24.
61. *Evita*, dir. Alan Parker, USA, 1996; *The Birdcage*, dir. Mike Nichols, USA, 1996.
62. See 'Before and Beyond any Word', in *Luce Irigaray: Key Writings*, p. 140.
63. See Marks, *Touch*, p. 2.
64. See Irigaray, 'The Sharing of Speech', in *The Way of Love* (London: Continuum, 2004), pp. 13–53 (p. 26).
65. See Bruno, prologue to *Atlas of Emotion: Journeys in Art, Architecture and Film* (London: Verso, 2002), pp. 1–11 (pp. 6–7).
66. Ibid. p. 2.
67. See Irigaray, 'Before and Beyond Any Word', in *Luce Irigaray: Key Writings*, p. 140.
68. I refer here to Chion's use of the term 'emanation speech' which conveys the essence of the character without 'words being completely heard or understood'. See Chion, *Audio-Vision*, pp. 177–83.
69. See Irigaray, *Everyday Prayers*, pp. 150–1.
70. For a further discussion on the role of mise en scène in *Dancer in the Dark* see, in particular, José Arroyo's article 'How Do You Solve a Problem Like von Trier', *Sight and Sound*, September 2000, available at <http://www.bfi.org.uk/sightandsound/feature/53> (accessed 25 March 2011).
71. See Bruno, 'Travelling Domestic: The Movie "House"', in *Atlas of Emotion*, pp. 75–109 (p. 102).
72. See Trotter, 'Lynne Ramsay's *Ratcatcher*: Towards a Theory of Haptic Narrative', *Paragraph: A Journal of Modern Critical Theory*, special issue on 'Cinema and the Senses', ed. Emma Wilson, 31:2 (July 2008), pp. 138–58 (p. 139).
73. I refer here to Deleuze and Guattari's definition of the striated which relates to a distant vision and more optical space. See, in particular, '1440: The Smooth and the Striated', in *A Thousand Plateaus* (London: Continuum, 2004), p. 544.
74. One is reminded, in particular, of Julia Kristeva's theoretical concept of 'abjection' which calls into question borders. The borders disrupted by the micro-montage are those that separate the clean from the unclean since they represent both and hold the potential to be both at once, carrying the material traces of living skin, hair and other bodily matter concealed in their 'whiteness'. See Kristeva, *Powers of Horror: An Essay on Abjection* (New York: Columbia University Press, 1982).
75. See Rogers's 2000 review online, available at <http://thefilmexperience.net/Reviews/dancerinthedark.html> (accessed 29 March 2008).
76. This view is also supported by Jack Stevenson, whose book on von Trier makes clear that *Dancer in the Dark* was not intended to entertain. See Stevenson, *Lars von Trier*, World Cinema Series (London: BFI, 2002), p. 149.
77. See Irigaray, 'The Age of the Breath', in *Luce Irigaray: Key Writings*, p. 167.
78. For more views on Karen's silences see, in particular, Bainbridge, *The Cinema of Lars von Trier*, pp. 116–17, and Hanna Laakso's analysis of Bodil Jørgensen's performance in '*Idioterne*', in Tytti Soila (ed.), *The Cinema of Scandinavia*, Twenty Four Frames Series (London: Wallflower Press, 2005), pp. 203–14.
79. See Laakso, '*Idioterne*', in *The Cinema of Scandinavia*, p. 204.
80. See Irigaray, *An Ethics of Sexual Difference*, pp. 180–2.
81. See Catherine Fowler, *The European Cinema Reader* (London: Routledge, 2002), pp. 83–84.
82. See Beltzer, 'Lars von Trier', available at <http://archive.sensesofcinema.com/contents/directors/02/vontrier.html> (accessed 1 May 2010).

CONCLUSION

In the first chapter of this book, the films of Egoyan resonated with the cathartic dimensions of breathing central to Irigaray's thought. Egoyan's 'elemental topographies' presented new ways in which to explore the real and psychical perception of space to which breathing attunes the subject, and this led to questions of ambivalence that related to the viewer's perception of the film.

The ambivalent form of film viewing that emerged through my analysis of Egoyan's films was re-examined in light of the breathing, sexed bodies of Cronenberg's films in the second chapter of this book. The locus of breathing in Cronenberg's films led me to hypothesise a form of identification which was articulated through the film's body – a breathing body which responds, mimetically, to the diegetic bodies on screen.

While the films of Egoyan and Cronenberg presented ways in which to reflect on the issue of bodily identification with filmed subjects, as well as film form, in terms that relate to breathing, the last chapter of this book underlined the notion of sharing breath and the identificatory processes informed by the presence of breathing in film. The third chapter's analysis of von Trier's 'Gold Heart' trilogy and its suggestion of breathing according to inter-subjective relations stimulated my concept of breathing visuality, which sought to emphasise the effects of the film's form and its diegesis on the viewer and the involvement of their breathing as part of the film experience.

Although the final chapter of this book focused on the breathing film viewer, the introduction to this book began by raising more general questions about the absence and presence of the human body in contemporary art as well as film. My analyses of the films of Egoyan, Cronenberg and von Trier have made possible the exploration of the place of breath in cinema. Such a notion, as I have argued throughout, seeks to challenge conceptions of the sensible and sentient 'bodies' of film and the medium's debt to materiality prevalent in existing accounts of the embodied, filmic encounter. The 'bodies' that have come to represent the locus of breath in cinema have led me to question the extent to which breathing is involved in the representation of the human body in the film's content, form and the film experience as a whole. Indeed, my exploration of the role of breathing in the film experience has led me to raise questions about the film viewer's body and its significance as a breathing body. More broadly, the 'bodies' that I have discussed according to the locus of breath in film bear implications for the discipline of embodied film theory, as well as the wider field of visual studies. This conclusion will reflect on some of the most vital issues that were raised as a result of my investment in the notion of the breathing body in film.

What has been brought to light through my examination of the place of breath in cinema is the significance of breathing to film experiences that are especially intense, emotional and visceral. Breathing, whether it is evoked by the filmed subject on screen, the film's form or a combination of both, represents an embodied gesture that is of the mind as well as the body. While the filmed subject tends to evoke breathing through the presence of the body on screen in terms that relate to sound as well as the visual registering of bodily movement, the film's form suggests breathing through various styles of editing, framing and camera movements which portray a heightened state of bodily consciousness that I argue is crucial to Irigaray's theorisation of breathing. Bodily consciousness of breathing is most significant to the locus of breath in film and it is this dimension of my argument which might be seen to explore the question of the film's mind in terms of its restorative and spiritual resonances. In this respect, my exploration of breathing and its suggestion of bodily consciousness in the film experience is best understood not as an enquiry into the film's mind, but as a vital way in which to develop thought on the film's 'soul'. While theorists such as Marks and Sobchack have developed models of embodied theory which have been organised by a bodily relationship with the filmic image and the apparatus, my engagement with Irigaray's philosophy of breathing and its spiritual connotations has led me to raise questions about the nature of thought and feeling since both are entwined within a schema of embodiment that breathing comes to stand for as part of the film experience. In the three chapters of this book I have explored the thematic, contextual, visual and aural motifs which prompt various viewing responses and identification processes according to the surfacing of breathing and its evocation of bodily consciousness in each of the films I have discussed.

As we have seen, the place of breath in cinema can be traced in multiple ways and its role is multidimensional. However, according to Irigaray's tripartite schema, my engagement with breathing in the films of Egoyan, Cronenberg and von Trier has focused mainly on the ways in which breath emerges through the spatial, corporeal and inter-subjective dimensions of the filmic medium. In the first chapter of this book, Egoyan's figuring of breath according to spatiality is shaped by his elemental topographies of memory and loss. In *The Sweet Hereafter*, Egoyan situates breathing within the very heart of its narrative in order to awaken the viewer's mind and body to the presence of the lost children of the film whose bodies live on in the film's elemental imagery and formal composition, but such spaces are mapped out in more troubling ways in *Felicia's Journey*, where the boundaries between the inside, and interiority of the mind, and the outside of the body become blurred. Finally, the filmed, diegetic spaces of *Exotica* prompt a bodily response to the image which also relates to the psychical trauma of the film's protagonists. In the second chapter of this book which focused on Cronenberg's corporeal cinema, *Spider* foregrounds breathing as a kind of gendered suffering in the flesh that encompasses the senses as well as evoking a breathing consciousness. Such suffering of the body and mind is radically tested and re-viewed according to the sexed bodies of *Videodrome* and its breathing objects which engender breathing, desiring subjects. Following my engagement with the films of Cronenberg, von Trier's socially and ethically enquiring 'Gold Heart' trilogy enables an investigation into the viewer's breathing body and the ways in which it becomes implicated in the emotional and physical trauma of his narratives, responding in ways that might be described as an inter-subjective relation with the film. The three chapters of this book have collectively emphasised the connections between sensuous theory and the cultivation of embodied subjectivity that is central to Irigaray's philosophy of breathing. One of the most important achievements of this book has been my rethinking of haptic theory, especially in light of Irigaray's concept of the 'caress' as a mode of tactile perception appropriate to breathing.

The sensuality of breathing, or rather its particularly tactile resonance, is an issue that has been addressed in most of the films I have discussed and my theorisation of vocality has been most significant to this facet of my argument. The sound of the voice and its conceptualisation in terms of Irigaray's philosophy of breath and, especially, haptic theory has been key to my questioning of the roles of selfhood, autonomy and self-expression which come to suggest subjective, bodily consciousness – an issue that is central to the foregrounding of breathing in film. Selma uses her 'breathy' voice to liberate herself from responsibility and self-sacrifice, while the sound of Bess's breathing suggests an aural texture, presenting thought on the aurality of the filmic image which invigorates haptic theory and emphasises how vital sound is to haptic thinking. While these examples engage with Marks's model of haptic visuality, they also, most importantly, complicate her mimetic model of identification by positing a new mode of film viewing that I have termed 'breathing visuality'.

Breathing visuality describes images which evoke a kind of breathing space suggested through formal and contextual motifs, sounds and syntaxes, while the breathing film viewer refers to the real, lived body of the viewer. I have used these terms to distinguish between the abstract (symbolic) and the 'real' configuration of breathing in film viewing. Both concepts refer to an awakening of breathing bodies, but the breathing film viewer tends to privilege the real breaths of the viewer. In this sense, breathing visuality, following Marks's haptic visuality, turns the eyes into organs of respiration or, to risk taking this analogy further, stimulates a resuscitated vision, as Irigaray's thought has implied.[1] Breathing visuality does not affect the 'real' breathing of the viewer;

it is contemplative, patient, sensitive to an inner 'depth' of the film which tends to evoke a breathing body. Breathing visuality does not privilege the visual, nor does it substitute vision for breathing; it posits a movement between gaze and breath.

Also crucial to my model of breathing visuality is the discussion of the film's 'body' and its articulation, through various formal devices, of a visuality which corresponds with the filmed body in the diegesis and the central concerns and themes of films which bear implications for the kind of visuality that is generated. When we view Bess adrift and gasping, about to sacrifice herself for Jan, her heavy breathing and exhaling is underscored by the formal attributes of the film; the images lose focus as if to echo her desire for composure, relaxation and calmness that her diegetic sigh represents. Close-ups of Selma's body in motion pick up her erratic, breathy rhythms and notes of euphoria which are amplified by rapid editing. What is key to the type of embodied perception that breathing visuality represents is the involvement of the viewer as a breathing body, becoming attuned and sensitive to ways of hearing and seeing that are alive and open to the emergence of the breathing body as a diegetic and formal presence in the film experience. However, it is not the formal attributes alone that come to stand for breathing visuality. Rather, it is the combination of various formal attributes such as close-ups, depth of focus, sound, editing and zooming with particularly heightened emotional and visceral representations within the diegesis which may be co-ordinated in order to prompt reflection on the nature of breathing in the film. Above all, it is the viewer's proximity to a breathing, diegetic body on screen which tends to elicit a compelling kind of breathing visuality.

While the diegetic, breathing body and the viewer's breathing body have been important to my analysis of the locus of breathing in film, my discussion of the formal attributes of film have also led me to consider the medium's specificity as a differentiated 'body' in the film experience. In *The Sweet Hereafter*, the film's body bears comparison with an (im)material flow of breath which ultimately signifies the lost children of the film. In *Spider*, the syntax and rhythm of the images of Mrs Clegg, combined with her voice, open up the body of the film, creating a greater illusion of depth and orienting the viewer towards the image of Mrs Clegg and her open, breathing mouth – generating a sense of volume and air. Thus the film's breathing body has been explored in terms that relate to gender and, as *Spider* has shown us, it tends to emphasise an identification with a female subject on screen. Indeed, in *Breaking the Waves*, the film's 'body' is 'empathetic' to its heroine, complicit with her body, sighing when she sighs in the diegetic image. Yet the film's 'body' also closes off to air, as we have seen over the course of this book. In *Exotica*, *Spider*, *Felicia's Journey* and *Dancer in the Dark*, the film's 'body' works on various levels to create sensations of suffocation, nausea and claustrophobia which echo the trauma and psychical anxiety of the film's protagonists. This mode of perception is useful in trying to understand the sensuous implications of embodied narratives and images whose content is so traumatic that it spills over into the physical realm of experience. Such sensations elicited by the film's 'body' accord with what might be called 'phantom senses' in which viewers over-identify with the subjects of the film, caught up in its realm of suffering.

While I have argued that the locus of breathing in film relates to the filmic conception and (im)materialisation of the mind as well as the body, my reflection on the senses and the (in)visible presence of breathing, especially in chapter two, might be viewed as a new dimension of synaesthesia which refers to the feeling of sensation in one part of the body when another is stimulated. For Georgina Evans, the concept of synaesthesia is especially useful in order to map out the emotional geography of cinema in sensuous terms.[2] In some ways, *The Place of Breath in Cinema* may be seen to reflect an implicit interest in breathing as part of a synaesthetic realm of film experience since it is Irigaray's thought which likens breathing to a kind of 'touch' while, simultaneously, privileging modes of inner experience and the interiority of the thinking, embodied subject. Indeed, a project that was to expand upon the Irigarayan notion of breathing alongside the concept of synaesthesia might offer a worthwhile way in which to remap and reconfigure discourses of embodied knowledge. However, my project here was not to develop an analysis of the senses and breathing in film; my primary aim was to investigate and demonstrate the power and significance of breathing in relation to the specificity of the film experience.

This book is the only study to date within film theory, and indeed visual theory, to engage with the notion of breathing as its central point of enquiry. While the embodied discourses of Marks and Sobchack have been crucial to my synthesis of haptic and sensuous theory, the work undertaken here also unsettled the ground upon which their theories are based; it has set the stage for new theorisations of the sentient qualities of film, its manifestations and nuanced representations to be now rethought and re-viewed according to the place of breath in cinema.

Notes

1. See Irigaray, *An Ethics of Sexual Difference* (London: Continuum, 2004), p. 161.
2. See, in particular, Evans, 'Synaesthesia in Kieślowski's *Trois Couleurs: Bleu*', *Studies in French Cinema*, 5:2 (2005), pp. 77–86.

BIBLIOGRAPHY

Abram, David, 'Ethics in Place', <http://www.ethicsinplace.org/pages/paperabstracts.html> (accessed 2 September 2009).
Adams, Doug, 'An Interview with Mychael Danna', *Film Score Monthly*, January 1998, <http://www.mychaeldanna.com/Interviewsframe.html> (accessed 10 April 2009).
Adams, Parveen, 'Death Drive', in David Grant (ed.), *The Modern Fantastic: The Cinema of David Cronenberg* (Trowbridge: Flicks Books, 2000), pp. 102–22.
Anderson, Don, 'A Review of Anna Powell's *Deleuze and Horror Film*', *Rhizomes*, 11/12 (Fall 2005/Spring 2006), <http://www.rhizomes.net/issue11/anderson/review.html> (accessed 3 December 2010).
Armatage, Kay, and Caryl Clark, 'Seeing and Hearing Atom Egoyan's *Salomé*', in Monique Tschofen and Jennifer Burwell (eds), *Image and Territory: Essays on Atom Egoyan* (Waterloo, ON: Wilfrid Laurier Press, 2007), pp. 307–30.
Arroyo, José, 'How Do You Solve a Problem Like von Trier', *Sight and Sound*, September 2000, <http://www.bfi.org.uk/sightandsound/feature/53> (accessed 25 March 2011).
Atkinson, Michael, *Blue Velvet*, BFI Modern Classics (London: BFI, 1997).
Bachelard, Gaston, *Air and Dreams: An Essay on the Imagination of Movement* (Dallas: Dallas Institute of Humanities and Culture, 1988); Eng. trans. by Edith R. Farrell and C. Frederick Farrell from the French *L'Air et les songes* (Paris: José Corti, 1987).
Bainbridge, Caroline, *The Cinema of Lars von Trier: Authenticity and Artifice* (London: Wallflower Press, 2007).
Bainbridge, Caroline, 'Feminine Enunciation in the Cinema', *Paragraph: A Journal of Modern Critical Theory*, 25:3 (2002), pp. 129–43.
Bainbridge, Caroline, 'The Trauma Debate: Just Looking? The Work of Lars von Trier', *Screen*, 45:4 (Winter 2004), pp. 391–400.
Balázs, Béla, 'The Close Up', in *Theory of Film: Character and Growth of a New Art* (New York: Dover Publications, 1970).

Banks, Russell, *The Sweet Hereafter* (London: Picador, 1992).
Barker, Jennifer, *The Tactile Eye: Touch and the Cinematic Experience* (Los Angeles: University of California Press, 2009).
Baronian, Marie-Aude, 'History and Memory, Repetition and Epistolarity', in Monique Tschofen and Jennifer Burwell (eds), *Image and Territory: Essays on Atom Egoyan* (Waterloo, ON: Wilfrid Laurier Press, 2007), pp. 157–76.
Barthes, Roland, 'The Grain of the Voice', in *Image, Music, Text* (London: Fontana, 1997), pp. 179–89; Eng. trans. by Stephen Heath from the French *Le Grain de la voix* (Paris: Éditions du Seuil, 1981).
Barthes, Roland, *The Pleasure of the Text* (New York: Hill & Wang, 1975); Eng. trans by Richard Howard from the French *Le Plaisir du texte* (Paris: Éditions du Seuil, 1973).
Beard, William, *The Artist as Monster* (Toronto: University of Toronto Press, 2006).
Beltzer, Thomas, 'Lars von Trier', <http://archive.sensesofcinema.com/contents/directors/02/vontrier.html> (accessed 1 May 2010).
Beugnet, Martine, *Cinema and Sensation: French Film and the Art of Transgression* (Edinburgh: Edinburgh University Press, 2007).
Beugnet, Martine, 'Evil and the Senses: Philippe Grandrieux's *Sombre* and *La vie nouvelle*', *Studies in French Cinema*, 5:3 (2005), pp. 175–84.
Beugnet, Martine, 'Filming Obsession: Chantal Akerman's *La Captive*', in Martine Beugnet and Marion Schmid (eds), *Proust at the Movies*, Studies in European Cultural Transition Series (Aldershot: Ashgate Publishing, 2005), pp. 168–205.
Beugnet, Martine, 'The Practice of Strangeness: *L'Intrus* – Claire Denis (2004) and Jean-Luc Nancy (2000)', *Film-Philosophy*, 12:1, pp. 31–48, <http://www.film-philosophy.com/2008v12n1/beugnet.pdf> (accessed 5 August 2011).
Beugnet, Martine, and Elizabeth Ezra, 'A Portrait of the Twenty-First Century', *Screen*, 50:1 (Spring 2009), pp. 77–85.
Bolton, Lucy, 'The Camera as Speculum: Examining Female Consciousness in *Lost in Translation*, Using the Thought of Luce Irigaray', in Barbara Gabriella Renzi and Stephen Rainey (eds), *From Plato's Cave to the Multiplex: Contemporary Philosophy and Film* (Newcastle: Cambridge Scholars Press, 2006), pp. 87–97.
Bolton, Lucy, *Film and Female Consciousness: Irigaray, Cinema and Thinking Women* (Basingstoke: Palgrave Macmillan, 2011).
Boym, Svetlana, 'Between the Borders of Cultural Identity: Atom Egoyan's *Calendar*', *CineAction*, 32 (Autumn 1993), pp. 30–4.
Brenez, Nicole, 'The Body's Night: An Interview with Philippe Grandrieux', *Rouge*, 1 (2003), <http://www.rouge.com.au/1/grandrieux.html> (accessed 7 July 2009).
Briefel, Aviva, 'What Some Ghosts Don't Know: Spectral Incognizance and the Horror Film', *Narrative*, 17:1 (January 2009), pp. 95–108.

Brooks, Jodie, 'The Sound of Knocking: Jacques Becker's *Le Trou*', *Screening the Past*, 12 (2001), <http://www.latrobe.edu.au/screeningthepast/firstrelease/fr0301/jbfr12a.htm> (accessed 7 December 2011).
Brophy, Philip, *100 Modern Soundtracks*, BFI Screen Guides (London: BFI, 2004).
Brougher, Kerry, Michael Tarantino and Astrid Brown (eds), *Notorious: Alfred Hitchcock and Contemporary Art* (Oxford: Museum of Contemporary Art, 1999).
Browning, Mark, *David Cronenberg: Author or Filmmaker?* (Bristol: Intellect, 2007).
Browning, Robert, *The Pied Piper of Hamelin*, in *Robert Browning Selected Poems* (New York: Penguin, 2004), pp. 30–8.
Bruno, Giuliana, *Atlas of Emotion: Journeys in Art, Architecture and Film* (London: Verso, 2002).
Bukatman, Scott, *Terminal Identity: The Virtual Subject in Postmodern Science Fiction* (Durham, NC: Duke University Press, 1993).
Cartwright, Lisa, *Screening the Body: Tracing Medicine's Visual Culture* (Minneapolis: Minnesota University Press, 1995).
Celeste, Reni, 'In the Web with David Cronenberg: *Spider* and the New Auteurism', *CineAction*, 65 (Winter 2005), pp. 2–5.
Celeste, Reni, 'The Sound of Silence: Film Music and Lament', *Quarterly Review of Film and Video*, 22 (2005), pp. 113–23.
Chanter, Tina, *Ethics of Eros: Irigaray's Re-writing of the Philosophers* (London: Routledge, 1995).
Chappell, Crissa-Jean, 'Alain Resnais and Atom Egoyan', *Cinetext*, 2003, <http://cinetext.philo.at/magazine/chappell/resnais_egoyan.html> (accessed 10 September 2009).
Chion, Michel, *Audio-Vision: Sound on Screen* (New York: Columbia University Press, 1993); Eng. trans. by Claudia Gorbman from the French *L'Audio-vision (son et image au cinéma)* (Paris: Armand-Colin, 1991).
Chion, Michel, 'Immobile Growth', in *David Lynch* (London: BFI, 2006), pp. 45–77; Eng. trans. by Robert Julian from the French *David Lynch* (Paris: Cahiers du Cinéma, 1992).
Chion, Michel, *The Voice in the Cinema* (New York: Columbia University Press, 1998); Eng. trans. by Claudia Gorbman from the French *La Voix au cinéma* (Paris: Cahiers du Cinéma, 1982).
Connor, Steven, 'An Air that Kills', <http://www.bbk.ac.uk/english/skc/gas> (accessed 5 May 2011).
Connor, Steven, 'Architecture on Air', <http://www.bbk.ac.uk/english/skc/atmospheres.htm> (accessed 20 May 2007).
Connor, Steven, *Dumbstruck: A Ventriloquistory: A Cultural History of Ventriloquism* (Oxford: Oxford University Press, 2000).
Connor, Steven, 'Inebriate of Air: Gas, Magic and Omnipotence of Thought

in the Nineteenth Century', <http://www.bbk.ac.uk/english/skc/inebriate/inebriate.pdf> (accessed 11 December 2010).

Connor, Steven, *The Matter of Air: Science and Art of the Ethereal* (London: Reaktion Books, 2010).

Connor, Steven, 'Next-to-Nothing', *Tate Etc*, 12 (Spring 2008), <http://www.tate.org.uk/tateetc/issue12/air.htm> (accessed 12 September 2009).

Connor, Steven, 'On the Air', <http://www.bbk.ac.uk/english/skc/onair> (accessed 23 February 2008).

Connor, Steven, 'Oxygen Debt: *Little Dorrit*'s Pneumatics', <http://www.bbk.ac.uk/english/skc/dorrit> (accessed 11 December 2009).

Connor, Steven, 'The Vapours', <http://www.bbk.ac.uk/english/skc/vapours> (accessed 11 December 2009).

Connor, Steven, 'Windbags and Skinsongs', <http://www.bbk.ac.uk/english/skc/windbags> (accessed 14 June 2010).

Constantini, Gustavo, 'Leitmotif Revisited', <http://filmsound.org/gustavo/leitmotif-revisted.htm> (accessed 1 May 2009).

Cooper, Sarah, 'Mortal Ethics: Reading Levinas with the Dardenne Brothers', *Film-Philosophy*, 11:2 (2007), <http://www.film-philosophy.com/2007v11n2/cooper.pdf> (accessed 7 December 2010).

Cornea, Christine, 'David Cronenberg's Performing Cyborgs', *Velvet Light Trap*, 52 (Fall 2003), pp. 4–14.

Creed, Barbara, 'The *Crash* Debate: Anal Wounds, Metallic Kisses', *Screen*, 39:2 (1998), pp. 175–9.

Creed, Barbara, 'Dark Desires', in Steven Cohan and Ina Rae Hark (eds), *Screening the Male* (London: Routledge, 1996), pp. 118–33.

Creed, Barbara, *The Monstrous Feminine: Film, Feminism and Psychoanalysis* (London: Routledge, 1993).

Critchley, Simon, 'Calm: On Terence Malick's *The Thin Red Line*', *Film-Philosophy*, 6:48 (2002), <www.film-philosophy.com/vol6–2002/n48critchley> (accessed 20 March 2009).

Deleuze, Gilles, *Cinema 2: The Time Image* (London: Continuum, 2005); Eng. trans. by Robert Galeta and Hugh Tomlinson from the French *Cinéma II: L'Image-temps* (Paris: Les Éditions de Minuit, 1985).

Deleuze, Gilles, 'Hysteria', in *Francis Bacon: The Logic of Sensation* (London: Continuum, 2005), pp. 32–9; Eng. trans. by Daniel W. Smith from the French *Logique du sens* (Paris: Les Éditions de Minuit, 1969).

Deleuze, Gilles, and Félix Guattari, *A Thousand Plateaus* (London: Continuum, 2004).

Desbarat, Carole, et al., *Atom Egoyan*, trans. Brian Holmes (Paris: Éditions Dis Voir, 1993).

Dillon, Steven, *Derek Jarman and Lyric Film: The Mirror and the Sea* (Austin: University of Texas Press, 2004).

Dulac, Germaine, 'The Expressive Techniques of the Camera', trans. Stuart Liebman, in Richard Abel (ed.), *French Film Theory and*

Criticism Volume 1 (Princeton: Princeton University Press, 1988), pp. 305–13.

Durkheim, Émile, *The Elementary Forms of Religious Life*, 2nd edition (Guildford: George Allen and Unwin, 1976).

Egoyan, Atom, and Ian Balfour, *Subtitles: On the Foreignness of Film* (Cambridge, MA: MIT Press, 2004).

Elley, Derek, review of *Dancer in the Dark*, *Variety*, <http://www.variety.com/review/VE1117915827.html?categoryid=31&cs=1> (accessed 14 December 2011).

Epstein, Jean, 'Magnification', in Richard Abel (ed.), *French Film Theory and Criticism Volume 1* (Princeton: Princeton University Press, 1988), pp. 235–40.

Evans, Georgina, 'Synaesthesia in Kieślowski's *Trois Couleurs: Bleu*', *Studies in French Cinema*, 5:2 (2005), pp. 77–86.

Fowler, Catherine, *The European Cinema Reader* (London: Routledge, 2002).

Frampton, Daniel, *Filmosophy* (London: Wallflower Press, 2006).

Frampton, Daniel, 'Notes on Filmosophy: A Reply to Reviews', *New Review of Television and Film Studies*, 6:3 (2008), pp. 365–74.

Frank, Marcie, 'The Camera and the Speculum: David Cronenberg's *Dead Ringers*', *PMLA*, 106:3 (1991), pp. 459–70.

Gray, Henry, *Anatomy: Descriptive and Surgical* (London: John W. Parker and Son, 1860).

Gray, Henry, *Anatomy of the Human Body* (Philadelphia: Lea and Febriger, 1918).

Grimley, Daniel M., 'Hidden Places: Hyperrealism, Björk's *Vespertine* and *Dancer in the Dark*', *Twentieth Century Music*, 2:1 (2005), pp. 37–51.

Grodal, Torben, 'Cognitive Identification and Empathy', in *Moving Pictures: A New Theory of Film Genres, Feelings and Cognition* (Oxford: Oxford University Press, 2002).

Grodal, Torben, 'Frozen Flows in von Trier's Oeuvre', *Northern Lights: Authorship, Creativity and Intentionality in the Media*, 3 (2004), pp. 129–68.

Gruben, Patricia, 'Look but Don't Touch: Visual and Tactile Desire in *Exotica*, *The Sweet Hereafter*, and *Felicia's Journey*', in Monique Tschofen and Jennifer Burwell (eds), *Image and Territory: Essays on Atom Egoyan* (Waterloo, ON: Wilfrid Laurier Press, 2007), pp. 249–74.

Ham, Martin, 'Excess and Resistance in Feminised Bodies: David Cronenberg's *Videodrome* and Jean Baudrillard's *Seduction*', *Senses of Cinema*, 30 (2004), <http://www.sensesofcinema.com/2004/30/videodrome_seduction> (accessed 8 December 2011).

Homer, *The Odyssey: A New Translation*, trans. Ian Johnston (Arlington: Richer Resources Publications, 2006).

hooks, bell, '*Exotica*: Breaking Down to Break Through', in *Reel to Real: Race, Sex and Class at the Movies* (London: Routledge, 1996), pp. 27–33.

Hotchkiss, Lia M., '"Still in the Game": Cyber-transformations of the "New

Flesh" in D. Cronenberg's *eXistenZ*', *Velvet Light Trap*, 52 (2003), pp. 15–32.

Irigaray, Luce, 'The Age of the Breath', in *Luce Irigaray: Key Writings* (New York: Continuum, 2004), pp. 165–70.

Irigaray, Luce, 'Before and Beyond any Word', in *Luce Irigaray: Key Writings* (New York: Continuum, 2004), pp. 134–44.

Irigaray, Luce, *Being Two: How Many Eyes Have We?* (Rüsselsheim: Christel Göttert Verlag, 2000); Eng. trans. by Luce Irigaray with Catherine Busson and Jim Mooney from the French *À deux, nous avons combien d'yeux?*.

Irigaray, Luce, 'A Breath that Touches in Words', in *I Love to You: Sketch for a Felicity Within History* (New York: Routledge, 1996), pp. 121–8; Eng. trans. by Alison Martin from the French *J'aime à toi. Esquisse d'une félicité dans l'histoire* (Paris: Grasset, 1992).

Irigaray, Luce, *Elemental Passions* (London: Continuum, 1992); Eng. trans. by Joanne Collie and Judith Still from the French *Passions élémentaires* (Paris: Les Éditions de Minuit, 1982).

Irigaray, Luce, *An Ethics of Sexual Difference*, Continuum Impacts Series (London: Continuum, 2004); Eng. trans. by Carolyn Burke and Gillian C. Gill from the French *Éthique de la différence sexuelle* (Paris: Les Éditions de Minuit, 1984).

Irigaray, Luce, *Everyday Prayers* (*Prières quotidiennes*) (Nottingham: Nottingham University Press, 2004).

Irigaray, Luce, *The Forgetting of Air in Martin Heidegger* (Austin: University of Texas Press, 1999); Eng. trans. by Mary Beth Mader from the French *L'Oubli de l'air chez Martin Heidegger* (Paris: Les Éditions de Minuit, 1983).

Irigaray, Luce, 'Part IV: Introduction', in *Luce Irigaray: Key Writings* (New York: Continuum, 2004), pp. 145–9.

Irigaray, Luce, 'The Redemption of Women', in *Luce Irigaray: Key Writings* (New York: Continuum, 2004), pp. 150–64.

Irigaray, Luce, *Sexes and Genealogies* (New York: Columbia University Press, 1987); Eng. trans. by Gillian C. Gill from the French *Sexes et parentés* (Paris: Les Éditions de Minuit, 1978).

Irigaray, Luce, 'Speaking of Immemorial Waters', in *The Marine Lover of Friedrich Nietzsche* (New York: Columbia University Press, 1991); Eng. trans. by Gillian C. Gill from the French *Amante marine* (Paris: Les Éditions de Minuit, 1991).

Irigaray, Luce, *Speculum of the Other Woman* (Ithaca: Cornell University Press, 1985); Eng. trans. by Gillian C. Gill from the French *Speculum de l'autre femme* (Paris: Les Éditions de Minuit, 1974).

Irigaray, Luce, 'Spirituality and Religion', in *Luce Irigaray: Key Writings* (New York: Continuum, 2004), pp. 145–86.

Irigaray, Luce, *This Sex Which Is Not One* (Ithaca: Cornell University Press,

1985); Eng. trans. by Catherine Porter from the French *Ce sexe qui n'en est pas un* (Paris: Les Éditions de Minuit, 1977).

Irigaray, Luce, 'The Way of Breath', in *Between East and West: From Singularity to Community* (New York: Columbia University Press, 2002), pp. 73–92; Eng. trans. by Stephen Pluháček from the French *Entre Orient et Occident: De la singularité à la communauté* (Paris: Grasset, 1999).

Irigaray, Luce, *The Way of Love* (London: Continuum, 2004); Eng. trans. by Heidi Bostic and Stephen Pluháček from the French *La Voie de l'amour*.

Jackson, Kevin, 'Odd Man Out', *Sight and Sound*, January 2003, <http://www.bfi.org.uk/sightandsound/feature/72> (accessed 8 December 2011).

Jameson, Frederic, 'Totality as Conspiracy', in *The Geopolitical Aesthetic: Cinema and Space in the World System* (London: BFI, 1992), pp. 9–82.

Johnson, David, 'Writing and Directing *The Sweet Hereafter*: A Talk with Atom Egoyan', *Scenario: The Magazine of Screenwriting Art*, 3:4 (1997), pp. 42–6.

Johnston, Sheila, 'Lars von Trier's Funny Turn', <http://www.telegraph.co.uk/culture/film/starsandstories/3671331/Lars-Von-Triers-funny-turn.html> (accessed 14 December 2011).

Kaufman, Anthony, 'David Cronenberg on *Spider*: Reality Is What You Make of It', *Indiewire*, 2003, <http://www.ralphfiennes-jenniferlash.com/article.php?id=89> (accessed 8 December 2011).

Keathley, Christian, *Cinephilia and History, or The Wind in the Trees* (Indianapolis: Indiana University Press, 2006).

Kirkeby, Per, 'The Pictures between the Chapters in *Breaking the Waves*', in *Breaking the Waves: Lars von Trier* (London: Faber and Faber, 1996).

Klinger, Barbara, 'The Art Film, Affect and The Viewer: *The Piano* Revisited', *Screen*, 47:1 (2006), pp. 19–41.

K-Punk, 'She's Not My Mother', <http://k-punk.abstractdynamics.org/archives/003227.html> (accessed 5 June 2010).

Krier, Theresa M., 'From Aggression to Gratitude: Air and Song in the *Parlement of Foules*', in *Birth Passages: Maternity and Nostalgia, Antiquity to Shakespeare* (New York: Cornell University Press, 2001), pp. 109–38.

Kristeva, Julia, *Powers of Horror: An Essay on Abjection* (New York: Columbia University Press, 1982).

Laakso, Hanna, '*Idioterne*', in Tytti Soila (ed.), *The Cinema of Scandinavia*, Twenty Four Frames Series (London: Wallflower Press, 2005), pp. 203–14.

Laine, Tarja, 'Lars von Trier, *Dogville* and the Hodological Space of Cinema', *Studies in European Cinema*, 3:2 (November 2006), pp. 129–41.

Laine, Tarja, 'Triadic Communality', in *Shame and Desire: Emotion, Intersubjectivity, Cinema* (Oxford: Peter Lang, 2007), pp. 70–3.

Leaman, Oliver, *Key Concepts in Eastern Philosophy* (London: Routledge, 1999).

Lévi-Strauss, Claude, *A World on the Wane* (New York: Athenaeum, 1975);

Eng. trans. by John and Doreen Weightman from the French *Tristes Tropiques* (Paris: Plon, 1955).

Lloyd, Mike, 'Life in the Slow Lane: Rethinking Spectacular Body Modification', *Journal of Media and Cultural Studies*, 18:4 (2004), pp. 555–64.

Lonergan, Bernard J. F., et al. (eds), *The Collected Works of Bernard Lonergan: Philosophical and Theological Papers 1958–1964* (Toronto: University of Toronto Press, 1996).

Lorraine, Tamazin E., *Irigaray and Deleuze: Experiments in Visceral Philosophy* (Ithaca: Cornell University Press, 1999).

Lumholdt, Jan (ed.), *Lars von Trier: Interviews* (Jackson: University Press of Mississippi, 2003).

Lyotard, Jean-François, 'Scapeland', in *The Inhuman: Reflections on Time* (Stanford: Stanford University Press, 1992), pp. 182–90; Eng. trans. by Geoffrey Bennington and Rachel Bowlby from the French *L'Inhumain. Causeries sur le temps* (Paris: Galilée, 1988).

McCormack, Patricia, 'Phantasmatic Fissures: *Spider*', *Senses of Cinema*, 27 (2003), <http://www.sensesofcinema.com/2003/feature-articles/spider> (accessed 8 December 2011).

McGrath, Patrick, *Spider* (London: Viking, 1991).

McLuhan, Marshall, *McLuhan: Hot and Cool*, ed. G. E. Stearn (New York: Dial, 1967).

Mai, Joseph, 'Corps-Caméra: The Evocation of Touch in the Dardennes' *La Promesse* (1996)', *Contact!*, special issue of *L'Esprit Créateur*, ed. Martin Crowley, 47:3 (2007), pp. 133–44.

Makarushka, Irena S. M., 'Transgressing Goodness in *Breaking the Waves*', *Journal of Religion and Film*, 2:1 (April 1998), <http://www.unomaha.edu/jrf/breaking.htm> (accessed 3 May 2011).

Margulies, Ivone, *Nothing Happens: Chantal Akerman's Hyperrealist Everyday* (Durham, NC: Duke University Press, 1996).

Marks, Laura U., 'Asphalt Nomadism: The New Desert in Arab Independent Cinema', <http://www.sfu.ca/~lmarks/writings/files/Asphalt%20Nomadism.pdf> (accessed 8 December 2011).

Marks, Laura U., *Enfoldment and Infinity: An Islamic Genealogy of New Media Art* (Cambridge, MA: MIT Press, 2010).

Marks, Laura U., 'The Haptic Transfer and the Travels of the Abstract Line: Embodied Perception from Classical Islam to Modern Europe', in Christina Lammer and Kim Sawchuck (eds), *Verkörperungen/Embodiment* (Vienna: Löcker Verlag, 2007), pp. 269–84.

Marks, Laura U., 'Haptic Visuality: Touching with the Eyes', *Framework: The Finnish Art Review*, 2 (2004), <http://www.framework.fi/2_2004/visitor/artikkelit/marks2.html> (accessed 7 June 2009).

Marks, Laura U., *The Skin of the Film: Intercultural Cinema, Embodiment and the Senses* (Durham, NC: Duke University Press, 1999).Marks, Laura U., 'Thinking Multisensory Culture', *Paragraph: A Journal of Modern*

Critical Theory, special issue on 'Cinema and the Senses', ed. Emma Wilson, 31:2 (July 2008), pp. 123–37.

Marks, Laura U., *Touch: Sensuous Theory and Multisensory Media* (Minneapolis: University of Minnesota Press, 2002).

Maura, Monika, 'The Colour of Pomegranates (a.k.a. Sayat Nova)', <http://www.kamera.co.uk/reviews_extra/pomegran.php> (accessed 15 November 2006).

Merleau-Ponty, Maurice, *The Phenomenology of Perception* (London: Continuum, 2002); Eng. trans. by Colin Smith from the French *Phénoménologie de la perception* (Paris: Gallimard, 1945).

Morris, Gary, 'The Passion of Joan of Arc on DVD', *Bright Lights Film Journal*, 27 (January 2000), <http://www.brightlightsfilm.com/27/joanofarc.html> (accessed 3 October 2011).

Mulvey, Laura, *Death 24x a Second: Stillness and the Moving Image* (London: Reaktion Books, 2006).

Mulvey, Laura, *Fetishism and Curiosity* (London: BFI, 1996).

Mulvey, Laura, 'Visual Pleasure and Narrative Cinema', *Screen*, 16:3 (Autumn 1975), pp. 6–18.

Naficy, Hamid, *An Accented Cinema: Exilic and Diasporic Filmmaking* (Princeton: Princeton University Press, 2001).

Nair, Sreenath, *Restoration of Breath: Consciousness and Performance* (Amsterdam: Rodopi, 2007).

Nancy, Jean-Luc, 'Icon of Fury: Claire Denis's *Trouble Every Day*', trans. Douglas Morrey (2001), *Film-Philosophy*, 12:1 (2008), <http://www.film-philosophy.com/2008v12n1/nancy.pdf> (accessed 20 July 2008).

Ostrawoska, Dorothy, and Graham Roberts, 'The Element of Childhood from Children's Television to Dogme 95', in *European Cinemas in the Television Age* (Edinburgh: Edinburgh University Press, 2007).

Owen, Lesley, and Kenneth Mackinnon, *Smoking in Films: A Review* (London: Health Education Authority, 1997).

Pallasmaa, Juhani, *The Architecture of Image: Existential Space in Cinema* (Helsinki: Rakennustieto, 2000).

Pallasmaa, Juhani, 'The Significance of Shadow', in *The Eyes of the Skin: Architecture and the Senses*, 2nd edn (Chichester: John Wiley and Sons, 2005), pp. 46–8.

Pence, Jeffrey, 'Cinema of the Sublime: Theorizing the Ineffable', *Poetics Today*, 25:1 (2004), pp. 29–66.

Pevere, Geoff, 'Difficult to Say: Atom Egoyan Interviewed by Geoff Pevere', in *Exotica* (Toronto: Coach House Press, 1995).

Plant, Sadie, 'On the Matrix: Cyberfeminist Stimulations', in Gill Kirkup et al. (eds), *The Gendered Cyborg: A Reader* (London: Routledge, 2000).

Powrie, Phil, 'The Haptic Moment: Sparring with Paolo Conte in Ozon's *5x2*', *Paragraph: A Journal of Modern Critical Theory*, 31:2 (2008), pp. 206–22.

Quinlivan, Davina, 'Material Hauntings: The Kinaesthesia of Sound in

Innocence (Hadzihalilovic, 2004)', *Studies in French Cinema*, 9:3 (2009), pp. 215–24.

Quinlivan, Davina, 'Review: Caroline Bainbridge, *The Cinema of Lars von Trier: Authenticity and Artifice*', *Film-Philosophy*, 12:1 (2008), <www.filmphilosophy.com/2008v12n1/quinlivan.pfd> (accessed 12 June 2011).

Quinlivan, Davina, 'Von Trier's Breath Control: The Sound and Sight of Respiration as Hyper-realist Corporeality in *Breaking the Waves* (1996)', in Lúcia Nagib and Cecilia de Mello (eds), *Realism and the Audio-Visual Media* (Basingstoke: Palgrave Macmillan, 2009), pp. 152–63.

Quinlivan, Davina, and Will Brooker (eds), *Star Wars*, <http://www.oxfordbibliographiesonline.com/view/document/obo-9780199791286/obo-9780199791286-0059.xml> (accessed 29 October 2011).

Rawson, Nancy E., 'Olfaction', in E. Bruce Goldstein (ed.), *The Blackwell Handbook of Perception* (London: Blackwell Publishing, 2004), pp. 567–600.

Rio, Elena del, 'The Body as Foundation of the Screen: Allegories of Technology in Atom Egoyan's *Speaking Parts*', *Camera Obscura*, 38 (1996), pp. 94–115.

Robbins, Helen W., 'More Human Than I Am Alone', in Steven Cohan and Ina Rae Hark (eds), *Screening the Male* (London: Routledge, 1996), pp. 134–50.

Rodowick, D. N., *The Virtual Life of Film* (Cambridge, MA: Harvard University Press, 2007).

Rogers, Nathaniel, review of *Dancer in the Dark*, *The Film Experience*, <http://thefilmexperience.net/Reviews/dancerinthedark.html> (accessed 29 March 2011).

Romney, Jonathan, *Atom Egoyan*, World Directors Series (London: BFI, 2004).

Romney, Jonathan, '*Felicia's Journey*', *Sight and Sound*, 9:10 (October 1999), pp. 34–5, <http://www.bfi.org.uk/sightandsound/review/215> (accessed 7 May 2009).

Romney, Jonathan, 'This Green Unpleasant Land', *Sight and Sound*, 9:10 (October 1999), pp. 34–5.

Sarat, Austin, 'Imagining the Law of the Father: Loss, Dread and Mourning in *The Sweet Hereafter*', *Law and Society Review*, 34 (2000), pp. 5–46.

Saunders, Theresa, 'Both/And Holiness and Mental Illness', in *Celluloid Saints: Images of Sanctity in Film* (Atlanta: Mercer University Press, 2002), pp. 201–3.

Shambu, Girish, 'The Pleasure and Pain of "Watching": Atom Egoyan's *Exotica*', *Senses of Cinema*, 13 (2001), <http://www.sensesofcinema.com/2001/13/exotica> (accessed 8 December 2011).

Shaviro, Steven, *The Cinematic Body: Theory out of Bounds* (Minneapolis: University of Minnesota Press, 1993).

Shaviro, Steven, '*Eastern Promises*', *The Pinocchio Theory*, <http://www.shaviro.com/Blog/?p=601> (accessed 11 October 2008).

Shaviro, Steven, '*Spider*', *The Pinocchio Theory*, <http://www.shaviro.com/Blog/?p=76> (accessed 5 May 2010).

Shaviro, Steven, 'Untimely Bodies: Towards a Comparative Film Theory of Human Figures, Temporalities and Visibilities', <http://ftp.shaviro.com/Othertexts/SCMS08Response.pdf> (accessed 1 February 2009).

Silverman, Kaja, *The Acoustic Mirror: The Female Voice in Psychoanalysis and Cinema* (Bloomington: Indiana University Press, 1988).

Smets, Jo, 'Memory can be a terrifying thing', <http://www.writemen.com/pages/writing-print-article-Spider-E.html> (accessed 5 October 2011).

Sobchack, Vivian, *The Address of the Eye: A Phenomenology of Film Experience* (Princeton: Princeton University Press, 1992).

Sobchack, Vivian, *Carnal Thoughts: Embodiment and Moving Image Culture* (Berkeley: University of California Press, 2004).

Sobchack, Vivian, 'Embodying Transcendence: On the Literal, the Material and the Filmic Sublime', *Material Religion*, 4:2 (July 2007), pp. 194–203.

Sobchack, Vivian, 'Thoughts on Seeing (most of) *The Descent* and *Isolation*', *Film Comment*, July–August 2006, pp. 40–1.

Sobchack, Vivian, 'What My Fingers Knew: The Cinesthetic Subject, or Vision in the Flesh', *Senses of Cinema*, 5 (2000), <http://www.sensesofcinema.com/2000/5/fingers> (accessed 7 December 2011).

Stevenson, Jack, *Lars von Trier*, World Cinema Series (London: BFI, 2002).

Syed, Soraya, 'The Art of the Pen', <http://www.artofthepen.com/home.html> (accessed 10 October 2010).

Taylor, Jeremy, *The Living Labyrinth: Exploring Universal Themes in Myths, Dreams, and the Symbolisms of Waking Life* (Mahwah, NJ: Paulist Press, 1998).

Thomsen, Brad, *Lars von Trier: Interviews*, ed. Jan Lumholdt (Jackson: University Press of Mississippi, 2003).

Thomson, Claire, 'A Cinema of Dust: On the Ontology of the Image from Dreyer's Thorvaldsen to Ordrupgaard's Dreyer', <eprints.ucl.ac.uk/4963/1/4963.pdf> (accessed 2 December 2010).

Thomson, Claire, 'It's All About Snow: Limning the Posthuman Body in Tarkovsky's *Solaris* and Vinterberg's *It's All About Love*', *New Cinemas: Journal of Contemporary Cinema*, 5:1 (April 2007), pp. 3–22.

Thomson, Michael, '*eXistenZ*: bio-ports/boundaries/bodies', *Legal Studies*, 21:2 (2001), pp. 325–43.

Travers, Peter, review of *Dancer in the Dark*, <http://www.rollingstone.com/movies/reviews/dancer-in-the-dark-20001006> (accessed 14 December 2011).

Trier, Lars von, *Breaking the Waves: Lars von Trier* (London: Faber and Faber, 1996).

Trotter, David, 'Lynne Ramsay's *Ratcatcher*: Towards a Theory of Haptic Narrative', *Paragraph: A Journal of Modern Critical Theory*, special issue on 'Cinema and the Senses', ed. Emma Wilson, 31:2 (July 2008), pp. 138–58.

Tschofen, Monique, and Jennifer Burwell (eds), *Image and Territory: Essays on Atom Egoyan* (Waterloo, ON: Wilfrid Laurier Press, 2007).

Vasseleu, Catherine, *Textures of Light: Vision and Touch in Irigaray, Levinas and Merleau-Ponty* (New York: Routledge, 1998).

Watkins, Liz, 'Light, Colour and Sound in Cinema', *Paragraph: A Journal of Modern Critical Theory*, 25:3 (2002), pp. 117–28.

Weese, Katherine, 'Family Stories: Gender and Discourse in Atom Egoyan's *The Sweet Hereafter*', *Narrative*, 10:1 (2002), pp. 131–51.

Wells, H. G., *The Invisible Man* (London: Penguin, 2005).

Whitford, Margaret (ed.), *The Irigaray Reader: Luce Irigaray* (London: Blackwell Publishing, 1991).

Whitford, Margaret, 'The Same, the Semblance and the Other', in *Luce Irigaray: Philosophy in the Feminine*, 2nd edition (London: Routledge, 1995), pp. 101–22.

Williams, Linda Ruth, 'The Inside-Out of Masculinity: David Cronenberg's Visceral Pleasures', in Michele Aaron (ed.), *The Body's Perilous Pleasures: Dangerous Desires and Contemporary Culture* (Edinburgh: Edinburgh University Press, 1999), pp. 30–48.

Wilson, Donald, and Richard Stevenson, *Learning to Smell: Olfactory Perception from Neurobiology to Behaviour* (Baltimore: The Johns Hopkins University Press, 2006).

Wilson, Emma, *Atom Egoyan*, Contemporary Film Directors Series (Champaign: University of Illinois Press, 2009).

Wilson, Emma, *Cinema's Missing Children* (London: Wallflower Press, 2004).

Winters, Laura, 'A Gentle Interpreter of Human Fallibility', *The New York Times*, 23 November 1997, p. 17.

Žižek, Slavoj, 'Femininity between Goodness and Act', <http://lacan.com/frameXIV3.htm> (accessed 4 May 2011).

FILMOGRAPHY

Adoration. Dir. Atom Egoyan. Canada, 2009.
Alien. Dir. Ridley Scott. UK, 1979.
Aliens. Dir. James Cameron. USA, 1986.
Alien 3. Dir. David Fincher. USA, 1992.
Alien Resurrection. Dir. Jean-Pierre Jeunet. USA, 1997.
Antichrist. Dir. Lars von Trier. Denmark/Sweden/France/Poland/Norway/Netherlands, 2009.
The Birdcage. Dir. Mike Nichols. USA, 1996.
Black Narcissus. Dir. Michael Powell and Emeric Pressburger. UK, 1947.
Blue. Dir. Derek Jarman. UK, 1993.
Blue Velvet. Dir. David Lynch. UK, 1986.
The Boss of It All. Dir. Lars von Trier. Denmark/Sweden/Iceland/Italy/France/Norway/Finland/Germany/Spain, 2006.
Brasiconoscopio. Dir. Mauro Giuntini. Brazil, 1995.
Breaking the Waves. Dir. Lars von Trier. Denmark/Sweden/France/Netherlands/Norway/Iceland, 1996.
The Brood. Dir. David Cronenberg. Canada, 1979.
Calendar. Dir. Atom Egoyan. Canada, 1993.
Chott El-Jehrid (A Portrait of Light and Heat). Dir. Bill Viola. USA, 1979.
The Colour of Pomegranates. Dir. Sergei Paradjanov. Armenia, 1968.
Crash. Dir. David Cronenberg. Canada, 1997.
Dancer in the Dark. Dir. Lars von Trier. Spain/Argentina/Denmark/Germany/Netherlands/Italy/UK/France/Sweden/Finland/Iceland/Norway, 2000.
Dead Ringers. Dir. David Cronenberg. Canada/USA, 1988.
The Descent. Dir. Neil Marshall. UK, 2005.
Dogville. Dir. Lars von Trier. Denmark/Sweden/UK/France/Germany/Netherlands/Norway/Finland, 2003.
Eastern Promises. Dir. David Cronenberg. UK/Canada/USA, 2007.
Element of Crime. Dir. Lars von Trier. Denmark, 1984.
Epidemic. Dir. Lars von Trier. Denmark, 1987.
Europa. Dir. Lars von Trier. Denmark, 1990.

Event Horizon. Dir. Paul W. S. Anderson. UK/USA, 1997.
Evita. Dir. Alan Parker. USA, 1996.
eXistenZ. Dir David Cronenberg. Canada/UK, 1999.
The Exorcist. Dir. William Friedkin. USA, 1973.
Exotica. Dir. Atom Egoyan. Canada, 1994.
Family Viewing. Dir. Atom Egoyan. Canada, 1987.
Felicia's Journey. Dir. Atom Egoyan, Canada/UK, 1999.
Festen. Dir. Thomas Vinterberg. Denmark, 1998.
5x2. Dir. François Ozon. France, 2004.
The Fly. Dir. Kurt Neumann. USA, 1958.
The Fly. Dir. David Cronenberg. USA, 1986.
The Idiots (Idioterne). Dir. Lars von Trier. Denmark/Sweden/France/Netherlands/Italy, 1998.
L'Intrus (The Intruder). Dir. Claire Denis. France, 2004.
It's All About Love. Dir. Thomas Vinterberg. Denmark, 2003.
La Jetée. Dir. Chris Marker. France, 1962.
The Kingdom (Riget). Dir. Lars von Trier. Denmark, 1994.
The Last Temptation of Christ. Dir. Martin Scorsese. USA, 1988.
Lost Highway. Dir. David Lynch. USA, 1977.
M Butterfly. Dir. David Cronenberg. USA, 1993.
Magnolia. Dir. Paul Thomas Anderson. USA, 1999.
Manderlay. Dir. Lars von Trier. Denmark/Sweden/Netherlands/France/Germany/UK/Italy, 2005.
Medea. Dir. Lars von Trier. Denmark, 1988.
Melancholia. Dir. Lars von Trier. Denmark/Sweden/France/Germany, 2011.
Naked Lunch. Dir. David Cronenberg. Canada/UK/Japan, 1991.
Next of Kin. Dir. Atom Egoyan. Canada, 1984.
Now, Voyager. Dir. Irving Rapper. USA, 1942.
La Passion de Jeanne d'Arc (The Passion of Joan of Arc). Dir. Carl Theodor Dreyer. France, 1928.
Perfume: The Story of a Murderer. Dir. Tom Tykwer. Germany/France/Spain/USA, 2006.
A Portrait of Arshile. Dir. Atom Egoyan. Canada/UK, 1995.
Rabid. Dir. David Cronenberg. Canada, 1977.
Rosetta. Dir. Jean-Pierre and Luc Dardenne. France/Belgium, 1999.
Salomé. Dir. William Dieterle. USA, 1953.
Scanners. Dir. David Cronenberg. Canada, 1981.
Scream. Dir. Wes Craven. USA, 1996.
Seeing Is Believing. Dir. Shauna Beharry. Canada, 1991.
Shivers. Dir. David Cronenberg. Canada, 1975.
The Silence of the Lambs. Dir. Jonathan Demme. USA, 1992.
Solyaris. Dir. Andrei Tarkovsky. Soviet Union, 1972.
The Sound of Music. Dir. Robert Wise. USA, 1965.
Speaking Parts. Dir. Atom Egoyan. Canada, 1989.

Spider. Dir. David Cronenberg. Canada/UK, 2002.
Stars Wars. Dir. George Lucas. USA, 1977.
Star Wars Episode III: The Revenge of the Sith. Dir. George Lucas. USA, 2005.
Stranded. Dir. María Lidón, Spain, 2002.
Sunshine. Dir. Danny Boyle. UK/USA, 2007.
Supernova. Dir. Walter Hill. USA/Switzerland, 1999.
The Sweet Hereafter. Dir. Atom Egoyan. Canada, 1997.
Taxidermia. Dir. György Pálfi. Hungary/Austria/France, 2006.
The Thin Red Line. Dir. Terence Malick. USA, 1998.
Three Colours: Blue. Dir. Krzysztof Kieślowski. Poland, 1993.
Le Trou (The Hole). Dir. Jacques Becker. France, 1960.
True North. Dir. Isaac Julien. USA, 2004.
2001: A Space Odyssey. Dir. Stanley Kubrick. UK, 1968.
Videodrome. Dir. David Cronenberg. Canada, 1986.
Wings of Desire. Dir. Wim Wenders. Germany, 1987.
Zidane: A 21st Century Portrait. Dir. Douglas Gordon and Philippe Parreno. France, 2006.

INDEX

Adoration, 74
Alien, 23–4
Anderson, Don, 38n53
Antichrist, 128, 164n11

Bachelard, Gaston, 28–9
Bainbridge, Caroline, 166n43
Balázs, Béla, 165n20, 165n29
Barker, Jennifer, 133
Baronian, Marie-Aude, 41
Barthes, Roland, 15–16, 46, 75, 138–9
Beugnet, Martine, 93, 120n12
The Birdcage, 148
Black Narcissus, 82
Blue, 53
Blue Velvet, 24–5
Bolton, Lucy, 30
The Boss of It All, 164n11
Brasiconoscopio, 54
Breaking the Waves, 12, 131–45, 171
breathing
  consciousness, 17, 170
  corporeality, 28
  film viewer, 125–6, 129, 140, 148, 155, 157–8, 160, 163, 168, 170
  subjectivity, 17, 22, 140
  visuality, 126, 129, 133–4, 137, 146, 148–50, 156–8, 160, 162–3, 168, 170–1
Brenez, Nicole, 93
The Brood, 95–6
Brooks, Jodie, 4
Brophy, Philip, 114, 140
Bruno, Giuliana, 45, 50, 69, 151, 155

Calendar, 73
Celeste, Reni, 56
Chion, Michel, 107, 136, 140–1, 167n68

Chott El-Jehrid (A Portrait of Light and Heat), 54
The Colour of Pomegranates, 63
Connor, Steven, 13–14, 16, 103–4
Cooper, Sarah, 38n67
Crash, 91, 106
Creed, Barbara, 2–3, 95, 106
Critchley, Simon, 82–3

Dancer in the Dark, 146–56
Dead Ringers, 90
Deleuze, Gilles, 20, 37n47, 38n53, 57–8, 117, 156
  and the crystal image, 49
Dillon, Steven, 50, 60
Dogville, 129, 164n11, 164n16

Eastern Promises, 110
Egoyan, Atom, 49
Element of Crime, 12, 126–30, 134, 145
Elemental topography, 52, 53, 59, 60, 72, 84, 91
Epidemic, 127–8
Epstein, Jean, 165n31
Europa, 127, 129
Evans, Georgina, 172
Event Horizon, 23
Evita, 148
The Exorcist, 24
Exotica, 12, 77–83, 170–1

Family Viewing, 74
Felicia's Journey, 65–77
Festen, 130
5x2, 138
The Fly (Dir. Kurt Neumann), 113
The Fly (Dir. David Cronenberg), 96, 113
Frampton, Daniel, 21, 38n65, 120n10

Grimley, Daniel M, 146, 155
Guattari, Félix, 20, 37n47, 57–8, 156

hooks, bell, 35n13, 78

The Idiots (Idioterne), 12, 157–61
L'Intrus (The Intruder), 93
Irigaray, Luce
    and breathing, 27–30
    and the caress, 28, 31–2
    and film, 29–30
    and inter-subjectivity, 140–5

La Jetée, 23, 25–6, 93, 99

The Kingdom (Riget), 155
Kirkeby, Per, 142
K-Punk, 95, 101, 103
Kristeva, Julia, 95, 167n74

Laakso, Hanna, 160
Laine, Tarja, 124, 130, 164n16
The Last Temptation of Christ, 19, 116
Lloyd, Mike, 13–15, 16, 20, 118
Lost Highway, 38n65
Lyotard, Jean-François, 28–9, 56

M Butterfly, 121n25
Magnolia, 8–9, 11, 22–3
Manderlay, 129, 164n11
Marks, Laura U., 11, 12, 17, 19–21, 137–8, 148, 149, 162–3, 169, 170, 172
    and Irigaray, 28, 142
McCormack, Patricia, 110
McGrath, Patrick, 95, 104–5, 122n39
Medea, 128–9, 158, 160–1
Melancholia, 128
Mulvey, Laura, 2, 24, 63

Naked Lunch, 94, 102
Next of Kin, 43, 74
Now, Voyager, 111

La Passion de Jeanne d'Arc (The Passion of Joan of Arc), 135
Pence, Jeffrey, 141, 165n29
Perfume: The Story of a Murderer, 101
Pevere, Geoff, 76
A Portrait of Arshile, 41–2, 44–6, 56–7, 74, 84
Powrie, Phil, 138

Rabid, 91
Rio, Elena del, 74

Rodowick, D. N., 35n15
Romney, Jonathan, 43, 89n96
Rosetta, 23, 26, 38n67

Salomé, 69, 75
Scanners, 113
Scream, 23–4, 27
Seeing Is Believing, 21, 41, 54
Shambu, Girish, 79–80
Shaviro, Steven, 91, 100, 110
Shivers, 96, 121n25
The Silence of the Lambs, 23–4, 27
Silverman, Kaja, 107
Sobchack, Vivian, 11–12, 15, 17–22, 30–4, 37n51, 50–1, 82, 92–3, 105, 115, 125, 137, 169, 172
Solyaris, 23
The Sound of Music, 153
Speaking Parts, 74
Spider, 12, 34, 85, 91–112, 116, 119, 125, 170, 171
Stars Wars, 4–6, 8, 9, 11, 13, 15, 21, 22, 23, 24, 25, 35n11
Star Wars Episode III: The Revenge of the Sith, 35n12
Stranded, 23
Sunshine, 23
Supernova, 23
The Sweet Hereafter, 12, 45–65, 69, 71, 78, 81, 84, 92, 95, 116, 125, 127, 169, 171

Taxidermia, 91
The Thin Red Line, 82
Three Colours: Blue, 61
Trier, Lars von, and the *Europa* trilogy, 127
Trotter, David, 156
Le Trou (The Hole), 4
True North, 55
2001: A Space Odyssey, 23

Vasseleu, Catherine, 11, 28, 36n28
Videodrome, 12, 112–19, 125, 133, 170

Weese, Katherine, 49
Whitford, Margaret, 10, 72
Williams, Linda Ruth, 90
Wilson, Emma, 43–4, 61, 78–9, 89n95, 89n96, 127, 143
Wings of Desire, 23, 25, 27

Zidane: A 21st Century Portrait, 23, 26
Žižek, Slavoj, 164n13

EU representative:
Easy Access System Europe
Mustamäe tee 50, 10621 Tallinn, Estonia
Gpsr.requests@easproject.com